Improper Influence

Improper Influence

Campaign Finance Law,
Political Interest Groups,
and the Problem of Equality

Thomas Gais

Ann Arbor

THE UNIVERSITY OF MICHIGAN PRESS

Copyright © by the University of Michigan 1996
All rights reserved
Published in the United States of America by
The University of Michigan Press
Manufactured in the United States of America
⊗ Printed on acid-free paper

1999   1998   1997   1996   4   3   2   1

A CIP catalog record for this book is available from the British Library.

Library of Congress Cataloging-in-Publication Data
Gais, Thomas, 1952–
    Improper influence : campaign finance law, political interest
groups, and the problem of equality / Thomas Gais.
        p.   cm.
    Includes bibliographical references and index.
    ISBN 0-472-10631-7 (hardcover : alk. paper)
    1. Campaign funds—Law and legislation—United States.
2. Political action committees—United States.   3. Pressure groups—
United States.   I. Title.
KF4920.G35   1996
342.73′078—dc20
[347.30278]   95-43821
                                                           CIP

To Juanita Lewis Gais and in memory
of Frederick Sandford Gais

Contents

Figures

Tables

Abbreviations

Newspaper names are abbreviated in text as follows:

LAT   *Los Angeles Times*
NJ   *National Journal*
NYT *New York Times*
WP   *Washington Post*

Acknowledgments

Rick Hall, John Kingdon, Ned Gramlich, Larry Mohr, Fred Gais, and two anonymous reviewers read early versions of this book and provided superb comments and criticisms. I am especially thankful for Larry's encouragement and guidance throughout this project. I have also benefited from discussions with Michael Malbin, Tim Cook, and John Jackson. Dick Nathan, Director of the Rockefeller Institute of Government, also contributed to this study by creating a wonderful scholarly environment where I made the final revisions to the manuscript.

I shall always be thankful to Cathy Johnson for her patience and support. Mark Peterson has given me several pep talks over the years, some that go back quite a long time, but which I still remember and appreciate. I also wish to thank Linda Walker for allowing me to use these data and for her interest in and excitement over the completion of this project.

This study relies heavily on the ideas and data of my late teacher and friend, Jack L. Walker. I do not know whether Jack would have agreed with my conclusions, since I did nearly all this work after his death. But though I am sure that he would have disagreed with at least some of my conclusions, I think and hope he would have appreciated the point of view in this book—that we have to be careful about enacting any models regarding the appropriate forms of political organization in American politics, since none of those models fit particularly well. Jack loved American politics and all its messiness and mutability. He relished mapping out the diversity in the system and discovering all the particular reasons for it. And though he truly believed in reform and constitutional change, I think that he felt very deeply that we had to understand this complexity and its functions before trying to purge it of any political activities that we deemed to be excessive, unseemly, or even outright wrong.

At least that's what I thought he felt. Like American politics, it was hard to pin Jack down. I remember those morning appointments in May when Jack and I would get together after winter semester in the old IPPS director's office in the corner of Rackham, with its tall windows open to another lovely (and well-deserved) Ann Arbor spring. We would usually sit at a corner of a table—a small section from which Jack had cleared away teetering stacks of papers and books—and we would talk for hours about the ideas we needed to work on and the data we needed to collect. I would then go back to my office, look over my notes, and find at least a dozen distinct projects and not a word on where to start; and when I'd go back to him for guidance, I'd usually end up with several more. There was nothing orderly about Jack's mind, but then there have been very few political scientists who have given us so much to think about. For that and many other things I shall always be grateful to him, and I, like many others, will surely miss him for a very long time.

CHAPTER 1

Introduction

Frustration with the unruliness of American political institutions and allegations that they distort or misrepresent the people's will are long and strong threads in the nation's political tradition. Yet even the most vigorous critics of forty years ago might have been shocked at the charges now leveled against American politics, and the criticisms are nowhere harsher than in the perceived relations between "special interests" and U.S. elections. Congress is accused of being sold to the highest bidders; elected officials are viewed as beholden to greedy hordes of organized interests; and policy processes in the executive branch as well as the legislature are seen as unresponsive to the needs of ordinary citizens and moved, if at all, by the demands of vested interests, armed with enormously wealthy political action committees (PACs).

What is ironic about these perceptions of a system out of control is the fact that no other aspect of American politics has been the target of such thorough reform as campaign financing and the participation of interest groups in elections. By 1974, amendments to the Federal Election Campaign Act had established regulations covering nearly all aspects of interest group involvement in elections, including their registration, their internal organization, their record keeping and reporting, the scope of their memberships, the maximum size of contributions to their funds, the permissible sources of support, their relationships with and contributions to candidates, their internal communications with members, their connections with sponsoring institutions, and their communications with the public. These regulations were enacted in the widespread American belief, deeply rooted in Progressive thought, that organized groups, if left unchecked, wielded enormous political power by giving money to politicians or their campaigns, and that the only hope of controlling their power was by subjecting their political activities to public disclosure and strict regulation. Yet, despite the reforms, many political observers have claimed that the distorting effects of "special interests" have worsened in recent years. Not only are organized groups still believed to control too much money and to be too important in formulating government policies; such groups, especially when they are organized as PACs, are viewed as unrepresentative of, even alien to, the interests of most citizens.

What accounts for the apparent failure of the campaign finance regulations to produce the kind of broadly representative system of civic-minded contributors that the reformers wanted? Journalists have often argued that the reforms have been poorly enforced, perhaps because the Federal Election Commission (FEC) has been a flawed enforcement agency from the start (Jackson 1990). Many reformers have claimed that the reforms did not go far enough—that more stringent constraints should have been placed on interest group activities and that public funding was needed to reduce the power of private money (U.S. House Committee on House Administration 1991, 119–23). And some scholars have pointed out that though the original reforms had a certain coherence, the Supreme Court made so many changes that the resulting hodgepodge of regulations created loopholes that aggressive special interest groups were able to exploit (Sorauf 1992, 238–42).

If the reforms have in fact failed, and I believe that they have, each of these explanations probably has some merit. Yet I think that a more important reason why the reforms did not establish a more representative system was because the laws themselves made no allowance for the enormous difficulties of organizing people for collective action. The reformers focused on the problems of suppressing political action and ignored the difficulties of building a broad-based system of group representation. A primary goal of the reforms was to create a more egalitarian system of campaign financing, one in which the concerns and interests of large publics were not "drowned out" by the vast resources of small groups of wealthy individuals and economic institutions. As the Supreme Court interpreted the reforms in *FEC* v. *Massachusetts Citizens for Life*, the regulations sought to ensure that the money raised and spent on political activities would "reflect popular support for the political positions of the committee" rather than the arbitrary or "unfair" distribution of "resources amassed in the economic marketplace" (1986, 257–58). The laws were expected to produce this result by ensuring that most of the financial support for a group's electoral efforts was raised through voluntary contributions by private individuals in small amounts. This "grassroots" model of electoral mobilization was viewed as congenial to a wide array of citizen and other broad-based interests, while it was seen as an important constraint on the electoral activities of unions and corporations. The model was enforced through a variety of means, including limits on the size of contributions to PACs and candidates; the requirement that unions, corporations, and associations established "separate segregated funds" to raise money for contributions and expenditures; restrictions intended to ensure that contributions to political committees were voluntary; and limits on the direct use of institutional resources to support electoral activities.

Yet, I will argue, a campaign finance system that enforces dependence on small contributors cannot produce an egalitarian system of group representation, since the ability of interest groups to mobilize small contributors is itself unequally distributed. The laws prescribed an organizational form with which many groups could not comply. What was worse, the groups that were least able to conform to this "grassroots" model were not the corporations, unions, or other economic institutions that the reformers had hoped to constrain. Instead, they included the groups that sought to represent the concerns of large groups of citizens not linked together by occupational or institutional ties and that already faced the greatest barriers to political mobilization. The laws actually enhanced the importance of an institutional base for group mobilization; and rather than establishing a broader, more egalitarian system of group representation, the regulations limited the variety of interest groups that were effectively organized in elections and campaign financing.

These unintended effects are understandable in light of Mancur Olson's work on the problem of collective action (1965, 1982). His theory suggests that small contributors are hard to organize around their common interests, even if they fully agree with one another on public issues and believe that an electoral organization would advance their cause. Given their incentives to act as free riders, their mobilization around collective goals is costly and usually depends on the use of individualized rewards and sanctions. This "by-product" method of political organization is not, however, easily deployed by certain groups. It is not hard to use when an interest group has an institutional base, like a corporation or labor union. Institutions can reduce the costs of finding and communicating with potential contributors; they can encourage contributions through a host of mechanisms, such as peer pressures, frequent interaction, and institutional rules or conventions; and they can ensure a greater correspondence between the private goods needed to elicit contributions and the collective goals of the group. Citizen groups and others without an institutional base do not enjoy these advantages and face many obstacles in establishing an effective political organization by providing and manipulating selective goods or services, and some of the campaign finance laws have exacerbated these problems. To ensure that the contributions were "voluntary"—that is, based on purely political motives—associations were prohibited from making any membership benefits contingent on whether or not an individual contributed to an affiliated PAC; and the disclosure and record-keeping require-ments in the campaign finance laws greatly increased the costs of raising money from many small contributors.

The difficulty of mobilizing small contributors has led many interest groups, outside the arena of electoral politics, to secure financial sup-port from patrons or large contributors who support the organization's aims, often in exchange for special honors or control over the group's goals, agenda, or activities (Walker 1991). This is particularly true for citizen groups and groups representing nonprofit institutions, groups that have accounted for much of the growth of the American interest group system in recent decades. These groups have succeeded in repre-senting a wide range of often diffuse and encompassing interests by raising money from a wide variety of patrons, such as large individual donors and benefactors, public and private foundations, corporations making tax-deductible gifts, and governments offering grants, contracts, and tax subsidies. Yet the campaign finance and tax laws regulating group involvement in elections severely limit the ability of such groups to use many of their traditional patrons to establish or fund electoral organizations. Again, the consequence is that the regulations governing interest group involvement in elections are not neutral in their impact on different types of groups. Rather than preventing economic institutions from using their resources for electoral purposes, the reforms estab-lished a small-contributor model of political mobilization with which only institutionally based groups could readily comply. And far from creating a legal framework that was congenial to their spontaneous orga-nization, the laws prevented citizen and other groups from using, for electoral purposes, the same political patrons that had long been so important to their formation and maintenance in nonelectoral settings. In essence, the reforms required that all groups wanting to finance cam-paigns had to overcome the "large group" problem found in the theory of collective action. But neither the reforms nor the other laws affecting group participation in elections provided neutral and widely accessible methods of solving that problem. The result is a small and highly biased system of interest group participation in elections—a system that, when compared to other forms of political organization, is dominated by busi-ness and labor groups and underrepresents citizen interests and occupa-tional interests in the nonprofit sector.

These biases in group representation have important repercussions for the party system and in the representation of policy views. The laws tend to disadvantage groups that support liberal policies, that are inter-ested in certain noneconomic issues, and that support Democratic admin-istrations, while groups that are able to form and maintain strong PACs tend to support more conservative policies, are primarily interested in economic issues, and are more likely to support Republican administrations. These findings undermine several of the assumptions that have shaped campaign finance reforms in recent years: that the equal participation of citizens is directly related to the equal representation of political interests; the distinction between contributions and expenditures regarding their importance to First Amendment questions; and the expectation that restrictions on fund-raising have their primary effect on the wealthiest, most aggressive groups. These findings also suggest a fundamental tension between the nation's need to establish a system of campaign financing that commands and maintains legitimacy among the nation's citizens and the need to have a system that is open, adaptive, and broadly representative—between the ideal forms of group organization and mobilization and the eclectic and unexpected ways in which real groups raise their money.

This study analyzes the tensions between the current regulatory regime and the problems of collective action by examining political action committees in American national politics. As I define them, PACs are organizations created by interest groups to raise or spend money for the purpose of influencing federal elections. They include *segregated funds*—which are financial accounts created and administered by a corporation, labor union, association, or other parent group, and which are funded by voluntary contributions from the connected organization's employees, members, stockholders, or officers—and *independent* or *nonconnected political committees*—which have no direct connection with a parent group and may raise money from the general public. All PACs are required by law to have treasurers, maintain records, and report their activities to federal and state agencies; and though not legally required to do so, the larger PACs often have additional officers, governing boards, and staff.

The term *political action committee* is itself an informal one that is not found in federal statutes or administrative code, and its origins lie in the American labor movement, when the Congress of Industrial Organization (CIO) established the CIO-PAC in 1943 and the National Citizen's Political Action Committee (NC-PAC) in 1944 (Cantor 1982, 2, 23). These early organizations were financial accounts created and administered by union officials but were separate from the union's general revenues. Rather than getting money for campaign contributions from union dues, the PAC funded its activities through voluntary contributions from members and officers, who presumably intended that their contributions be used for electoral purposes. This financial segregation was crucial, since the CIO formed its PACs to evade the 1943 wartime

prohibitions against contributions by labor organizations to federal candidates, prohibitions that were made permanent by the Taft-Hartley Act
of 1947 and that paralleled the 1907 ban on corporate contributions and
electoral activities. The ambivalence of the judiciary regarding the con-
stitutionality of these statutes and the weak enforcement of the laws by
the federal executive seemed to legitimize segregated funds as a form of
labor participation in federal elections, and the number of national labor
PACs grew to 17 by 1956 and 37 by 1968.

Although a few business and professional groups like the American
Medical Association and the National Association of Manufacturers had
established PACs in the 1960s, the great diffusion of PACs beyond the
labor movement only began after the enactment of the Federal Election
Campaign Act (FECA) of 1971 and its 1974 amendments. Partly in
response to the demands of labor leaders, the 1971 reforms clarified the
authority of unions and corporations to use general treasury funds to
establish and maintain "separate segregated funds," which could be used
to finance federal campaign contributions and expenditures (Epstein
1980, 112–14).[1] The advantages to corporations of establishing such
funds were then enhanced by the Watergate-inspired amendments of
1974, which created contribution limits that were much stricter for
individuals—the traditional channel for business money (Handler and
Mulkern 1982, 58–59)—than for most PACs. After the Federal Election
Commission issued a 1975 advisory opinion that laid out specific guide-
lines for corporations wanting to establish PACs and solicit employees
and stockholders, corporate PACs grew in number from 89 in 1974 to
433 in 1976;[2] and they continued their rapid expansion at least until 1980,
when they numbered 1,204 (Sabato 1984, 10–13). PACs also spread
among corporations without capital stock—such as membership associations and cooperatives—especially after the 1976 amendments to the
FECA authorized such organizations to solicit their members for voluntary contributions to a segregated fund (Cantor 1982, 48). Finally, independent or nonconnected PACs—that is, nonparty political committees
that were not formally affiliated with any parent organizations—began
to proliferate in the late 1970s, when their numbers swelled from 165 in
1978 to 574 in 1980. Thus, by the early 1980s, PACs had grown suffi-
ciently in number and variety to constitute the primary method by which
organized interest groups participated in national electoral politics.

The development of the PAC system has given us an opportunity to
ask several questions about the representative character of groups involved in national elections. Some of the questions I ask in this study are
descriptive, such as: What kinds of interests are represented by PACs,
and what kinds of interests are weakly represented or even excluded?

How does the pattern of representation found in the PAC system differ from that found in other forms of interest group advocacy? How does the PAC system respond to partisan change, and does it represent interests that are congruent with or antagonistic to the interests represented by the party system? I also address the more difficult, explanatory questions, such as: What accounts for the PAC system's particular scope and biases? And to what extent can these differences be attributed to the regulations governing PACs, campaign financing, and interest group involvement in elections?

The Significance of PACs

Answering these questions is important for three reasons. First, knowing why some groups form strong and effective PACs and others do not helps us understand the overall distribution of political interests in the PAC system. That distribution, in turn, influences the distribution of electoral advantages among candidates and may affect certain patterns of legislative behavior. Second, at the level of individual groups, having a PAC may affect a group's capacity to achieve its own political goals. If some groups cannot establish viable PACs—and if they face situations where campaign contributions are useful—then the PAC system selectively handicaps groups as they compete with one another for access and other political advantages. Third, a lot of effort, resources, and hope have been invested in campaign finance reform as a way of making national politics more representative of large numbers of citizens and less vulnerable to the dominance of wealthy individuals and economic institutions. If we find, however, that the laws do not have these effects, then that effort should be either abandoned or redirected.

It is not hard to see why PACs are important at the aggregate level—they constitute a large part of the federal campaign finance system. In the 1992 elections, they contributed $180.4 million to congressional candidates, over 27 percent of candidates' total receipts. House candidates were particularly reliant on PACs—which provided nearly one-third of their receipts in 1992—while PACs supplied Senate candidates with about one-fifth of their total funds. However, these figures surely understated the role of PACs. PAC officials also helped raise individual contributions by sponsoring fund-raisers or by "bundling" together individual donations before handing them over to a candidate (Sorauf 1995). PACs also spent money independently of candidates, often by creating advertisements and buying broadcast time in support or opposition to a candidate—but without any explicit coordination or consultation with the candidates themselves. In the 1992 elections, independent expenditures totaled $10.4 million. And some PACs carried out still other activities that did not show up as contributions to candidates, such as advocating the election or defeat of candidates to their members (i.e., internal communications), sponsoring get-out-the-vote drives, or giving money to party organizations.

The large role of PACs in financing national elections is important because money has significant effects in federal elections. Campaign spending increases a candidate's chances of winning (Goidal and Gross 1994; Green and Krasno 1988, 1990; Jacobson 1980, 1985, 1990; Kenny and McBurnett 1992), largely by allowing candidates to get their message across to potential voters (Jacobson 1992). The impact of money is thus strongest for candidates who are not already well known to citizens, such as challengers, open-seat candidates, and first-term incumbents. However, some studies show that even veteran incumbents reap significant, though smaller, advantages from campaign expenditures (Goidal and Gross 1994).

If the distribution of campaign money has important electoral consequences, knowing what kinds of interest groups form large, effective PACs will help us understand what kinds of candidates enjoy significant electoral advantages. This is so because different PACs—especially those representing different interests—contribute to different candidates. PACs usually give to candidates who support their interests and ideological views; and they vary in the importance they place on other factors—such as incumbency or assignments to specific legislative committees—when making contributions. Thus, biases in the PAC system ultimately affect how money is distributed among candidates. In particular, I argue in this study that because of selective barriers to PAC formation and viability, most PAC money comes from certain types of interest groups, while other types contribute very little (see chapters 3 through 5). Since these broad categories of groups are empirically correlated with policy interests and positions (chapter 6) and partisan support (chapter 7), these biases in the PAC system may have important effects on which candidates receive a lot of money and which do not—and thus on the electoral fortunes of candidates of different parties and issue positions.

The general contours of the PAC system may also influence the behavior of candidates. Most of the research on this issue deals with the effects of PAC contributions on roll-call voting in the U.S. House of Representatives; and though the results are mixed and often hard to reconcile (Smith 1995), they do suggest that aggregate contributions made by large numbers of PACs can have an important impact on legislative outcomes. Kau, Keenan, and Rubin (1982) analyzed roll-call votes on several economic issues in 1979 and found that contributions from broad categories of PACs—such as business, labor, and medical organizations—were often significant causal factors. Wilhite and Theilmann (1987) concluded that contributions from labor PACs as a whole had an important impact on floor votes sought by unions, measured by the AFL-CIO's ranking of congressional members. And Saltzman (1987) found that union contributions were directly related to prolabor votes in the House, while contributions from corporate PACs reduced members' probability of supporting labor. Thus, if PACs overrepresent some political interests and underrepresent others, there may be significant consequences for general patterns of legislative voting.

However, although large numbers of PACs may influence roll-call voting, campaign contributions appear to be a weak political resource from the point of view of individual groups. In studies analyzing the effects of a few PACs—such as those affiliated with a single organization or interest group—contributions often show little or no impact on floor votes. Grenzke (1989), for example, investigated contributions by PACs affiliated with ten major interest groups, including labor unions like the AFL-CIO and business associations like the Association of General Contractors. When she estimated the impact of each group's contributions on roll-call votes important to their interests, she found no significant effects. Chappell (1982) came to similar conclusions. After analyzing the effects of PAC contributions to House members on roll-call votes on seven issues between 1974 and 1977, he was "unable to conclude that contributions [had] a significant impact on voting decisions" (83). Like Grenzke's, his conclusions were based on several separate analyses, each involving a small number of PACs.

That a few PACs are unlikely to have much impact on floor votes makes sense in light of what political scientists have long known about these decisions—that they are typically dominated by members' ideological views, perceptions of their constituencies, personal voting histories, and party affiliations (Kingdon 1989). These are powerful forces that a few contributions are unlikely to override. However, some members might adjust their general voting patterns in ways that make it possible for them to draw on rich pools of potential contributors. They may, for example, put together a financial constituency early in their career that is compatible with their own ideological views and constituent interests—but that takes into account the macrolevel distribution of interest groups involved in the campaign finance system. It is therefore not unreasonable to expect that legislators' voting behavior is responsive to the aggregate distribution of PACs, even though it is hard to find evidence at the microlevel of specific quid pro quo relationships between legislators and individual PACs.

Yet even at the microlevel, small numbers of PACs may sometimes affect votes. If these effects occur, however, they appear to be contingent, in the sense that they occur in some circumstances but not in others. Some argue that PACs are more likely to sway legislators when members would otherwise have no strong preferences on an issue. Fleisher (1993), for example, found that PAC contributions from committees affiliated with defense contractors were related to pro-defense positions on House floor votes but that the magnitude of the effects varied considerably among members. Although ideology dominated the decisions of most members, he also discovered that PAC contributions had a much larger impact on members whose ideological views were middle-of-the-road. These effects were even stronger on "close" votes— that is, those decided by less than 50-vote margins in the House.

Other researchers have explored other contingencies. Davis (1993) also believed that PAC influence was constrained by the "wide array of competing pressures to which legislators are subject" (205). But rather than looking for different impacts among legislators, Davis looked for overall political situations where these competing pressures were weak. He argued that PAC contributions should have the greatest impact on roll calls where "issue visibility, partisanship, and opposition are limited, PAC contributors serve institutional sponsors concerned with a narrow range of policy, and legislators' ideological concerns are not activated" (208). He felt that these conditions were present in the 1970s and early 1980s on issues relating to the airline and railroad industries; and he claimed that PAC contributions from these industries did indeed affect votes on these issues. The effects of contributions appeared to be particularly strong for legislators who did not sit on committees that had jurisdiction over the issues, that is, legislators who probably had weaker predispositions about the vote. Stratmann (1991) made a similar argument. He estimated that contributions from agriculture PACs had a strong impact on floor votes on the 1985 farm bills, and he claimed that these effects were abetted by the fact that farm subsidy bills do not evoke a lot of opposition from voters or "numerous competing groups" (607).

These studies thus argue that the key to knowing whether contributions affect legislative votes lies in the kinds of issues in which PACs are engaged. PACs may exert a lot of influence over legislative votes if they organize around issues that do not elicit public attention, involve opposing groups and coalitions, or evoke intense partisan or ideological divisions. But if PACs are found where conflicts are intense, where the parties are divided, and where large publics are engaged, then their contributions are less likely to swing many decisions on the floor. By examining the correlates of PAC formation, we can determine whether PACs are even in the position to exercise the kind of unchecked influence often described in the accounts of journalists and reform groups— or whether their impact is usually circumscribed by a large number of competing political forces.

Although arguments about the contingent effects of contributions on legislative voting are not obviously unreasonable, they do run counter to a widespread observation about PAC contributions—that PACs usually contribute to legislative supporters, not fence-sitters (McCarty and Poole 1993; Grier and Munger 1993; Saltzman 1987; Poole and Romer 1985; Wright 1985; Chappell 1982; Welch 1982). If PACs are most likely to influence legislators with weak or contradictory predispositions, they apparently have not gotten the message. But rather than assuming that PACs are behaving irrationally, some researchers have reconsidered what PACs are trying to get. The most plausible argument along these lines is that contributions buy access—that is, that contributions encourage legislators to devote more time and energy to the group's concerns. What form this time and energy takes surely varies: it could range from a group receiving more extensive opportunities to make its concerns and arguments known to legislators or their staff up to encouraging legislators to become active coalition builders in support of a group's goals.

This argument has the virtue of conforming with what we already know about the legislative process. Legislators are pressed for time and exercise considerable discretion in deciding how to use it—what to pay attention to, what to ignore, and what activities to engage in (Bauer, Pool, and Dexter 1963). We also know that legislators' choices about how they spend their time and energy can affect policy processes. Policy arguments and interpretations are critical to interest groups in securing the support of legislators, and presenting this information effectively can take a lot of time (Smith 1984; Hansen 1991). Securing the *active* support of at least a few legislators is also very important, since a large part of coalition building involves legislators convincing their colleagues to support bills (Kingdon 1989; Matthews and Stimson 1975), because influence over committee and subcommittee decisions usually requires considerable work by members or their staff (Hall 1987; Fenno 1973; Johnson 1992), and because the growing complexity of the legislative process and fluidity of political coalitions means that groups are in even greater need of members of Congress to shepherd, or block, legislation

(Ornstein, Peabody, and Rohde 1993; Dodd and Oppenheimer 1993; Sinclair 1989).

The argument also makes sense of the tendency for PACs to give to sympathetic legislators. Campaign contributions by a few PACs are unlikely to lead members to switch their votes. Most floor votes are easy calls for legislators, since the factors most important to their decisions—personal policy preferences, the positions of their party leaders, the opinions of their constituents, and their own voting histories—reinforce each other in the vast majority of votes (Kingdon 1989). Yet there are many ways in which legislators can advocate the interests of their constituents or their own policy views, and it is not unreasonable for members of Congress to act as advocates for the subset of interests and views that also help to solve their fund-raising problems. By giving to already sympathetic legislators, interest groups may thus transform passive supporters into active policy advocates whose time and energy permit them to penetrate an increasingly complex and crowded legislative process.

Not much research has been done on the question of contributions and access, but the little that has been done generally supports the idea. Hall and Wayman (1990) found that PAC contributions were related to increased levels of committee participation by members of Congress on three fairly salient issues: dairy price supports, job training, and natural gas regulation. Committee participation included such activities as attending meetings, participating in votes, speaking, authoring legislation, offering amendments, or negotiating behind the scenes. PAC contributions had the effect of increasing the level of participation by members who were already predisposed to support the group's interests. Wright (1990) also found that contributions facilitated access. In his analysis of congressional committee votes, he discovered that a lobbying organization was more likely to contact a legislator who had received a contribution from its affiliated PAC. This was especially true in the Ways and Means Committee, where relations between lobbyists and legislators were more formal and less frequent, in contrast to a "subgovernment" committee like House Agriculture, where relations were informal and access was less difficult. Langbein (1986) also found evidence—albeit weak and indirect—that total PAC contributions to House incumbents were related to overall group access to legislators, measured by the time that House members spent in their offices with representatives of organized interest groups during a typical workweek. And in studies that relied heavily on interviews, several scholars reported that access was usually cited by PAC officers as their primary goal in making contributions, at least among committees affiliated with organizations involved in legislative lobbying (Clawson, Neustadtl, and Scott 1992; Sabato 1984).

Nearly all the studies of the effects of PAC contributions on recipients' behavior have focused on legislative processes. Yet PACs may exert at least as much influence, if not more, on recipients' activities in campaigns. Candidates must make so many decisions in campaigns and their choices are subject to such weak institutional constraints that we would expect that the need to raise campaign money would influence many of their activities, such as what issues to emphasize, which ones to ignore, and whose endorsements to seek. That would be particularly true for nonincumbents, who are usually strapped for money and have fewer options when seeking funds (Malbin 1993). Thus, PACs are probably able to—and some probably want to—exert some influence over the conduct of campaigns. Many citizen groups may use campaigns to bring issues before the public and increase voters' awareness of certain problems or potential solutions—awareness that not only serves the group's political aims but may also enhance the group's visibility and its capacity to mobilize more members. Groups may also use their perceived influence over the conduct of campaigns to create electoral lessons—that is, interpretations of how voters respond to various issues and policy positions. For example, pro-life PACs may use congressional elections to shape politicians' beliefs about the risks and advantages of taking sides on the abortion issue. They may do so by getting involved in congressional elections where the candidates are deeply and publicly divided over the issue and where their favored candidate is likely to win (Hershey and West 1983). If their candidate wins, other pro-life candidates may give the abortion issue greater emphasis in their campaigns, and pro-choice candidates may play down their positions. Because these interpretations spread quickly among politicians—even if groups only influence a few elections in a vivid way—the groups' participation in a few elections may affect the conduct of other campaigns and ultimately their access to legislators.

However, few of these conclusions are really firm. Although I have only referred to the better studies in a large and growing literature, even these analyses do not resolve all the problems of methodology and theory that threaten conclusions about the relationship between contributions, elections, and legislative behavior.[3] Nonetheless, it is reasonable to conclude that the aggregate distribution of PACs is very important in understanding the distribution of money and electoral advantage in national elections. This same macrolevel distribution also seems to be related to certain patterns of legislative voting. And contributions by small numbers of PACs appear to influence *some* legislative and campaign behaviors, in *some* circumstances.

These findings give us good enough reason to be concerned about biases in the PAC system—and so they justify this study. They also help us understand why interest groups might want to form PACs in some situations but not in others. In chapter 4, I develop a model of group incentives to establish a PAC, based on the following assumptions: (1) that campaign contributions are a weak political resource from the point of view of individual groups; (2) that this weakness limits the goals that groups can reasonably expect to attain—that is, that groups cannot expect to expand legislative coalitions by changing legislators' preferences on votes or affecting the overall outcome of legislative elections, though they may be able to increase access to sympathetic legislators by direct contributions or by intervening in selected elections and creating highly visible "examples" of how their organizations and the issues they advocate can influence specific campaigns and elections; (3) that because of contributions' weakness as a resource and because electoral participation is costly, interest groups make campaign contributions only when other resources (like strong and widespread constituency ties, institutionalized advocacy, and a political consensus in support of their aims) cannot ensure political success; and (4) that groups are most likely to think that these preferred resources are absent or inadequate in policy areas that are unsettled, conflictual, and institutionally complex. I argue that although many interest groups have little interest in forming PACs, motivational factors alone cannot account for the scope and bias of the PAC system. Many groups with apparently strong incentives do not establish strong, effective PACs, and this is largely due to the highly selective impact of institutional constraints.

Finally, the representativeness of the PAC system is worth studying even if we are unsure whether campaign contributions exert any effect over electoral or legislative processes. Many citizens, reform groups, and legislators are acting on assumptions regarding that representativeness and the capacity of our institutional reforms to shape it. Laws have been enacted based on practical—though not always well articulated—theories about the capacity of our institutions to enforce a particular structure in our politics. These practical theories may assume, for example, that we can produce a competitive, open, and broadly representative system of campaign financing based on a large number of small contributors or that we can purge our politics of "special" or "vested" interests simply by regulating their participation in campaigns and elections.[4] By examining the representativeness of the PAC system, the reasons for its particular biases, and its relations with other forms of interest group activity, we can determine whether these assumptions make any sense and therefore justify the costs of the reforms—costs that not only include administrative and enforcement activities but also encompass possible burdens on rights to free speech and assembly.

Analytical Strategy

How will these issues be addressed? Implicit in any statement about the representative character of a political institution is a comparison with some standard. Most studies of legislative representation, for example, compare the policy preferences or behavior of legislators with the preferences of their constituents or some part of their constituencies, such as those who identified with the legislator's party or who voted for the legislator in the last election. However, though a comparison between PACs and their "constituencies" may be useful for certain purposes, I have chosen to compare PACs with other systems of organized interests. Two methods of comparison are used for this study: the PAC system as a whole is compared to the system of membership associations—such as trade and professional associations, citizen groups, and unions—involved in national policy making; and membership associations that have affiliated PACs are compared to associations that do not.

These comparisons have several merits. Membership associations resemble PACs in the sense that they are organizations with a voluntary membership, even though the terms *members* and *voluntary* must be stretched to encompass a wide range of roles and behaviors. Both types of organization therefore face comparable problems of resource mobilization and political action. Although there are many other ways in which political interests are represented and advocated in American national politics—such as by corporate public affairs officers or Washington counsel, certain think tanks and other advocacy-type research organizations, and Washington representatives retained by specific state or local governments or service agencies—these forms of representation often do not confront the same problems of collective action that PACs and membership associations do.

But though PACs and membership associations face similar problems of mobilizing resources among persons who have some ability to withhold their support, they differ in important ways. First, PACs are a highly regulated form of political action, since they are involved in elections and campaign financing and come under the elaborate array of federal regulations affecting campaign contributions, the organization of political committees, and other aspects of their behavior and structure. In contrast, membership associations are much less regulated, except in such areas as antitrust and tax law; and though regulations may have some impact on the associations' capacity to mobilize resources and represent certain interests, they are still weak constraints when compared to the detailed restrictions applying to the behavior and internal structure of PACs. Comparing PACs with associations therefore allows us to study the consequences of regulating political activities.

Second, although associations engage in a wide variety of political activities in advocating their interests, PACs are almost exclusively involved in elections and campaign financing. A comparison between these two organizational systems may thus be useful in understanding the factors leading interest groups to try to achieve their political goals through elections or campaign contributions rather than by litigation, administrative lobbying, public education, or legislative lobbying. This sort of analysis is crucial because many analyses and proposed reforms focus on the electoral activities of interest groups as posing special problems for American politics—indeed, as creating problems of representation, or misrepresentation, that deserve special attention and perhaps more stringent regulation. But unless we understand more precisely how groups represented in electoral activities differ from or resemble interest groups involved in other forms of political advocacy, we cannot say whether the growth of the PAC system constitutes a major shift in the types of interests involved in national politics.

Third, the system of membership associations is a useful standard in assessing the range of interests represented by PACs because it is a much older system, one that has been evolving at least since the latter decades of the nineteenth century, and thus offers us a good basis for determining whether the PAC system represents a major departure from or a continuation of the more traditional system of interest representation. Success in mobilizing interests for collective action depends on a host of factors, but one of the most important is time (Olson 1982). A good standard for evaluating the scope and bias of the PAC system should therefore be a system that has had the time to develop with few exogenous interruptions—and thus to encompass a wide range of political interests, including those that face the greatest barriers to collective action.

The age and relatively unrestricted nature of the system of membership associations means that it is likely to include a wider range of interests than the PAC system, even though PACs and associations both face the same basic problems of collective action. Comparing the two systems therefore allows us to see which types of interests are well represented in the PAC system, which are poorly represented, and which are missing altogether. And if we have data on the various factors that might account for these differences—such as the impact of regulations on different groups or the importance of parties and elections for their goals—we can then analyze their causes. From this perspective, it is not necessary to assume that membership associations themselves constitute a perfectly representative collection of interest groups. Yet it is important for our analysis that membership associations encompass greater diversity with respect to the major types of interests represented, so that we can understand what types of groups that might be missing from the PAC system have shown themselves to be capable of vigorous and effective political action in other institutional settings.

Of course, this pragmatic approach cannot provide answers about the ultimate degree of bias in the PAC system, since it does not measure the amount of bias in the comparison group, that is, the system of membership associations. That some bias exists among associations may be taken for granted: surely their distribution would diverge at many points from the distribution of all collective interests found among all citizens. In fact, this bias is useful in some respects, since it helps to control for the *general* problems of collective action that interest groups face. For example, if collective action problems are particularly difficult for certain types of interest groups—whatever political activity they choose to engage in—then the differences that we find between PACs and membership associations are more easily attributable to obstacles or other factors unique to the PAC system, such as special motivations or institutional constraints.

These arguments might, however, suggest that a finding of bias among PACs is inevitable—that because PACs are specialized groups, comparisons with more general-purpose political organizations like membership associations will always show the former to be less inclusive. That may be true if we consider bias to be any situation where PACs are formed by a minority of all politically active organizations. But that is not the way bias is interpreted here. I use the term *bias* in a preliminary way in chapter 3 to summarize a situation where PACs are comparatively more common among groups that represent certain types of interests than among other groups. Yet for some purposes, even that sort of finding may not be viewed as important if the resulting pattern of PAC formation emerges solely from the different calculations of groups regarding the expected value of electoral participation. Thus, I develop a more refined notion of bias in chapter 4, such that a system displays bias where groups that have similar motivations to participate in elections or campaign financing—for example, because of the nature or level of political conflict they face—are *not* equally likely to have a PAC, especially when these inequalities vary across different types of political interests.

Unfortunately, this sort of precise description and diagnosis of the representative character of the PAC system is missing from the literature on PACs. Most discussions of the interests represented in the PAC system involve no comparisons at all. Such studies are usually descriptions of the marginal distribution of the interests represented by PACs or their institutional affiliations, and these descriptions typically use sui generis categories that make comparison with other forms of interest representation fairly difficult (Sabato 1984; Makinson 1990); and that is even true for the more sophisticated, theoretically informed classification schemes for PACs (Sorauf 1984a, 1984b) . Other studies make some attempt at comparison, but their conclusions are rather vague because the comparisons only involve aggregate data (Schlozman 1984). Finally, there are several studies on what types of corporations have affiliated PACs and what types do not (Grier, Munger, and Roberts 1991; Boies 1989; Masters and Keim 1985). Yet these analyses cannot evaluate the PAC system as a whole, since many PACs are not affiliated with corporations. Moreover, the comparison between corporations with PACs and those without does not reveal the unique *political* biases of the PAC system, since many of the corporations without PACs may have little or no political agendas. The comparison, in other words, may confound two biases: bias in the politicization of corporations, and bias in the use of PACs by corporations involved in politics.[5] To remedy these problems, this study compares PACs with other, explicitly political organizations; the comparisons use organization-level as well as aggregate data; and the analyses employ interest group classification schemes that are comprehensive and valid across different forms of group activity.

Data

The analyses in this study focus on PACs and membership associations in the period from 1979 to 1985, or roughly between the latter years of the Carter Administration and the beginning of the second term of the Reagan Administration. This particular time span was selected in part for opportunistic reasons. In 1980 and 1985, Professor Jack L. Walker of the University of Michigan conducted two comprehensive surveys of membership associations active in national policy making. The surveys were conducted by mail and included questions on a host of group characteristics, such as organization histories, resources, political activities, sources of financial support, memberships, staff backgrounds, policy positions, rela-

tions with various political institutions, and perceptions of political conflict. The data from these surveys were used in several important studies
of interest groups—including analyses of their formation and maintenance, their political activities, their relations with national political institutions, and their structure within policy communities—and culminated
in the posthumous publication of Professor Walker's *Mobilizing Interest
Groups in America* in 1991.

These surveys yielded two of the best pictures yet produced of
membership-based interest groups in American national politics, and
they therefore served our need in establishing standards for measuring
the representative character of the PAC system. To make these comparisons between PACs and membership associations, I created six data sets.
Two of these data sets were created by merging the survey data on
membership associations with concurrent campaign finance data on
PACs affiliated with the respondent organizations. For example, a data
set was created by determining whether each of the organizations that
responded in the 1980 Walker survey had registered any PACs with the
U.S. Federal Election Commission during the 1979–80 election cycle.[6] If
the association had one or more affiliated committees, the FEC data on
all those election committees were summarized and merged with the
association's survey-response data. The resulting data set allows us to
compare the associations that had affiliated PACs in 1980 with those that
did not and to analyze the relationships between various characteristics
of the association and its affiliated PACs, such as their number, size, and
partisanship in contributions. Similarly, a second data set was constructed by performing the same search and merger procedures for associations in the 1985 Walker survey, except for the fact that the relevant
PAC data came from the committees registered during the 1983–84
election cycle. The search procedures themselves were quite comprehensive, relying on a variety of governmental and commercial sources to
determine whether an association had an affiliated PAC.[7]

Although these two data sets are quite useful in helping us understand what kinds of associations have PACs and what kinds do not, they
suffer important limitations in generalizing about interest representation
among PACs, since most PACs are not connected with associations in
the two surveys. There are several reasons for this incomplete coverage.
First, many associations failed to respond to the surveys. The response
rate for groups in the 1980 survey was 62 percent, while the rate for
associations in the 1985 survey was 55 percent, meaning that about four
out of ten groups that were identified as having an interest in national
policy making were not in the surveys. Second, many associations and
labor unions, even though some of them have PACs, were not included

in the original samples. Some of them may have been too small, too sporadically involved in national politics, or overly local or regional in their base to be included in the national surveys; or there may also have been oversights in the survey samples themselves. Third, many PACs are not affiliated with the types of organizations surveyed. The surveys did not include corporations, which typically establish almost half of all PACs. Nor did they include independent or "nonconnected" PACs, which are committees not affiliated with any association or other parent organization.

To remedy this problem of coverage, I used two other data sets that included *all* nonparty political committees registered with the FEC in the 1979–80 and 1983–84 election cycles. In the aggregate, these two data sets can be compared in the aggregate to the two surveys of membership associations to measure differences in their representative qualities. But to make these comparisons, we need to use a classification scheme that is applied consistently in all four data sets. I thus coded all registered PACs according to the typology of occupational roles, a classification scheme of interest groups derived from their membership base. Because this typology was used to great advantage in analyzing membership associations—particularly as it delineated important differences in the sources of support they relied on to establish and maintain themselves—I believed that it would also be useful in understanding the biases and special characteristics of PACs. Details regarding this typology are discussed in later chapters, but it should be emphasized that the use of this coding scheme means that the PAC system can be directly compared to other forms of interest representation, and that we thereby avoid the problem of using different measures for different systems. The information sources and procedures used to code these data are described in appendix B.

From these four basic data sets, two others were constructed. First, the PAC-affiliation data obtained for the 1980 and 1985 Walker surveys were used to construct a similar merging of PAC information with association data in the 1980–85 Walker panel study, which included all associations that Walker surveyed in 1980 and was able to resurvey in 1985. Second, the two data sets including all PACs registered in 1979–80 and 1983–84 were merged. The resulting data set gives us a panel study of PACs, including their financial activities and their membership base according to the typology of occupational roles.

Taken together, these data cover the period from 1980 to 1985, a period that has important advantages. By the 1980 elections, the PAC system finished its transitional stage, during which corporations, associations, and other organizations that had been involved in elections completed the transfer of their electoral programs to the newly formalized legal mechanism, the "separate segregated fund," or PAC. Thus, the 1980 elections were probably the first time in which the PAC constituted the primary method by which interest groups participated in elections. Much of the growth among PACs before 1980 was attributable not to a real expansion in the number of groups or institutions participating in elections but rather to a formalization of interest group involvement in elections (Epstein 1980).

If the time of our initial observations was fortuitous, the time of our second observations was no less so. Our readings of the PAC and interest group systems span a particularly volatile and divisive political period, as the Reagan Administration moved aggressively to change long-standing policies in many areas, including housing, economic regulation, education, environmental regulation, transportation, defense, and others. It was a time when many interest groups that had aligned themselves with the Democratic Party or its programs felt threatened, a time when electoral and partisan change penetrated interest group politics more than it had for many years. Observing the changes among PACs and other forms of interest representation thus gives us a chance to see how these larger political forces affect group strategies and resources.

Preview of Chapters

I argue in chapter 2 that the problems of collective action imply not only that certain types of interest groups are likely to remain latent, unorganized, or ineffective but also that certain types of support coalitions are hard to mobilize in support of a collective endeavor. In particular, coalitions of small contributors are extremely difficult to organize. Yet the regulations and institutional conditions affecting interest group participation in elections and campaign financing force groups to rely on such contributors. The result is a small, narrowly based system of interest groups involved in campaign financing and elections, since few groups are able to mobilize effectively under these legal constraints. The groups that are able to overcome these barriers are those that have direct access to institutions—such as corporations, unions, and associations—including their patronage, benefits, and power. Thus, the system of groups involved in financing campaigns is likely to have little autonomy, in the sense that it is unable to extend the institutional basis of politics and instead depends on access to existing institutions. The smallness of the PAC system, its limited scope, and its lack of autonomy are described in chapter 3. Chapter 4 continues the argument by showing both the importance and the limits of motivational factors in accounting for which groups do or do not have PACs, while chapter 5 demonstrates that institutional constraints interact with motivational factors to inhibit certain kinds of groups from establishing committees. Chapter 6 indicates that the selective effects of these institutional constraints produce considerable bias in the representation of policy preferences; and chapter 7 shows that the same constraints create an unbalanced system with respect to the political parties. These findings are applied to discussions of campaign finance reform in chapter 8. In general, I argue that the current regulations governing group participation in elections and campaigns inhibit or exclude many of the support coalitions that have been critical in creating a broadly representative system of interest groups *outside* the electoral arena, and that the campaign finance reforms, which sought to establish more of a "grass roots" style of politics, actually produced greater inequality and rigidity in the representation of interests. I argue that it is not only ironic that the most regulated form of political activity is among the least inclusive. It is also common sense.

CHAPTER 2

Collective Action, Institutions, and Bias in the PAC System

A central goal of the campaign finance reforms enacted in the wake of the Watergate scandals was to eliminate the corrupting influence of very large contributors, like those that had played such prominent roles in supporting Nixon's reelection campaign in 1972. Large contributions were attacked as creating a politics of "barter and purchase" and undermining egalitarian ideals. As one of the strongest proponents of reform argued, "All citizens should have equal access to decision-making processes of government, but money makes some citizens more equal than others" (Gardner 1972, 55). By establishing a new system of campaign financing with limits on giving and spending by individuals, clearer restrictions on corporations and labor unions, partial public funding, full disclosure, and vigorous enforcement, the reforms seemed intended not only to "eliminate corruption and the appearance of corruption" (*Buckley* v. *Valeo* 1976) but also to establish a new sort of political system, a broadly representative one based on widespread participation by small donors, volunteering their money for the advancement of broad public purposes.

It is, however, impossible to create a broadly representative system of campaign financing through such restrictions, if by "representative" one means a system that effectively organizes a large, diverse, and unbiased collection of the interests that have significant stakes in American national elections. Small individual contributors, acting out of purely political motives, simply cannot provide enough money to support most political interests, particularly when those interests seek to achieve their goals in increasingly costly electoral arenas. The result of the legal restrictions is therefore an undermobilization of political interests involved in national elections; and the groups that succeed in mobilizing resources for electoral activities are a biased subset of all groups with stakes in national elections, since they are the groups that the regulations have selectively allowed to secure support from other sources.

The Problem of Collective Action

The problems created by the restrictions on contributions become clear when the laws are viewed in light of certain fundamental difficulties in mobilizing support for political action. If leaders try to raise money for their political organizations—including PACs, which seek political influence by funding campaigns—Mancur Olson (1965, 1982) has argued that they will not win much support by advocating the common interests of a large group of citizens and soliciting support from those who would gain from the organization's political success. The problem lies in the incentives for members of the group to withhold their contributions to the organization and act as free riders. If the success or failure of the group is little affected by a member's participation and if the political goods that interest groups seek cannot be feasibly withheld from those who do not participate, so that the fruits of a successful lobbying or election campaign are enjoyed by all group members if they are enjoyed by any, it would not be cost-effective for an individual to contribute more than a trivial amount to the political effort. The incentives are the same for group members whatever their expectations about the behavior of others. If they expect other members not to contribute, they should keep their money and avoid playing the sucker. But if they expect other members to behave irrationally and support an effort to achieve their common goals, they should withhold support and hope for a political free lunch (Hardin 1982, 25–28). Assuming that citizens' decisions to participate in group politics reflect these cost-benefit calculations, such groups will fail to sustain political organizations advocating their common interests.

The force of this theory comes from its generality. The argument does not depend on the diversity of interests among members and usually does not depend on the stakes that each person perceives in the political struggle. The incentives are strong for individuals to act as free riders even if the members agree completely on political goals and even if each person expects to gain a lot from the group's political success. What is crucial for the argument is the small expected impact of each person's participation. When one's own contribution counts as no more than a drop in the bucket, there is little in the way of rational (i.e., instrumental) calculations to motivate even a passionately interested group member. To the extent that individual contributions are small—relative to what is needed to achieve political success—the incentives not to contribute are strong.

There are, however, circumstances when political organizations can be expected to form and survive. If a person has so much at stake in the political outcome that he or she is willing and able to make a large contribution and if that contribution is large enough to have a significant marginal effect on the success of the political effort, it is reasonable for that person to contribute to an organization advocating his or her political interests. Small groups may fit these conditions. In a concentrated industry—such as automobile manufacturing—the failure of any one firm to support a political effort would mean a large reduction in the amount of resources available for political action. Note, however, that it is important not only that the group be small but also that the contributions be "large" relative to what is needed in a particular political system to achieve its goals. Even when a group is small, members may find that their participation would be of little utility if, for whatever reasons, they were individually unable to make contributions large enough to have a perceptible effect on the group's chances for success.

The same logic suggests that groups with "large members"—or members who would receive a very large share of the anticipated benefits of collective action—may be able to secure adequate support for effective political action, regardless of the size of the overall group. A very large corporation may expect to reap such large benefits from a change in the regulations affecting the entire industry that it would be willing to absorb all or most of the costs of an effective lobbying campaign, even if the industry as a whole is composed of many firms. (An example might be Microsoft in the personal computer software industry.) The lesser firms will not contribute, since their stakes in the outcome would be so small that the largest contributions they would be willing to make would have an imperceptible impact on the political struggle; and they expect in any case that the larger firms will foot the bill. The small exploit the large, as the latter are forced to accept responsibility by virtue of their unique capacity to make a significant and gainful contribution (Sandler 1992, 54–58; Olson and Zeckhauser 1966).

Groups may also be mobilized for political action if contributions from members are induced by the manipulation of selective rewards or punishments and if the total contributions provide enough revenues to pay for the selective incentives and leave a surplus for political activities (Sandler 1992, 58–60). Olson calls this organizational strategy the "by-product theory" of groups, which means that the political activities of the organization are incidental to the transactions involving private goods supplied by the organization in exchange for contributions from individual members. Political activities are essentially a way of using the organization's slack resources. A political party or interest group may, for example, sponsor a rock concert (performed by politically sympathetic musicians who charge less than their usual rate), charge admission, and use the profits for campaign contributions; an organization seeking support from the elderly may offer discounts on drugs, insurance, travel, or other consumer goods that appeal to their target population and then use the profits for its lobbying activities; or a professional society may support a policy research and advocacy staff from revenues produced from conferences providing members with unique opportunities to develop contacts and reputations with their peers.

The Special Roles of Patrons and Institutions

These two solutions to the problem of collective action—that is, the "large member" and "selective incentive" methods—form the basis of other, more elaborate strategies for mobilizing support. Reliance on political "patrons" is one variant in the use of selective incentives to elicit support for political activities, though the concept shares some characteristics of the "large member " idea. The term *patron* refers to a special supporter or financial guardian of the organization, a person who assumes responsibility for paying or underwriting a large share of an organization's costs, usually in exchange for special status or control over its activities (Walker 1983, 1991; Cigler and Nownes 1995; also see Friedman 1962, 17, 168). Patrons need not be individuals; they may be corporations, government agencies, churches, private foundations, or other institutions. They may have personal stakes in the group's political goals, though unlike a "large member," those stakes are not sufficient to justify the large sums they in fact provide. Their motivation comes not only from the gains of making a significant and perceptible contribution to the group's success—like a large member—but also from gaining a privileged position within the organization, either control over the organization's goals or tactics, or special recognition of the patron's role in supporting the organization and its mission. A private foundation, for example, may be willing to support a black civil rights group if the group focuses its agenda on the problems of inner-city schools; or a wealthy individual may help establish an environmental group in exchange for that group's commitment to rely on public education to achieve its political goals rather than on protests, lobbying, or electioneering. These privileges and honors are selective benefits that group leaders may distribute in close proportion to the amount of support that patrons provide, yet these particular benefits differ from many other sorts of selective goods. They raise special problems for the organization because they are "positional goods," goods that lose value as they are more widely shared (Hirsch 1977). Special privileges, honors, and powers decline in value—and in their capacity to elicit support—precisely as they become less special, less distinctive, less in a class by themselves. The extreme depletability of such benefits means that organizations have only a few special honors or unique decisional roles to parcel out, and that the number of patrons for a particular organization can never be large.

The logic of collective action also implies that a critical ingredient for the mobilization of political interests is support from or affiliation with an institution serving purposes other than political representation, such as a firm, government agency, or nonprofit organization (Salisbury 1984). These institutions facilitate mobilization not only by acting as patrons or large members—since they can often act as unified "persons" despite their size and complexity—but also by making it possible for Olson's by-product theory of groups to work. This latter function is important because the by-product theory is incomplete, in the sense that it does not state the sufficient as well as the necessary conditions for collective action. Although Olson's by-product theory has led some scholars to look for the origins of political organizations in political entrepreneurs—who are viewed as having the capacity to create autonomous political organizations out of the "profits" generated by the supply of selective benefits to group members—this bootstrapping model of political organization does not explain how any "profits" are generated or why they are used for political ends. These questions may, however, be answerable if one interprets the by-product theory as a kind of political piggybacking onto existing institutional structures rather than as a general formula for making political organizations from scratch.

We can begin to see the importance of institutions by recognizing that the manipulation of selective goods to support political goals really depends on some sort of market imperfection, constraint, or intervention— some special advantage that the political organization enjoys in supplying selective or private benefits (see Olson 1965, 133 n. 2; Hardin 1982, 33). If a political organization exchanges consumer or other private goods for support, firms that do not divert resources to political activities can provide the same goods or services at a lower cost and force the organization to lose market share or reduce the surplus available for politics. One important way to overcome this problem is to secure governmental grants of power over a class of private activities, and these powers are typically delegated to institutions. Union shop laws, occupational licensing procedures, and professional and institutional accreditation methods give control to particular organizations over entry into jobs, professions, or industries; and that control can be used by union or professional organizations to elicit support in the form of membership dues. Governments may also provide market advantages by means of direct or indirect subsidies—such as tax exemptions for nonprofit organizations—that allow these institutions to build up a surplus that may be used for political activities or that permit them to supply members with publications, insurance benefits, and other selective benefits at a lower cost than can profit-motivated firms.

Although many economic institutions do not have publicly enforced protections or subsidies, they can often generate a surplus to spend on political activities, since most are organized to produce and supply private goods efficiently, and since few of them actually face perfectly competitive markets. Indeed, behavioral studies suggest that even small firms in fairly competitive markets, such as retail stores, can produce a considerable amount of organizational "slack" (Cyert and March 1963). However, it is probably much more difficult for an organization that is primarily political in purpose—or a political "entrepreneur" without an existing institutional base—to produce and supply private goods to members and rake off a portion of their contributions for political purposes. Political entrepreneurs cannot easily acquire the organizational efficiency or market power required to produce an adequate surplus without access to a well-developed economic institution and its resources. The American Association of Retired Persons, for example, one of the most successful examples of a politically active membership organization that built up support on the basis of selective benefits, did not develop its benefits package by itself but instead relied on the market power already acquired by the Continental Casualty Company and the National Retired Teachers Association. It exploited a significant market inefficiency by focusing on the unmet insurance needs of the elderly; it required a large investment by at least one individual patron; and it only slowly and cautiously built up its political activities (Pratt 1976, 89–90). Even such success stories demonstrate that creating a political organization by supplying selective incentives is an extremely difficult task.

Institutions also have advantages in mobilizing political interests that go well beyond their strength in the market. Economic, governmental, and social institutions may be viewed as elaborate structures of relationships that may be used to apply selective benefits or injuries in order to elicit contributions to political causes. Peer pressures within a labor union or a corporation's management team, implicit threats or promises of reward by a corporation's leadership to its employees, or even a psychological identification with the institution and its role in the polity may all be conceived as a kind of social surplus—or power—that can be used to draw contributions from members in support of the institution's political activities. Institutions also reduce the costs of mobilization by allowing group leaders to exploit existing information networks, while noninstitutionalized interests must absorb all the costs of communicating with and getting the attention of potential supporters.

Finally, institutions can often draw on a ready base of specialized knowledge about public policies and problems—knowledge acquired by persons who have an occupational interest and responsibility in dealing with such areas—and can thus exploit a kind of joint production efficiency in the generation of knowledge about public issues. For example, while a citizens' environmental group may have to hire a scientific consultant to estimate the dangers of a new manufacturing process, the manufacturer and its trade association can draw on their own ample supply of scientists and analysts in developing competing estimates. Or professionals who serve certain clients through their work in government agencies or nonprofit organizations—such as gerontologists and social workers who serve the elderly poor—may also use their expertise and contacts for purposes of political advocacy by articulating the problems and public significance of their clients. Unlike the typical interpretation of Olson's by-product theory as suggesting the possibility of an autonomous political organization that maintains itself through essentially private-market transactions (see, for example, Moe 1980; Salisbury 1969), a more reasonable conception is to suppose that political activities grow out of institutions whose structures generate politically useful expertise as a by-product of their work, whose systems represent powerful social relations and communication networks that can be used to elicit member contributions, or whose market niches are such that surplus resources are routinely produced.

Institutions also solve another problem confronted by interest groups seeking to use selective incentives to mobilize political support. Underlying the by-product thesis is the assumption that the distribution of citizens' tastes for private goods will at least roughly correlate with the distribution of their preferences on public issues. If no such correspondence exists, it would be hard for interest group leaders to generate a surplus and use it for effective political action. A group of citizens who share public viewpoints yet have diverse private tastes would not allow a political organization to enjoy the efficiencies of scale and specialization needed to create a surplus from the production and distribution of private goods. Nor would the organization have an easy time mobilizing resources for effective political action if it sought support from citizens who had the same tastes in private goods but disagreed with one another on public issues. Conflicting views among group members on public affairs undermine the legitimacy of the organization's claims to represent its members, and competition with firms providing similar private goods creates incentives for the organization to play down its political activities so as not to alienate any customers.

Institutions reduce the problems caused by uncorrelated preferences on public and private goods by creating greater correspondence. Economic institutions, like corporations and labor unions, not only control private benefits that can be supplied or withheld from their members. They are also important units in public policy. All those who work within a particular union, profession, or corporation are similarly affected by at least some policies, thereby inducing greater agreement on public affairs. Agreement is enhanced by socialization within the institution, growing out of members' interactions with each other and their shared experiences. Finally, institutions of all kinds tend to recruit members selectively and create some homogeneity within their ranks.

Institutions also facilitate political mobilization by concentrating responsibility for political issues into the hands of a smaller number of persons. Authority and responsibility within institutions can thus create small interest groups out of large ones. By organizing a large number of persons into hierarchical structures of nested groups, institutions can exploit the characteristics of small groups and concentrate responsibility for collective goals at many different levels (Sandler 1992, 60–61). Institutions, in other words, are often composed of small "chunks," within which the smaller number of persons, the more intense interactions among members, and the stronger selective incentives controlled by the subgroups help to focus responsibility for collective aims. The frequent interaction among persons within these chunks may even give rise to "conventions" of cooperation that are generalized and applied to a wide variety of activities, including various forms of political participation (Hardin 1982). As each chunk, or subgroup, forms a unit for collective action at higher levels, the hierarchical structure may be used to overcome the free-rider problem.

This capacity of institutions to emphasize collective goals through organizational structures also helps to overcome an important deficiency in the by-product theory: the fact that there is nothing to compel a group leader to use profits generated from the provision of selective benefits for collective political purposes. A group's leadership might just as easily plow the profits back into producing more selective benefits or even skim off any surplus for the leadership's private needs. In the absence of any structural factors enforcing a focus on the collective or political needs of the group, the by-product theory ultimately depends on happenstance—the probability that the leaders' personal motives and interests lead them to devote resources to political rather than nonpolitical purposes. However, institutions can provide the missing incentives by forcing the leaders to be responsible and accountable for the group's long-term collective goals. A similar function is performed by political patrons or large members, whose motivations are either based on or strongly related to the group's collective purposes, and whose contributions to the group are large enough to make the group's leadership accountable to their demands. Thus, an institutional base, patrons, or large members are generally needed to complete the by-product theory and overcome its dependence on the private motives and interests of the group leaders.

These elaborations on the theory of collective action imply that effective collective action is unlikely unless an interest group can rely on large members or patrons for support or unless it can rely on one or more institutions to mobilize support among small contributors or members. Since patrons and large members are large contributors—in the sense that each must contribute enough to have a perceptible effect on the group's expected political success—a corollary of this conclusion says that where large contributors are not available and the group must depend on small donations, its organizational success depends on whether it can exploit the power and resources of an economic, governmental, or social institution for political purposes. Conversely, a group's prospects for organization are less dependent on access to institutions if it can draw support from a wide variety of patrons or large members. Olson's basic argument means that it is nearly impossible for an interest group without an institutional base or affiliation to establish and maintain a strong and enduring political organization by securing all its support from small contributors. But as I argue in the next section of this chapter, though this insight has been evolving for nearly three decades, its full implications for the design and reform of political institutions have not been taken seriously, nor have they been fully understood.

In empirical studies, we can see the importance of patrons, large members, and institutions in supporting political action. Salisbury (1984), for example, found that institutions were nearly ubiquitous in his surveys of interest representatives in Washington. And in one of his most comprehensive discussions, Jack Walker (1991, 185–96) classified most forms of interest representation in the U.S. into three categories: (1) trade or other occupationally based organizations, such as corporations and farm associations, that represent their own professional interest; (2) social movements, such as the women's movement, that represent citizen or nonoccupational interests; and (3) third-party representatives, such as those found among many groups interested in policies affecting children or handicapped people, who claim to represent and advocate the interests of other persons, typically people whose physical, social, or economic status makes it hard for them to represent themselves. Walker's analyses show that patrons and institutions are critical in each of these three modes of representation. The first and third modes clearly depend on the existence of an occupational base in economic or governmental institutions. That base not only helps to define the group and facilitate communication and the development of shared preferences in public and private goods but also allows political efforts to draw directly on institutional resources and occupational expertise and thus to rely on institutions as political patrons.

Yet even social movements show considerable dependence on patrons and institutions. Groups representing emergent citizen interests often depend a great deal on support from large gifts from individuals, foundation grants, and government sponsorship of conferences, contracts, or other forms of support (Cigler and Nownes 1995). The modern women's movement, for example, owes much to the National Organization for Women, which grew directly out of government patronage through its sponsorship of the President's Commission on the Status of Women in 1961 and the fifty state commissions set up in its aftermath (Freeman 1975, 52–53); and women's organizations, despite their large memberships, still get much of their funding from government grants and contracts, corporations, and especially foundations (Gelb and Palley 1987, 39–48). The importance of patrons is even greater among groups that face important barriers to political participation. As Henry Pratt concluded in his study of the elderly as a political constituency, "the initial push toward what later was to become a true social movement . . . [came] not from the aged themselves but from government agencies and officials whose work obliged them to deal regularly with an aging clientele" (1976, 41). Although exceptions may exist (see Bosso 1995), political organization is very difficult without access to individual or institutional patrons able to absorb a large share of the costs of political action or without a preexisting base of institutions to structure, facilitate, or support political mobilization.

Reforms, Institutions, and Collective Action

The theory of collective action therefore implies that it is hard to organize political interest groups by relying on the voluntary actions of small and independent contributors, where "small" means contributions that have an imperceptible or nearly imperceptible impact on the provision of the collective good. Successful political organization usually depends on the group's ability to draw on large contributors—whether they be patrons or large members—or on its capacity to exploit institutional structures or resources to elicit small contributions.

These conclusions, however, diverge rather sharply from the ideas that underlie campaign finance reforms and other regulations affecting interest group involvement in U.S. elections. The reforms of the 1970s were clearly an attempt to establish a campaign financing system based on the donations of small individual contributors, by means of public disclosure, ceilings on contributions, and other measures. As concurrent changes in American politics and government inflated the costs of success in elections and policy processes, these ceilings were effectively lowered, diminishing even further the potential impact of each contribution. Although there are ways of evading these limits, these institutional changes have generally prevented any individual contribution—either to or in behalf of a political interest group involved in elections—from having a perceptible impact on the group's success. This enforced system of small contributions magnifies the importance of access to institutional resources for the mobilization of political interests; and since this access is itself highly regulated and very selective, many political interests are prevented from organizing effectively for electoral action, so only a limited and biased system of interest groups is involved in national elections and campaigns.

Although legal limits on the size of contributions are hardly new to American politics, their effective enforcement is. A 1940 amendment to the Hatch Act forbade any individual from contributing more than $5,000 to a national committee or federal candidate. Yet contributors could channel nearly unlimited amounts of money to candidates or political committees by giving to many state or local groups that would then pass the money along in the organization's name (Mutch 1988, 32–35; Bauer and Kafka 1984, chap. 1, 5; Heard 1960, 347–48). Even when contributors breached the ceilings, their violations were rarely detected or enforced, since the disclosure requirements were incomplete (covering only election years) and generally ignored, and the Justice Department initiated few legal actions (Mutch 1988, 24–29; Heard 1960, 357–67). Large contributors—and the interest groups they supported—faced few constraints and were probably encouraged in this complex, informal, *sub-rosa* system of campaign financing; and the low costs of congressional campaigns before the 1960s made it even easier for a single individual or institution to make a contribution large enough to have a significant electoral effect.

However, this system was largely destroyed by the mid-1970s by the enactment of fairly comprehensive and enforceable ceilings on contributions. These restrictions constituted the core of the Federal Election

Campaign Act amendments of 1974, which limited individual contributions to $5,000 per year when given to "multicandidate" political action committees, $1,000 per election when given directly to federal candidates, and $20,000 per year when provided to the national parties. Individual citizens were also prohibited from contributing more than $25,000 per year to all candidates and committees. Political parties and most PACs were allowed to contribute up to $5,000 to a candidate per election, though party committees could also make coordinated expenditures of higher amounts. Just as important, these new contribution limits were made effective by treating affiliated committees as one for the purpose of contribution limits, by defining contributions broadly to include many forms of support, by requiring comprehensive record keeping and disclosure of contributions, and by establishing an agency, the Federal Election Commission, to collect disclosure reports, make them available to the public, and enforce the regulations. Finally, the reforms have discouraged some large contributors by giving the media and public interest groups a better opportunity to publicize their activities. The laws require political committees to collect considerable information on all persons whose contributions exceed $200 in a calendar year, including the contributor's name, address, and occupation and the name of his or her employer; and these reports are filed with the Federal Election Commission and made available to reporters at virtually all major newspapers and wire services, which frequently publish stories on candidates and their war chests. Although the potential for publicity has not dissuaded the most strongly motivated contributors from making large donations, it has made such contributions politically riskier and less frequent.

The laws and enforcement practices of the FEC leave some room for large contributors, but despite the claims by some journalists and watchdog groups that "fat cats" have returned to dominate American campaigns, the channels for large contributions are of limited use to most political interest groups. Surely the most widely used exception was the one created by the Supreme Court in *Buckley* v. *Valeo* (1976), when it overturned the FECA's limits on candidates' use of their own money in campaigns as an unconstitutional restriction on free speech. Although only about 6 percent of the funds raised by congressional candidates between 1980 and 1990 came from their own pockets (Jacobson 1992, 65), that figure understates the electoral importance of personal funds, since such funds are more widely used by nonincumbents, who often take out personal loans that they hope to repay from contributions from other sources after the election. Nonetheless, these personal contributions rarely solve the broader problems of group mobilization. The patron must be the candidate, a role that many political patrons are unwilling or unable to accept; and many candidates are not interested in representing or mobilizing a particular group or set of political interests. Ross Perot may have performed the classic role of political patron in 1992 with his strong issue orientation and his establishment of a new citizens' organization, United We Stand America, but his emphasis on political mobilization is hardly commonplace among candidates.

Most potential group patrons or large members are also unable to do much with the "soft money" exception enacted in the 1979 amendments to the FECA. To strengthen state and local party organizations and grassroots activities, contributions to these organizations were exempted from federal ceilings if the money was used for volunteer registration activities and get-out-the-vote drives, as well as for campaign materials, such as bumper stickers or brochures. These exemptions have opened up a loophole through which many large contributions have been funneled into federal campaigns (*NJ*, 17 October 1992, 2350; Drew 1983). Some states allow their party organizations to accept large contributions and even contributions from corporate or union treasuries, and these contributions have been used to support presidential candidates and some Senate races. For example, the Archer-Daniels-Midland Corporation gave over $1 million to the GOP for the 1992 elections, and almost $300,000 to the Democratic Party (Makinson and Goldstein 1994). Although federal laws prohibit these funds from being used in support of specific federal campaigns—or from being used for advertising or other nongrassroots activities—there are obviously opportunities for spillover effects, such as when a bumper sticker or brochure says, "Vote Republican"; and due to fairly lax disclosure and allocation rules, it may be easy in some states to take advantage of these opportunities (Boyle and Reyes 1986). Yet these channels are not very useful for most interest groups and group patrons. The money goes to the party, while most groups want to give to specific candidates; the funds typically benefit presidential candidates rather than congressional candidates, the usual target of most interest group activities; and soft money does not allow large contributors to act as group patrons, that is, persons or institutions that absorb the high costs of mobilizing new political interests within the electoral system.

The effects of the reforms on reducing the importance of large contributions in federal campaigns have been reinforced by the growing costs of federal elections. Average spending by congressional candidates has grown roughly fivefold since the current system of contribution limits went into effect in 1976; mean expenditures in House campaigns rose from $73,316 in 1976 to $409,836 in 1992, while average spending in Senate races increased from $595,449 to $2,891,488 over the same period (Ornstein, Mann, and Malbin 1994). These costs have grown in part because of the continuing decline of party loyalties in the electorate since the mid-1960s, a trend that has made the campaign more important by forcing candidates to build personal coalitions without the aid of a strong political base (Alford and Brady 1993). At the same time, the means by which candidates reach voters have become ever more costly, as autonomous candidate organizations have replaced party organizations and adopted expensive services and technologies like television advertising, polling, direct mail, computerized phone banks, professional staffs, and public relations consultants (Luntz 1988; Ginsberg 1984). The rapidly rising cost of television time has hit Senate campaigns especially hard, since Senate candidates typically spend four out of every ten dollars on electronic advertising (Morris and Gamache 1994). Winning elections has also become particularly expensive for candidates trying to unseat congressional incumbents, due to the growth of institutional resources available to members of Congress—such as personal staff, in-house media resources, franking privileges, and casework—and of the willingness of members to use them (Jacobson 1992). In the few races where a House incumbent actually lost in 1992, challengers spent an average of $444,359, up from $144,720 in 1976.

The legal limits on contributions, the greater publicity of campaign financing, and the increasing costs of electoral success have thus created a new institutional context in which large contributions to candidates or electorally active interest groups are less and less feasible. Although Richard Nixon was able to get most of the money he needed for his first congressional race in 1948 from a small circle of wealthy California businessmen (Morris 1990), and though Lyndon Johnson was able to rely so heavily on the Brown brothers to sustain his own campaigns in his early congressional career (Dallek 1991), such small, intimate financial coalitions are no longer possible, even in House elections. PACs are also unable to rely on large contributors, if "large" means a contributor whose support makes a significant difference in the group's chances for success. According to one study, if an individual gave a PAC the entire $10,000 that he or she may contribute during a single election cycle and if the committee gave that entire amount to an incumbent candidate, the individual's contribution would have increased the candidate's chances of winning by only 0.04 percent.[1] Even if the contribution were made to a nonincumbent candidate—whose expenditures yield a larger electoral impact—the $10,000 would have only increased his or her chances of winning by 0.10 to 0.35 percent. Yet even these small effects must be qualified. These estimates are based on 1980 data and are surely diminished by inflation. More important, however, helping a single candidate is hardly enough to ensure an interest group's political success. The declining powers of committee chairs and party leaders over recent decades have produced a more complex and decentralized policy process in the American Congress, a trend that means an interest group seeking power over national policies through campaign contributions must influence the election or secure the support of a larger number of legislators.[2] The ceilings on campaign contributions to PACs and candidates— particularly in the context of increasingly expensive campaigns and policy processes of greater and greater complexity—have thus sharply reduced the potential importance of any one contributor and have forced interest groups wanting to participate in elections to raise their money in "small" amounts that have no perceptible effect on the group's overall success or failure.

Although individuals can only give small contributions to PACs, interest groups can spend considerable sums to advance their political aims. A PAC can only give $5,000 per election per candidate or $10,000 over the entire election cycle. But the limit is not as restrictive at the group level, since there are no limits on the amount that a PAC can give in the aggregate, while individuals are limited to $25,000 per year. Moreover, a single interest group—such as an industry—may have many PACs, including corporate committees, trade association PACs, and even nonconnected committees supported by industry executives. An interest group can therefore exert a significant impact on elections and policy processes that individual members of the group typically cannot.

The limited effects of an individual's contribution to a group's electoral activities prevent the group from relying on certain solutions to the problem of collective action. A large member, of course, must be free to make a large contribution. Limits on the size of contributions reduce the resources available to the interest group by preventing the large member from giving until the marginal costs of the contribution equal the expected marginal returns. The interest group would not, in other words, reap the full benefits of the large member's substantial stakes in the group's political objectives. Indeed, if the limits are especially low, the restrictions may even eliminate contributions from group members no matter how great their stakes in the political outcome, since a single contribution cannot then have more than a trivial effect on the group's chances for political success. Members may have private reasons to support the group's activities, but any incentives related to the group's political goals are undermined by the impotence of their individual contributions.

Neither is it possible to rely on individual patrons if funds must be raised from a large number of small contributors. Because patrons seek goods that lose value as they are distributed more widely—such as special honors and control over the organization's activities—the number of contributors attracted by these inducements cannot be large. Patrons must be able to impose their own personal imprimatur on the organization, and this sort of benefit cannot be widely distributed without creating too much conflict over the organization's agenda, activities, or goals. Because an organization cannot have more than a handful of patrons, limits on the maximum size of individual contributions sharply reduce the total amount of money an interest group can raise from this strategy.

Interest groups can mobilize small contributors, but it is a costly and difficult task when individual support does not depend on rational calculations. Small contributors may be mobilized by appeals that provide purposive benefits, benefits that accrue to individuals who value participation in a political cause for its own sake. As James Q. Wilson has long argued (1973), at least some citizens are willing to contribute time and money to political groups because they enjoy the articulation and advocacy of positions on controversial issues. But while there is no doubt that there are citizens who find intrinsic value in political involvement and that purposive benefits would suffice to motivate some citizens to contribute some money to some political groups or candidates, the fundamental problem of collective action does not disappear. Because the value of participation to an individual depends on so many variables—such as personality, experience, education, life cycle, and political circumstances—it will vary enormously among persons within a latent interest group and for each person over time. Interest group leaders who seek to mobilize support therefore need to sample widely within a group until they find citizens who value participation in its cause. But because demographic and other readily identifiable personal characteristics are only weakly related to a person's willingness to support a particular purposive benefit, group leaders must usually spend a lot of time and money winnowing through a large number of potential contributors before they finally find a reasonably reliable group of supporters (Rothenberg 1992). Witness, for example, the very low return rates and the high initial costs that ideological groups face when mobilizing support through direct-mail fund-raising (Latus 1984).

Even when citizens motivated to support a group are found, there is no guarantee that their contributions will sustain an effective political effort. Groups searching for supporters often keep their dues or contribution requests low enough to give the largest number of people a chance to try the group out, in the hope that new members will eventually increase their financial support after they have had a chance to experience membership (Rothenberg 1992). But there is no guarantee that they will. Small and infrequent expressions of support might satisfy an individual's desire for involvement just as well as large and recurrent contributions, and their support might die away altogether in response to even small changes in the political system that make a collective good less salient or a collective bad less of an immediate threat. Imperfect knowledge about who within a group is most likely to provide support on the basis of purposive benefits, coupled with the lack of any clear and stable relationship between contributors' behavior and the collective good, means that political mobilization on the basis of purposive benefits is usually unstable and ineffective. Exceptions to this rule certainly exist, but such groups must usually survive a long and costly period of experiential searching among potential contributors (Rothenberg 1992)—a period during which patrons, and their ability to absorb the initial costs of mobilization, are obviously invaluable.

The problems and costs of mobilizing small contributors are exacerbated by other campaign finance regulations designed to ensure public disclosure and accountability. The campaign finance laws include a host of record-keeping requirements and reporting obligations that impose considerable organizational costs on virtually all PACs. For example, a PAC must appoint a treasurer and forward all contributions to his or her office within 10 or 30 days of receipt, depending on the amount of the contribution; it must keep an account of every contribution, the name and address of persons contributing more than $50, and the name and address of any person to whom a disbursement is made; and it must preserve receipts for all disbursements over $200 and keep all records for at least three years. The committee must register with the FEC, including an updated statement of organization and all its depositories. It must compile comprehensive reports of total and, in many cases, itemized contributions and expenditures; it must list outstanding debts and obligations as well as its cash on hand; it must report rebates, refunds, interest, or any other offset to operating expenditures over $200; it must file these reports either every month or on a quarterly basis; and if it chooses to report on a quarterly basis, it must also submit special preelection and postelection reports and semiannual reports during nonelection years. These requirements are invaluable in creating the most open and accountable campaign finance system in the world, yet they also impose substantial administrative costs on groups wanting to engage in campaign activities, costs that are much greater than those required of groups employing other political tactics, such as legislative lobbying, administrative lobbying, public education, or litigation.

These administrative requirements apply immediately to new groups and thereby raise the initial costs of electoral mobilization. Although they are not insurmountable by themselves, these record-keeping and disclosure costs can be hard to overcome in tandem with the already high initial costs of locating and attracting small contributors. High entry costs, in turn, create special problems for collective action. Since some of these costs must be paid before the group is fully organized, the group must find a way of mobilizing support *even before* supplying any amount of the collective good. That task seems to require patrons or large members, whose large contributions can get the group over the initial threshold needed to begin mobilization. But the regulations governing interest group involvement in elections do not exempt individuals from contribution limits when paying the often substantial costs of group formation and thus seem to block growth within the PAC system.

The considerable costs and difficulties of mobilizing small contributors can, however, be overcome by the one remaining strategy for collective action—by relying on institutions to absorb the costs of mobilization or manipulate selective incentives needed to encourage small contributors. By stripping away the capacity of groups to draw on the concentrated resources of a small number of individuals—be they patrons or large members—the constraints governing the campaign finance system leave the power to provide and mobilize effective support to institutions, with their resources and preexisting structures of values and incentives. But the importance of institutions in mobilizing support creates other problems for representation, because the rules give some institutions considerable flexibility in deploying their resources for electoral purposes yet place strong constraints on others. Corporations, for example, are able to use many of their institutional resources to establish and administer affiliated PACs, to hold meetings, and to communicate with and solicit contributions from their stockholders and employees. However, charitable organizations, schools and universities, churches, private foundations, government agencies, and many other not-for-profit institutions face severe constraints in using their resources for electoral purposes—constraints found not only in the campaign finance reforms but also in our tax laws, rules governing government contracts, and civil service regulations. Of course, there are very good reasons for restricting or even prohibiting the involvement of these latter institutions in electoral politics, such as preventing corruption in the administration of government programs or the use of taxpayers' money for the advocacy of special interests, though it is curious why strong legal restrictions are imposed on the sources and levels of support for electioneering but not on those for litigation, legislative lobbying, administrative lobbying, public education, or any other political activity.

Whatever the reasons for the regulations, it is important to recognize their effects on the mobilization of interests in elections. Many of

these governmental or private nonprofit institutions have been historically critical in establishing and maintaining a wide range of politically
active groups that have countered the strength of business corporations
in American politics in legislative, judicial, and public arenas (Walker
1991, 28–33). This is so, in part, because the private nonprofit and
governmental sectors tend to respond to and institutionalize demands
that are quite different from the private demands met by profit-sector
institutions; that is, they tend to be more responsive to collective interests or other demands for goods generating external benefits and costs
(Weisbrod 1988, 90). To the extent, then, that these institutions are
prevented from aiding and subsidizing groups involved in *electoral* activities, the array of interests organized in our electoral system will be much
smaller and less inclusive than the interest group system as a whole, and
many of the demands and conflicts important in American politics will
be channeled away from the electoral arena.

The laws governing the electoral activities of interest groups therefore appear to have a suppressive effect on group mobilization and
representation, yet the impact is hardly evenhanded. By forcing groups
to mobilize small contributors, by eliminating access to individual patrons, by allowing only some institutions to use their resources to support electoral activities, and by raising the costs of organization, the
regulations are likely to produce a highly biased or selective system of
representation, one that magnifies the importance of access to the few
institutions—such as business corporations and labor unions—that have
the capacity and legal opportunities to mobilize resources for political
purposes as a by-product of their other activities and structures. The
regulations may be particularly oppressive for two types of groups: those
that involve citizen interests that cut across existing occupations and
other institutional structures, such as concerns about civil rights and the
environment; and those interests that are typically represented by third-
party advocates in the nonprofit sector, such as organizations of professionals serving children, the mentally impaired, the poor, or other disadvantaged groups.

In fact, the inhibitory effects of campaign finance reforms and other
laws on the mobilization of citizen interests and third-party representatives are good examples of a more general principle at work: that nearly
any restriction on the size or sources of support for collective action will
have the greatest impact on the mobilization of diffuse or otherwise
disadvantaged interests. While the organization for collective action
may be problematic in all circumstances, it is particularly difficult for
large and uninstitutionalized groups, since such groups cannot rely on
their individual members to provide a stable base of support. These

latter groups must rely instead on an unpredictable mix of ad hoc, incidental sources of support to supplement or even substitute for support from their members. Thus, the representation of such interests will emerge from evolving arrangements with a complex array of sources outside the membership proper, such as individual and institutional patrons or third-party representatives. Yet it is precisely the formation of these sorts of complex, unpredictable, incidental, and ad hoc coalitions that the laws prevent. The result is a truncated system of interest representation, one that is not only much narrower than the theoretical universe of "interests" or "groups" in a political system but also much smaller and less inclusive than the interests represented in other, less regulated forms of political activity.

The biased distribution of constraints and opportunities for mobilizing interests in elections should have important political ramifications. The system of PACs may be expected to be more conservative than other forms of interest representation, since many of the traditional sources of support for progressive groups—such as nonprofit institutions, government agencies, and individual patrons—are generally prevented from playing the same dominant role in supporting electoral efforts. We may also expect that groups in the PAC system will place greater emphasis on economic issues than do groups active in other political arenas, since it is economic institutions like corporations and trade associations that have the greatest opportunities to apply their resources to elections. The dominance of certain institutions within the PAC system may also help account for some of its general behavioral characteristics, such as its limited partisanship and the unwillingness of many committees to fund nonincumbents. Rather than viewing these characteristics as necessary or inherent in the PAC system, we may instead see them as stemming from the regulatory barriers imposed on group participation in elections.

We can see, then, that these and other representational problems in the PAC system may grow out of a fundamental discrepancy between the apparent ideals of the reforms and the ways in which interest groups in the U.S. are actually able to overcome the collective action dilemma and organize for effective political action. While the reforms attempt to enforce greater equality in participation among individuals in campaigns and elections, a broadly representative system of organized interest groups requires considerable asymmetry among individuals in their assessments of costs and benefits as well as in their contributions. And though the reforms and other relevant laws seem to uphold individualism and voluntarism by restricting the political involvement of many institutions, by minimizing direct and indirect subsidies, and by ensuring

that citizens control as much as possible the political use of their resources, the logic of collective action argues that political representation
often depends on nonmarket subsidies and interventions and on the
capacity of a wide array of institutions to use their powers to mobilize
political support. And while many of the reforms are designed to ensure
that individuals make their contributions exclusively in support of
broad, public objectives, effective political action often depends on political support that emerges indirectly, incidentally, or epiphenomenally.
A broadly representative system of interest groups is hard to achieve
under any circumstances, and it is certainly difficult to attain in a system
where the laws and other institutional constraints ignore what we already know about the real difficulties of political organization. Perhaps
the ideals that underlie the constraints are worth their representational
costs, but those costs should at least be understood and weighed.

CHAPTER 3

The Size and Scope of the PAC System

The difficulty of organizing small contributors, and the need to do just that under the current campaign finance laws, suggests that effective electoral organization will depend on the ability of groups to rely on patrons or other sources of support not directly constrained by the campaign finance laws or on institutions that reduce the costs of organization and provide the incentives and structures needed to activate small contributors. The PAC system thus has little autonomy, in the sense that it is very difficult for a truly independent committee to bootstrap itself into a strong, viable organization. These limitations imply that the PAC system will be relatively small and weak, especially when compared to less constrained forms of political organization, and that it will be highly biased, since the availability of an institutional base and legal access to patrons for electoral activities are distributed unequally. Indeed, these characteristics are closely and directly related; the PAC system is small in part because it excludes many groups from effective participation, and it is biased because the restrictions on mobilization fall most heavily on certain types of groups.

Claims that the PAC system is small and organizationally weak obviously do not resonate with the most commonly held views of organized group involvement in American elections—or with the assumptions underlying the current laws and most proposals for stricter reforms—which are more likely to presume that PACs are powerful organizations controlling enormous sums of money that would explode out of control unless strict regulations held them in check and that they constitute the primary method by which interest groups secure and exercise political power. Yet those who sketch such pictures of the PAC system usually look at it in isolation. I take a different approach in this chapter. I not only examine the connections between PACs and institutions and the organizational strengths and weaknesses of different kinds of committees. I also compare PACs with other forms of interest representation in American politics to assess the size, strength, and representative character of the system. Only then do the limits of the system become clear.

The Institutional Basis of the PACs

If it is hard to mobilize small individual contributors, we should expect that successful PACs will rely on other sources of support, particularly from institutions. In fact, we can see this institutional dependence in the predominance of "separate segregated funds" within the PAC system, a legal concept that allows some interest groups to tap the resources of nonelectoral organizations for electoral purposes. Federal law authorizes corporations, labor organizations, membership organizations, cooperatives, trade associations, and corporations without capital stock to act as "connected organizations" and establish "separate segregated funds" (2 U.S.C. §§ 441b(b)(2) and (4)(C); 11 C.F.R. §§ 100.6 and 114.1(a)(2)(iii)). These funds are essentially financial accounts that hold voluntary contributions from members, employees, or stockholders of the connected organization and that may be used to support federal candidates or parties through contributions or expenditures. The law allows the connected organization to use its general treasury funds to pay the costs of establishing and administering the separate segregated fund as well as of soliciting contributions, where general treasury monies include those "obtained in commercial transactions and dues monies or membership fees" (11 C.F.R. § 114.5(b)). These establishment, administration, and solicitation costs can thus be absorbed by a flexible array of funding sources: market earnings in the case of corporations; or member dues in the case of unions, trade associations, or membership organizations.[1]

What constitutes "establishment, administration, and solicitation costs" is not always clear, but the provision permits connected organizations to give considerable aid to their PACs. The Federal Election Commission interprets the terms as including "the cost of office space, phones, salaries, utilities, supplies, legal and accounting fees, fundraising and other expenses incurred in setting up and running a separate segregated fund" (11 C.F.R. § 114.1(b)). Virtually any administrative overhead expense can be absorbed by the connected organization, including the substantial costs of mailing solicitations to stockholders, employees, or union members; of maintaining comprehensive accounting records and meeting the reporting requirements of the FEC; of providing the salaries, travel expenses, and clerical support of PAC operatives and officers; and of retaining the lawyers and accountants needed by PACs to ensure compliance with federal election and tax laws and to represent the connected organization in case of legal actions or audits.

Separate segregated funds (SSFs) can also use nonmonetary resources to secure support. Corporate and union committees can employ checkoff systems such that contributions are automatically withheld from employees' pay, so long as employees give their approval and any devices for raising contributions for a corporate PAC are made available to its unions. SSFs may also use the connected organization's in-house publications for solicitations and their premises for meetings of PAC officers and contributors.

Perhaps even more important, corporations, labor unions, and incorporated trade associations and many membership organizations may spend an unlimited amount of money from their general treasuries on "partisan communications" with their members, employees, stockholders, or families (11 C.F.R. § 114.3). These communications may include inviting candidates or party representatives to the organization's premises, meetings, conventions, or other functions; establishing and operating phone banks in support of particular candidates or parties; and conducting partisan registration and get-out-the-vote drives (11 C.F.R. § 114.3(c)). Such communications need not be explicit solicitations for financial support. An organization may make these communications even if it has not established an SSF, but fund-raising by an SSF is surely facilitated by the capacity of an organization's leaders to use an unlimited amount of its treasury funds and facilities to interpret political events, raise political issues, and emphasize the organization's political significance.

There are certainly limits to what connected organizations may do for their PACs, but the limits are not always clear or easy to enforce. Connected organizations may not use the establishment, administrative, and solicitation process "as a means of exchanging treasury monies for voluntary contributions" by directly or indirectly reimbursing a PAC contributor with a bonus, expense account, or other form of compensation (11 C.F.R. § 114.5(b)). Yet this prohibition is not always strictly interpreted. The corporation, union, or association may sponsor a raffle or other fund-raising device involving a prize—paid out of the organization's general revenues—so long as the prize is not "disproportionately valuable." SSFs are also prohibited from obtaining contributions by the use or threat of physical force, job discrimination, or financial reprisal (11 C.F.R. § 114.5(a)(1)). But that is a difficult prohibition to enforce. Oral solicitations only require oral assurances that all contributions are voluntary, so it might be hard for an employee or member to prove otherwise; and some solicitations, such as those involving middle managers, may be construed as inherently coercive (Bauer and Kafka 1984, chap. 9, 49).

The ability of SSFs to rely on sources of support not subject to contribution limits and regulations—and the difficulties of raising support within the purview of those restrictions—suggests that SSFs ought to dominate the PAC system, and that is exactly what we find. We can see this predominance by examining the distribution and growth of PACs according to a typology used by the FEC and based on legal distinctions regarding PAC affiliations. Five of the six categories in the typology are SSFs. All such funds must report their affiliations to the FEC when the PAC is registered, and the FEC uses these categories in its reports to create the following typology for "nonparty political committees":

> *Corporations:* committees identifying themselves as being connected to a corporation, such as the Amoco PAC; the Bear, Stearns and Co. PAC; and the Tenneco Employees Good Government Fund
>
> *Labor organizations:* committees reporting a connection with a labor organization, including the National Education Association PAC, the Machinists Non-Partisan Political League, and N-CAP (Nurses Coalition for Action in Politics)
>
> *Trade/member/health organizations:* committees indicating a connection with a trade association or membership organization or involved in the "health-related field," such as the Realtors Political Action Committee, the National Rifle Association's Political Victory Fund, the American Medical Association PAC, or the Tooling and Machining PAC of the National Tooling and Machining Association
>
> *Cooperatives:* committees reporting a connection with a cooperative, mostly agricultural cooperatives, such as the Associated Milk Producers' Committee for Thorough Agricultural Political Education and the Michigan Blueberry Growers Association PAC
>
> *Corporations without capital stock:* committees affiliated with a corporation without capital stock, including various financial institutions and nonprofit organizations, such as the Commodity Futures Political Fund of the Chicago Mercantile Exchange, the Massachusetts Mutual Fund Life Insurance Company PAC, and the National Women's Political Caucus Campaign Support Committee

The remaining PACs are defined largely by what they are not. They are political committees that are not authorized by a candidate to spend or receive funds in his or her behalf, are not part of the official structure of a political party, and are not SSFs. Although there is no unique statutory name for these organizations, the FEC calls them "no connected organization" committees. They include many types of organizations, from ideological groups like the National Conservative Political Action Committee or the liberal National Committee for an Effective Congress, to more narrowly focused citizen groups like the National Right to Life PAC or the Council for a Livable World, to business organizations like the Auto Dealers for Free Trade PAC.

SSFs clearly outnumber committees without a connected organization. Table 3.1 shows that since 1986 about 72 percent of the "nonparty" committees registered with the FEC have been SSFs. That is a decline from 1978, when 87 percent of committees were formally connected to corporations, unions, or other organizations. But most of the decline occurred in a brief period in the early 1980s when nonconnected PACs grew quickly: in the 1980 elections, when conservative ideological and partisan groups mobilized against the Carter Administration and the Democratic Congress; and then in the 1982 elections, when a wide variety of liberal groups rallied against the aggressively conservative early Reagan Administration. Since then, the distribution of PACs has held fairly steady. Corporations, corporations without capital stock, agricultural cooperatives, and nonconnected committees added SSFs throughout the 1980s, though at a much slower pace after Reagan's first term; and the slowest growth rates during that time occurred among SSFs attached to labor unions and the organizations classified under the FEC's "Trade/Member/Health" designation.

SSFs control an especially large share of PAC contributions to

TABLE 3.1. Percentage of PACs Registered during Each Election Cycle, by Legal Affiliations, 1978–92

Legal Affiliation	Election Year							
	1978	1980	1982	1984	1986	1988	1990	1992
All separate segregated funds	87	83	75	74	72	72	72	71
Corporate	42	45	42	42	42	42	42	41
Trade/member/health	28	23	18	17	17	18	17	18
Corps without stock	1	2	3	3	3	4	3	3
Cooperatives	1	1	1	1	1	1	1	1
Labor	14	12	11	10	9	8	8	8
All nonconnected	13	17	25	26	28	28	28	29
Total percent	100	100	100	100	100	100	100	100
Total number	1,949	2,785	3,722	4,347	4,596	4,832	4,677	4,729

Source: Federal Election Commission.

candidates, as table 3.2 demonstrates; and despite the big shifts in the number of different kinds of PACs during the 1980s, changes in the sources of PAC contributions have been fairly small. Corporate committees provided 36 percent of all PAC contributions in the 1992 elections, the same share they accounted for in 1980. Labor committees lost a little ground, as their contributions went from 24 percent of the total to just under 22 percent. And committees without connected organizations started the 1980s with a very small share—9 percent of all PAC contributions—expanded through all the 1986 elections, and then fell back during Reagan's last years and the Bush Administration. The nonconnected PACs thus expanded in number during periods of partisan conflict and policy change but did not sustain their strength beyond those years, while the SSFs maintained their importance in contributing to campaigns even during periods of relative political quiescence and gridlock.

The dominance of SSFs is, however, only one aspect of the institutional underpinnings of the PAC system. To see more, we need a different typology. PACs may have a strong economic base even if they are nonconnected committees, and that base may confer critical advantages in mobilizing electoral resources. It is also possible that some institutions are better represented than others. There are legal differences in the ability of different economic sectors—such as the division between profit and nonprofit institutions—to use their resources for electoral purposes,

TABLE 3.2.   Percentage of Contributions by PACs Provided by Committees of Different Legal Affiliations, 1978–92

Legal Affiliation	Election Year							
	1978	1980	1982	1984	1986	1988	1990	1992
All separate segregated funds	92	91	87	86	86	87	90	90
Corporate	28	36	34	35	35	35	36	36
Trade/member/health	32	28	26	25	25	26	28	28
Corps without stock	0	1	1	1	2	2	2	2
Cooperatives	3	2	2	2	2	2	2	2
Labor	29	24	24	23	22	22	22	22
All nonconnected	8	9	13	14	14	13	10	10
Total percent	100	100	100	100	100	100	100	100
Total contributions (in millions)	$32.4	$55.0	$76.6	$97.7	$120.4	$138.9	$144.0	$188.7

Source: Federal Election Commission.

and those distinctions may give rise to significant differences in their representation and strength within the PAC system, differences that may have important political implications. Finally, the FEC typology is sui generis and not very useful in answering questions about the *representativeness* of the PAC system in comparison with other forms of interest representation in national politics. Although the corporate and labor categories seem fairly straightforward and may be used for such comparisons, the other categories each encompass an enormous variety of groups and make it impossible to determine whether certain interests or institutions are well or poorly represented.

For these reasons, I coded all (or nearly all) PACs that were registered in the 1979–80 and 1983–84 election cycles according to a typology that closely resembles the one developed and used by Jack Walker and his colleagues in analyzing membership associations involved in national policy making (Walker 1983, 1991). The typology is helpful not only because it has been employed in other contexts and facilitates comparisons with other forms of interest representation but also because it is based on the theoretical expectation—which our argument shares—that institutions and institutional support are critical in understanding how political interests are mobilized and represented in American politics.

The typology is based on three distinctions regarding a group's membership base. First, I distinguish between groups whose memberships are based expressly on their occupational roles and groups that are open to members regardless of their occupation. An interest group whose membership is based on occupational roles has access to important institutional resources that are critical for political organization. These occupational roles facilitate communication by allowing groups to tap into institutionalized networks; they may homogenize and link together tastes in public and private goods; they often permit groups to use institutional structures to apply selective incentives to members or employees in order to encourage support; and they sometimes allow direct access to corporate, union, or other institutional treasuries. Interest groups without an occupational base must usually organize support from scratch—by creating new patterns of communication, by locating potential supporters with little guidance, by producing selective incentives without any initial market power, and by raising support with no readily available pool of institutional resources.

Second, among groups that have an occupational base, I separate labor organizations from interest groups whose members hold administrative, professional, or proprietary positions in institutions. If having an occupational base is critical for deploying the resources of economic institutions for political purposes, it is also important to distinguish occupationally based groups with respect to their control over institutions. Managers, owners, and professionals enjoy privileged access to the resources of their corporations or agencies due to their authority over employees, their direct control of the institution's programs and budget, and their dominance over information flows within the organization. Labor is typically excluded from operational control of the corporation or agency's treasury and policies and is faced with greater constraints than is management in exercising authority over members and encouraging their political support.

Third, among groups with an occupational base, I distinguish between those that draw members from institutions in the for-profit sector and those whose members work in the nonprofit sector. The profit and nonprofit sectors generally differ in their economic outputs and sources of financing, differences that have important implications for the representation and mobilization of political interests. Profit sector institutions generate wealth for their investors from sales revenues by efficiently satisfying the private demands of consumers. Such institutions should be in a particularly strong position to exploit the "by-product" method of political action by skimming off a portion of sales revenues raised from private-market transactions. In contrast, institutions in the nonprofit sector usually respond to wants or needs not perfectly accompanied by money demand. Many private nonprofit institutions supply collective goods, or "services that generate sizable 'external' benefits to persons who do not help to finance the organization's activities—for example, medical research, museums, wildlife sanctuaries, environmental protection, and aid to the poor" (Weisbrod 1988, 59–60). Other private nonprofit institutions offer "trust goods." Even though these goods may be private services—such as health care or day care—consumers may think that they cannot evaluate the quality of the services for themselves and thus seek some assurance that the organization "will take less advantage of [their] . . . informational handicaps than a for-profit seller would" (Weisbrod 1988, 60). Finally, government agencies provide both types of services as well as other, essentially private goods that are collectively supplied to groups of voters large and cohesive enough to succeed in national politics. Because the nonprofit sector responds to needs and wants that differ from the distribution of private demands backed by private budgets, it must often rely on other sources of financing, such as taxes, donations, and government subsidies. Nonprofit institutions not only represent distinctive political interests. They confront difficult problems of political action by virtue of the collective demands they are organized to meet, and their reliance on different sources of revenue means that when deploying institutional resources for political purposes, they often face very different constraints than those impinging on business organizations.

I used these three basic distinctions to produce a sevenfold typology of groups (see table 3.3). Three types of PACs were organized around administrative, professional, or proprietary positions or occupations. They included PACs with an occupational base in the profit sector, committees organized around occupations in the nonprofit sector, and a few PACs that spanned both sectors. Three other types of PACs organized workers or labor union members. They also included PACs with an institutional base in the profit sector, those whose members worked in the nonprofit sector, and PACs that drew members from institutions in both sectors. Finally, the seventh category included all committees without an explicit occupational base. These "citizen" PACs may have drawn a large share of their contributors from certain occupations, but these occupations were not actual criteria for inclusion and organization, and they were not part of the organization's description of itself and the interests it represented. In general, citizen PACs were organized around issues or causes that cut across economic specializations, such as interests in environmental preservation, civil rights and liberties, or the enforcement of "traditional" values and family structures.

Two of the seven categories were divided again to reveal important distinctions in their institutional foundations. Business PACs affiliated with single corporations were distinguished from committees with a broader institutional base in the profit sector, such as PACs representing industries, professions within the profit sector, or general business

TABLE 3.3. Typology of PACs, Based on the Occupational Roles of Contributors

Membership Base	Sector	Typology
Administrative, proprietary, professional	Profit	1a. Profit sector—corporate committees 1b. Profit sector—industry, sector, professional
	Mixed	2. Mixed sectors
	Nonprofit	3. Nonprofit sector
Labor	Profit	4. Labor—profit sector
	Mixed	5. Labor—mixed sectors
	Nonprofit	6. Labor—nonprofit sector
Citizen groups		7a. Citizen groups—party, candidate 7b. Citizen groups—issue only

organizations. We expect that transcorporate interests are harder to organize, not only because of the collective action problems created by their larger memberships, but also because such interests have less control over the most common and basic institutional unit of the profit sector, the corporation. PACs representing citizen or nonoccupational interests were also divided into two subcategories, based on our hypothesis that institutional affiliations were critical in mobilizing electoral resources. PACs that had formal or informal ties to political parties, elected officials, or candidates—usually presidential candidates and members of Congress—were able to tap into existing works of supporters and in some cases could rely on institutional resources, such as congressional travel allowances, easy access to the media, and legislative staff, not to mention control over public policy. The remaining citizen PACs were organized around issues, even though, as we shall see, many of these had ties with other organizations and institutions.

I estimated the linkages between PACs and these broad institutional sectors in the U.S. economy by coding all PACs registered in the 1980 and 1984 elections according to their membership base.[2] In the vast majority of cases, that was a fairly easy task, since most PACs were SSFs with formal connections to institutions, which must be identified in committees' names (11 C.F.R. § 102.14(c)), and whose address and treasurer were found in FEC records. Other PACs had no connected organization, but their names clearly identified the types of interests and contributors they represented, as does, for example, the name Auto Dealers for Free Trade PAC. The remaining 10–15 percent of the committees, nearly all nonconnected PACs, required more research before they were coded. Using PAC directories, lists of major PAC contributors, newspaper articles, lists of Washington representatives, and encyclopedias of associations, I was able to code with a fair amount of certainty nearly all registered committees in both election cycles.

These affiliation data are displayed in table 3.4 and show that the vast majority of committees had an occupational base; that this base was largely organized around administrative, executive, or professional positions; and that these positions were overwhelmingly in the profit sector. Business PACs accounted for 72 percent of all registered committees in 1980 and 65 percent in 1984. The drop was not caused by a decline in the number of business committees—the profit sector actually added 810 committees between 1980 and 1984—but was instead the result of a growth rate slower than the near-explosion of citizen PACs between 1980 and 1984, from 388 to 942. Most business PACs were corporate committees, which made up about half of all registered PACs in both elections, and over 90 percent of these corporate committees were SSFs.

In 1984, the 25 largest corporate committees in terms of contributions included aerospace companies, such as Lockheed and General Dynamics; companies in the energy industry, such as Amoco, Tenneco, Exxon, and Union Oil; electronics companies with large defense contracts, such as Litton, Harris, General Electric, and Westinghouse; automobile manufacturers, such as General Motors and Ford; and a variety of others, such as Philip Morris, Union Pacific, and E. F. Hutton. These are obviously large companies that are strongly affected by government policies and decisions—as government contractors, as companies vulnerable to trade regulations and agreements, or as corporations whose products and services are subject to intense regulation or government scrutiny. PACs affiliated with law and lobbying firms were also included

TABLE 3.4. The Number and Percentage of PACs according to Their Institutional Affiliations, 1980 and 1984 Elections

	1980 Elections		1984 Elections	
Institutional Affiliation	Number	Percentage	Number	Percentage
Administrative/proprietary	**2,058**	**73.9**	**2,924**	**67.9**
Profit sector—all	2,000	71.8	2,809	65.2
Profit—corporate	1,323	47.5	1,961	45.5
Profit—industry/professional/general	677	24.3	848	19.7
Mixed sector	16	0.6	34	0.8
Nonprofit sector	42	1.5	80	1.9
Labor	**337**	**12.1**	**444**	**10.3**
Profit sector	262	9.4	345	8.0
Mixed sector	26	0.9	26	0.6
Nonprofit sector	49	1.8	73	1.7
Citizen	**388**	**13.9**	**942**	**21.8**
Party/candidate	90	3.2	255	5.9
Issue	298	10.7	687	15.9
Total coded	2,783	100.0	4,310	100.0
Missing	2	—	38	—
Total	2,785	—	4,347	—

Source: Federal Election Commission/various sources for occupational codes (see app. B).

under this corporate category, such as committees established by Akin, Gump, Hauer and Feld, a Dallas law firm with a large Washington office; Arnold and Porter, the Washington law firm with a strong emphasis on lobbying services; and Wexler, Reynolds, Harrison and Shule, a lobbying and public relations firm.

The remaining business PACs—about 24 percent of all committees in 1980 and about 20 percent in 1984—drew contributors from more than one corporation and sometimes more than one industry. Many of these committees were affiliated with trade associations with organizational memberships, such as the American Bankers Association, the U.S. League of Savings Institutions, the American Hospital Association, and the Tobacco Institute. However, the largest committees in this category were typically connected to business associations of individual businesspersons, professionals, or sole proprietors, such as the National Association of Realtors, the Independent Insurance Agents of America, the American Medical Association, the American Dental Association, the Associated General Contractors of America, and the Association of Trial Lawyers of America. PACs connected to agricultural cooperatives were also included here—since their contributor base was in the profit sector—as were committees with sectorwide clienteles, such as PACs affiliated with the Chamber of Commerce and the National Federation of Independent Business or independent committees like the Business–Industry PAC, which was founded by the National Association of Manufacturers and has often provided political intelligence on candidates and races to other business committees. Finally, some of the more politically aggressive industries established nonconnected committees to augment their corporate and trade association PACs or sometimes to advocate a view that divides their industry. Examples included the Auto Dealers for Free Trade PAC, composed of American dealers with foreign-car franchises, and several committees established by independent oil companies, such as the Dallas Energy PAC, HOUPAC, Louisiana Energy National PAC, and the Intermountain PAC (Edsall 1984, 76). Many of the nonconnected business PACs were local or regional organizations, such as the Miami Cruise PAC, supported by a number of local travel agencies, or the Gulf Coast Association, composed of real estate agents in Mobile, Alabama.

In contrast to the large number of business PACs, less than 2 percent of all committees in both election years drew their contributors from administrative interests in the nonprofit sector. Nearly as revealing as the small number of committees from this sector was the composition of this group. The committees were mostly from the borderline segments of the nonprofit sector that relied primarily on service fees rather than gifts or donations, such as credit unions and health organizations (like the committees affiliated with state Blue Cross/Blue Shield organizations or the PAC formed by the American Federation of Home Health Agencies). Others included advocacy groups for rural electric cooperative systems, which, though nominally nonprofit, have an important base in the agricultural industry. Few came from the enormous governmental sector, religious institutions, nonhealth charitable organizations, and public or private educational institutions that have long constituted the unique core of the nonprofit sector. Even if all formally nonprofit economic institutions were included in the count—such as mutual insurance corporations and agricultural cooperatives—the size of the nonprofit sector would have increased to only 4.6 percent of all PACs in 1980 and 5.5 percent in 1984. Finally, an even smaller proportion of registered committees organized contributors across the profit and nonprofit sectors. Less than 1 percent of all PACs were classified in the mixed category in both 1980 and 1984. All but one of these committees were SSFs, and most were trade associations in the health field, including the American Hospital Association and such professional associations as the American Physical Therapy Association.

The proportion of registered PACs affiliated with labor organizations declined between 1980 and 1984 from 12.1 to 10.3 percent. The slow growth of committees representing labor in the profit sector accounted for most of the relative decline, while unions in the nonprofit sector grew much more quickly. What is most striking in comparing labor committees and PACs affiliated with administrative or managerial interests is the greater representation of the nonprofit sector among labor committees: about one out of six labor committees drew contributors from the nonprofit sector, mostly teachers and other government employees, compared to about one out of thirty among administrative/managerial/professional PACs. Nearly all the committees organized around labor interests were SSFs, a significant fact in light of what is missing in this category. There is a complete absence of committees organizing nonunionized workers, who have no statutory rights to establish their SSFs or to draw on the institutional resources of the organizations in which they work.

The final two categories of PACs differed from all the others by organizing contributors independent of their occupational roles. These "citizen" committees grew from almost 14 percent of all registered committees to nearly 22 percent between the 1980 and 1984 elections. Yet even many of these PACs depended on access to various institutions. The strongest growth occurred among PACs affiliated either with specific political leaders or with the political parties. Some PACs, such as

Robert Dole's Campaign America or Richard Gephart's Effective Government Committee, were established by senior members of Congress to curry favor with other members in efforts to win party leadership posts (*NJ*, 1 October 1994, 2268–73; Baker 1989; *NYT*, 16 June 1989, A11). Others, such as Reagan's Citizens for the Republic, were "testing-the-water" or "precandidacy" committees, which permitted potential presidential or congressional candidates to raise money to conduct polls, travel to party leaders, and try out speeches in front of various audiences before they declared their candidacies (Corrado 1992). Finally, some of these PACs, such as Jesse Helms' National Congressional Club or Jack Kemp's Campaign for Prosperity, were hybrids of ideological groups, party factions, and personal political machines.

The committees affiliated with the political parties were just as diverse. Some of the committees were extensions of state party organizations, such as the various committees affiliated with the North Carolina Democratic Party during the Hunt–Helms race in 1984, most of which were organized around specific regions or localities in the state. Some committees were closely affiliated with the national parties, such as GOPAC, the controversial Republican PAC that was launched in 1978 by the then-governor of Delaware, Pierre S. duPont, but that has since become a personal organization of Representative Newt Gingrich. And a few committees were established by insurgent groups, like the PAC created by Republican activists and elected officials who wanted to change the party's platform on abortion (*WP*, 29 April 1990, A16). Many of the committees were small organizations that were placed in this category because their names identified them with a major party *and* because their contributions were made to candidates of only one party.

The remaining citizen groups displayed no explicit connections with institutional leaders or major political parties and appeared to be organized exclusively around issues or nonoccupational social divisions. These groups grew rapidly between 1980 and 1984, from 10.7 percent to 15.9 percent of all PACs. They included New Right groups, such as the National Conservative Political Action Committee; environmental groups, such as the Sierra Club's PAC; gun lobbies, such as the National Rifle Association's Political Victory Fund; and PACs associated with traditional liberal organizations, such as the Americans for Democratic Action (ADA). About 95 percent of these citizen-issue PACs were nonconnected committees. The remainder were SSFs established and funded by membership associations like the NRA, the ADA, or the Sierra Club.

Yet even among these citizen PACs, the mobilization of contributors often relied on preexisting ties or other sources of support. Some of these committees were nonconnected but were at least informally affiliated with other organizations; for example, RUFF-PAC shared facilities with Howard J. Ruff Publications, a firm that published a conservative newsletter in California. A significant minority of nonconnected PACs were pro-Israel committees, perhaps providing as much as 20–25 percent of all contributions by citizen PACs (Makinson 1990, 74, 76). Most of these pro-Israel organizations drew their contributors from a single urban area and appeared to rely on community ties; examples include the Hudson Valley PAC, the Mid Manhattan PAC, the Garden State PAC, the Delaware Valley PAC, and the St. Louisans for Better Government Committee. Contrary to the common belief that most citizen PACs were national organizations that mobilized vast numbers of contributors across the country through direct mail, the contributor lists of many citizen committees showed considerable localism, and few were located in Washington, D.C.

The PAC system looks more balanced if we consider committee receipts instead of the number of organizations. Table 3.5 shows the total receipts for each of the nine types of PACs as well as for the summary categories. Citizen groups raised over 30 percent of all non-party committee receipts in 1980, and over 37 percent in the 1984 elections. Business PACs accounted for about 49 percent of all receipts in 1980 and only about 43 percent in 1984. Labor committees, which only numbered about one out of nine PACs, raised nearly one out of five dollars in the PAC system as a whole. Thus, even though the profit sector controlled about two-thirds of all committees, they raised less than half of all PAC receipts, not much more than citizen groups.

Yet these receipts did not always translate into *political* expenditures. Table 3.6 shows the distribution of PAC spending on specifically political activities, which include contributions to candidates, independent expenditures, and transfers to political parties. Profit sector committees accounted for well over half of all political expenditures; labor committees provided about one-fifth; and committees representing citizen interests made approximately one-fourth of all contributions, party transfers, and independent expenditures. The stronger showing of business groups and the weaker presence of citizen PACs in overall political expenditures stemmed from the apparent problems that citizen committees had in using their receipts for political expenditures. Although they raised $109.8 million in the 1984 elections, they spent only about a third of it, or $36.5 million, on candidates, independent expenditures, or party aid. In contrast, profit sector groups raised $125.7 million and spent $75.6 million—or three-fifths of their receipts—on political support. Thus, despite the large sums of money that citizen PACs raised, little of it actually went to candidates or parties—a problem that occupationally based groups did not have.

Organizational Strength and Weakness in the PAC System

The discrepancies between the large sums raised by citizen and non-connected PACs and the small amounts that such committees provided to candidates and parties are symptoms of a more general imbalance between different types of PACs—between the organizational strength of committees that rely on other organizations or institutions for support and the weakness of committees that raise all or most of their funds from

TABLE 3.5.   PAC Receipts according to Their Institutional Affiliations, 1980 and 1984 Elections (Receipts in Millions of Dollars)

	1980 Elections		1984 Elections	
Institutional Affiliation	Receipts	Percentage	Receipts	Percentage
Administrative/proprietary	**$70.3**	**50.2**	**$130.9**	**44.5**
Profit sector—all	68.8	49.1	125.7	42.7
Profit—corporate	34.7	24.8	69.8	23.7
Profit—industry/professional/general	34.0	24.3	55.9	19.0
Mixed sector	0.3	0.2	1.1	0.4
Nonprofit sector	1.2	0.8	4.2	1.4
Labor	**27.4**	**19.5**	**53.7**	**18.2**
Profit sector	20.2	14.4	37.7	12.8
Mixed sector	2.8	2.0	3.5	1.2
Nonprofit sector	4.4	3.2	12.5	4.2
Citizen	**42.5**	**30.3**	**109.8**	**37.3**
Party/candidate	16.3	11.6	32.6	11.1
Issue	26.2	18.7	77.3	26.2
Total coded	$140.2	100.0	$294.4	100.0
Missing	0.0	—	0.1	—
Total	$140.2	—	$294.5	—

Source: Federal Election Commission/various sources for occupational codes (see app. B).

sources regulated by campaign finance restrictions. The effect of this imbalance is a lack of autonomy in the PAC system. It lacks autonomy in the sense that much of the money needed for truly effective organizations must be raised from economic institutions, such as corporations and labor unions, or by membership associations that rely on a variety of financial sources for support. Yet it also lacks autonomy in the broader sense that PACs do not create wholly new collections of individuals or institutions as much as they build on other, external political groupings or institutional structures. The dependence of PACs on existing institutions and organizational structures becomes particularly evident when we examine the apparent exceptions, the citizen-interest PACs.

The weakness of citizen PACs is clear when we see how many of them fail to satisfy even the most minimal criteria for organizational viability. I chose four criteria as essential for effective political organization.

TABLE 3.6. PAC Contributions and Political Expenditures according to Their Institutional Affiliations, 1980 and 1984 Elections (Receipts in Millions of Dollars)

| Institutional Affiliation | 1980 Elections | | 1984 Elections | |
	Contributions/ expenditures	Percentage	Contributions/ expenditures	Percentage
Administrative/proprietary	**$41.4**	**57.2**	**$78.9**	**54.3**
Profit sector—all	40.7	56.2	75.6	52.0
Profit—corporate	21.9	30.3	43.6	30.0
Profit—industry/professional/general	18.8	25.9	32.0	22.0
Mixed sector	0.1	0.2	0.7	0.5
Nonprofit sector	0.6	0.8	2.6	1.8
Labor	**14.5**	**19.9**	**30.1**	**20.7**
Profit sector	11.1	15.4	20.6	14.2
Mixed sector	1.7	2.4	2.2	1.5
Nonprofit sector	1.6	2.2	7.2	5.0
Citizen	**16.6**	**22.9**	**36.5**	**25.1**
Party/candidate	7.8	10.8	6.6	4.5
Issue	8.8	12.1	29.9	20.6
Total	$72.5	100.0	$145.5	100.0

Source: Federal Election Commission/various sources for occupational codes (see app. B).

First, the PAC's total receipts were greater than $10,000. Committees with total receipts of less than $10,000 for a two-year election cycle are unlikely to have a perceptible political impact and are frequently unable to qualify as "multicandidate committees" and to take advantage of their higher contribution limits. Multicandidate committees are political committees that have received contributions from at least 50 persons, have made contributions to at least five federal candidates, and have been registered for at least six months (11 C.F.R. § 100.5(e)(3)). Only multicandidate committees may give candidates up to $5,000 per election. Other nonqualifying nonparty committees may give candidates only $1,000 per election, the same limit that applies to individuals.

Second, more than 20 percent of the PAC's disbursements were spent on contributions to candidates and parties or independent political expenditures. This criterion measures the PAC's capacity to translate its resources into politically valuable forms of support. Committees whose operating expenditures absorb nearly all the money they get from individual contributors may sometimes serve significant political purposes—such as the Chamber of Commerce's Political Victory Fund, whose staff and newsletter provides political intelligence and guidance to other business committees—but in most cases, such organizations are impotent, at least relative to groups that can invest most of the funds they raise into real electoral support. Although any threshold is arbitrary, I chose a 20 percent test: an organization that spends 80 percent or more of its total disbursements on operating expenditures or other activities not constituting direct political support is not considered to be an effective electoral organization.

Third, the PAC's current debts did not exceed its current cash assets at the end of the election cycle. An organization that finds itself in debt at the end of an election cycle not only must raise funds all over again in the upcoming cycle but also must raise funds to deal with its current debt. Most PAC's have little debt and some leftover cash when the elections are over, but a few do not. Strong and effective committees are defined as those whose debts owed at the end of the election cycle are less than the total of their cash on hand and the debts that they are owed by others.

Fourth, the PAC was able to survive for four or more years. Although some committees can exert political influence if they are active in only one or two elections, most need to be viewed as more or less permanent organizations to be treated seriously by members of Congress and other political actors. A candidate rarely needs any one PAC's contribution in a single election, but a long-term, stable ally is quite valuable and hard to replace. For example, in his study of agriculture policy, Hansen (1991) argued that gaining access to members of Congress depended in part on whether legislators expected that an interest group and its issues would persist. Longevity also allows committees to build politically important reputations—for example, for effective independent expenditures—and it permits interests to build from an existing organizational base rather than starting from scratch each election. My simple criterion is whether the same PAC registered and active in the 1980 elections was also active in the 1984 cycle.

On all four of these criteria, citizen PACs showed much less viability and effectiveness than did committees organized around occupational roles, business PACs were organizationally stronger than were other occupational categories, and corporate committees showed more strength than did other business committees. We can see these differences in table 3.7, whose first two columns show the percentage of committees meeting these criteria during the 1980 and 1984 election cycles for each type of PAC. Over half of the PACs based on administrative, proprietary, or professional roles in the profit sector had receipts over $10,000 in both 1980 and 1984, while only about one-third of the committees in the citizen-issue category reported receipts over that amount. Citizen PACs with a partisan or candidate base were also rather anemic; only 39 percent of them had receipts over $10,000 in 1984, a decline from 46 percent in 1980. Yet even some of the other, occupationally based categories showed a small proportion of financially significant committees. Most PACs with contributors in both the profit and nonprofit sectors were small—whether they were labor committees or groups organized around administrative, executive, or professional roles—suggesting that mobilizing electoral resources may be especially hard when an electoral organization must appeal to persons in very different institutional settings. Administrative committees in the nonprofit sector also tended to be small—only 40 percent had receipts over $10,000 in 1984—though that was not true for labor committees with a nonprofit base, which showed the highest percentages of committees with significant receipts in both election cycles.

PACs representing citizen interests were also less effective than occupationally based committees when we examined their capacity to translate receipts into politically targeted spending. Columns 3 and 4 of table 3.7 show that less than half of the citizen PACs were able to devote more than 20 percent of their total disbursements to independent expenditures or contributions to candidates or parties. Business, especially corporate, committees occupied the other end of the spectrum. Nine out of ten corporate PACs spent 20 percent or more of their disbursements on contributions or other direct political expenditures, while other business committees met the same criterion in about three out of four cases.

The administrative or professional committees in the nonprofit and mixed categories showed significantly lower percentages: about two out of three of these PACs reported political expenditures over the 20 percent threshold. Labor committees were generally less successful, and less stable, than other occupationally based PACs in satisfying this criterion. The largest category of labor committees—those organizing in the profit sector—showed a decline in the percentage of groups exceeding the 20 percent test between 1980 and 1984, from 57 percent to 50 percent. However, labor committees organized within the public and other parts of the nonprofit sector were more likely to devote a substantial share of their expenditures to explicitly political targets. In sum, operat-

TABLE 3.7. Measures of Organizational Strength of PACs, 1980 and 1984 Election Cycles

Contributor Base	Percent of Committees with Total Receipts > $10,000[a]		Percent of Committees Whose Support for Candidates and Parties > 20 Percent of Total Disbursements[b]		Percent of Committees Whose Debt/Asset Ratio[c] < 1.0		Percent of Committees Surviving[d]
	1980	1984	1980	1984	1980	1984	1980-84
	1	2	3	4	5	6	7
Profit sector—corporate	57	57	87	89	98	99	93
Profit sector—industry/ professional/general	51	53	74	79	97	98	89
Mixed sectors	44	47	69	61	100	100	81
Nonprofit sector	43	40	67	66	100	96	85
Labor—profit sector	52	56	57	50	100	99	85
Labor—mixed sectors	46	39	75	50	100	91	87
Labor—nonprofit sector	71	57	62	71	100	95	77
Citizen—party/candidate	46	39	47	45	87	83	67
Citizen—issue	31	34	49	47	76	83	66
N =	2,783	4,309	2,486	3,655	2,326	3,335	2,469

Source: Federal Election Commission/various sources for occupational codes (see app. B).

[a] All registered nonparty committees included, whether or not they reported receipts.

[b] Only includes nonparty committees reporting disbursements > 0 in each election cycle.

[c] Ratio equals (debt owed by committee)/[(cash on hand) + (debt owed to committee)], measured at the end of the election cycle. Only includes nonparty committees with receipts > 0 in each election cycle.

[d] Only includes nonparty committees reporting receipts > 0 in 1980 election cycle.

ing expenditures overwhelmed direct political support among most citizen PACs, while that problem was fairly rare among business committees, especially those connected to corporations. Other occupationally based committees, including labor PACs, fell between these two poles.

We see a similar though less complex pattern when we look at the percentage of committees having a debt/asset ratio over 1.0 (see table 3.7, columns 5 and 6). Again, the greatest differences are found between citizen PACs and committees with an occupational base. Nearly all the occupationally based PACs reported a positive balance of debt and cash at the end of both election cycles, while a significant minority of citizen PACs—between one out of eight and one out of four—showed a negative balance; that is, the debts they owed to others were greater than the sum of their cash on hand and the debts that they were owed.

The survival rates of PACs between 1980 and 1984 generally paralleled our other indicators of organizational strength (see table 3.7, column 7). Citizen PACs showed the lowest survival rates, even after I eliminated from consideration the committees that were registered with the FEC in 1980 but reported no receipts. Only about two out of three citizen PACs were able to raise money in both the 1979–80 and 1983–84 cycles, while about nine out of ten business groups survived and raised funds in both elections. Other occupationally based committees were not as durable as business PACs, but their survival rates were still high, ranging between 77 and 87 percent, exceeding the rates for committees without an occupational base.

To argue that citizen PACs are weak and volatile organizations may not seem credible after the 1992 elections, when the feminist PAC EMILY's List raised over $6 million from 24,000 contributors and provided even greater political support by giving them access to a national network of women contributors by bundling individual contributions (*NYT*, 20 December 1993, 1–19). But if the experience of conservative PACs after Reagan's first term is relevant, the women's groups may find that the boost they got after the Hill-Thomas hearings will be rather short-lived. Consider, for example, the three largest conservative citizen PACs in the 1980 elections, which were also the three largest PACs of *all* types—the Fund for a Conservative Majority (FCM), sponsored by the Young Americans for Freedom; Jesse Helms' National Congressional Club (NCC); and the National Conservative Political Action Committee (NCPAC). These three PACs raised $18.6 million in 1979–80; the Congressional Club and NCPAC each claimed to have had lists of over 300,000 contributors, aided by the direct-mail expert Richard Viguerie; and some in the media even gave them partial credit for handing control of the Senate over to the Republicans by helping to defeat such Democratic senators as George McGovern, Frank Church, John Culver, and Birch Bayh.

Their heyday, however, did not last very long. The receipts of all three groups either increased or stayed about the same through the very divisive 1982 elections, as we can see at the top of figure 3.1, which shows the committees' receipts for each electoral cycle from 1980 to 1992. The groups even expanded their total resources through 1984, as NCPAC's receipts grew to over $19.5 million and FCM's swelled to $5.5 million, easily counterbalancing the temporary decline in NCC's receipts to $5.7 million (perhaps as Helms' supporters sent more of their money directly to his reelection committee). But problems crept in as early as 1984, when NCPAC's debt soared to $4.2 million (see the bottom of figure 3.1). Helms' Congressional Club resumed its growth in receipts in 1986 as it fought in behalf of David B. Funderburk, who lost the Republican senatorial primary race, but the committee's debt increased over tenfold from $155,000 to $1.6 million. NCPAC and FCM's receipts began a precipitous decline during the 1986 elections, and neither NCPAC nor NCC were able to erase the debt they first acquired in the mid-1980s. In 1988, the Fund for a Conservative Majority filed for protection under Chapter 11 of the bankruptcy code (*NYT*, 19 May 1988, A25), and though it remained in existence through the 1992 elections, it gave only $2,000 to candidates. NCPAC hardly exists anymore except as a target for creditors: it raised only $2,118 from individual contributors in the 1991–92 cycle, it gave nothing to candidates, and it still had debts of over $3.9 million. Helms' Congressional Club, though still large, began in 1987 to plough nearly all its receipts into operating expenditures, mostly direct-mail solicitation, advertising, and administrative expenses (*NJ*, 27 February 1988, 537). In the 1992 elections, it spent only 3.3 percent, or $127,581, of its receipts on independent expenditures or contributions to candidates.

These are hardly isolated examples of the weakness and volatility of conservative citizen PACs. One of the oldest and most important of the conservative organizations, the Committee for the Survival of a Free Congress (now the Free Congress PAC), lost strength throughout the 1980s. By 1992, its receipts were only $67,658, less than one-third of its total debt, and nowhere close to the $1.6 million it raised in 1979–80. Only one pro-life PAC remained significant through the 1987–88 election cycle: the National Right to Life PAC, which accounted for 84 percent of the contributions made by all pro-life PACs in the 1988 elections (Makinson 1990, 78). In 1984, the onetime powerhouse Life Amendment Political Action Committee (LAPAC) had $261 in the bank and a debt of $38,000, which grew to $81,000 by 1986. The bank eventu-

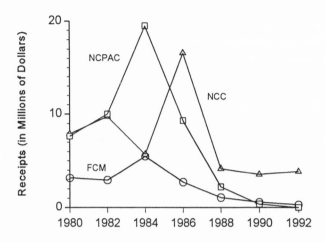

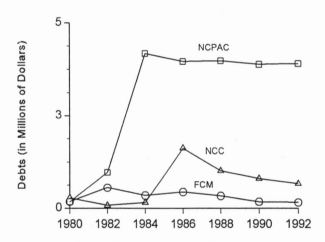

Fig. 3.1. The volatility of citizen PACs: Receipts and debts of the three largest conservative citizen PACs in the 1980 elections, 1980–92. FCM refers to the Fund for a Conservative Majority, NCC is the National Congressional Club, and NCPAC is the National Conservative Political Action Committee. (From Federal Election Commission.)

ally foreclosed on the executive secretary's house, and the committee devoted its meager resources to attacks on a couple of state representatives in Washington (*NYT*, 9 August 1987, 1–25). The American Security Council, a grassroots organization that specializes in defense and foreign policy issues, terminated its once sizable PAC; and though the conservative National Security PAC raised more than $10 million in the 1988 elections, a few months later it had just $14,751 on hand and was nearly $1.2 million in debt (*NJ*, 11 November 1989, 2747). Interestingly, one of the few bright spots for the conservative movement in recent years has appeared on the Religious Right, which has used religious institutions and government subsidies to nonprofit organizations in order to mobilize resources. The Christian Coalition, a nationwide organization started by Pat Robertson in 1990, seems to have flourished in its efforts to win local elections, build grassroots organizations, and conduct "in-pew" voter registration campaigns (*LAT*, 25 January 1992, F16). Yet some of its success may stem from its avoidance of the federal campaign finance laws and its retention, whether legitimate or illegitimate, of its tax-exempt status—as well as from its institutional (though nonoccupational) base in fundamentalist churches.[3]

Why are citizen PACs so weak? The basic problem seems to be the high costs of mobilizing small contributors coupled with the lack of any means for reducing or absorbing those costs. The only way to overcome the lack of an occupational or institutional base is to have access to patrons or large donors, which citizen PACs generally do not have. An organization that relies exclusively on small contributors without an institutional base may achieve considerable strength during tense and highly salient political circumstances (such as the Hill-Thomas hearings), but it is hard to sustain that level of effectiveness under more typical and mundane political conditions.

Consider, for example, the correlates of one of the more direct measures of organizational effectiveness, the proportion of disbursements going to contributions or independent expenditures. We expect that a PAC's capacity to translate receipts into politically effective contributions or independent expenditures is enhanced by three factors: (1) the existence of an occupational base, which reduces the costs of mobilizing individual contributors and often supplies important selective incentives; (2) the availability of a connected organization, which allows the PAC, as an SSF, to pay establishment, administrative, and solicitation costs out of revenues acquired from sources other than small contributors; and (3) the PAC's success in raising money from comparatively large (i.e., moderate-sized) contributors, who, though still hard to mobilize because their individual contributions are not large enough to overcome the collective action problem, are nonetheless easier to solicit than are small contributors.

I estimated the effects of these factors on the share of expenditures devoted to direct political support for PACs that reported receipts exceeding $10,000 in the 1980 or 1984 election cycles.[4] The PAC's occupational base was indicated as a series of dichotomous variables representing a simplified, five-category version of the typology: profit sector groups organized around administrative, professional, or proprietary positions; mixed sector groups representing similar positions; nonprofit sector groups organized around administrative or professional positions; labor groups of any economic sector; and citizen interests. Only the last four variables were included in the equation. The estimated coefficients for these variables thus represented the difference between these four types of groups and the profit sector's score, which was indicated by the intercept. Whether or not a PAC was an SSF was also represented as a dichotomous variable, while the committee's reliance on relatively large contributors was measured by the proportion of individual contributions raised in amounts greater than or equal to $500 per election cycle.

The estimated equations are displayed in table 3.8. The results for both election cycles suggest that a PAC's political effectiveness was strongly related to the occupational roles of its contributors. The intercept term represents the proportion of disbursements going directly to candidates or parties for profit sector PACs without an SSF and with no moderate-sized contributors: 0.519 (or 51.9 percent) of their disbursements went directly to candidates or parties in 1984. Nearly all the typology variables have negative coefficients, which means that committees not in the profit sector showed a lower proportion of direct political expenditures. For example, nonprofit sector PACs organized around professions or administrative roles may have been expected to invest 11.7 percent *less* of their disbursements to direct political action than otherwise comparable profit sector committees during the 1984 elections. Much larger differences were found between profit sector committees and labor or citizen PACs. In 1984, labor PACs were expected to give 29.8 percent less of their disbursements to candidates and parties than business PACs, while citizen PACs gave 24.9 percent less.

The equations also indicate that the levels of effectiveness attributable to different occupational roles might be reduced in two ways: by having a connected organization that absorbs the PAC's administrative and solicitation costs, or by raising the PAC's money in moderate rather than small contributions. In 1984, an SSF was expected to put 17.1 percent more of its disbursements into direct political support than a comparable nonconnected committee; and relying exclusively on moderate-sized contributions (i.e., over $500 per year) would have meant a boost of 23.3 percent over raising all funds in smaller amounts. The estimated equation for the 1980 elections yielded similar results: SSFs put an average of 12.5 percent more of their receipts into direct political support, and a PAC that relied exclusively on moderate-sized contributions was expected to invest 26.1 percent more of its receipts into contributions or independent expenditures than a PAC that only mobilized small contributors.

How do these differences help account for the organizational weakness of citizen PACs and the comparative strength of committees orga-

TABLE 3.8.   The Proportion of a PAC's Disbursements Going to Contributions and Other Political Expenditures as Related to its Membership Base, Reliance on Moderate-Sized Contributors, and Use of a Separate Segregated Fund

Independent Variables	Estimated Regression Coefficients for Political Expenditures as a Proportion of Total Disbursements in Each Election Cycle (Standard Errors in Parentheses)	
	1979-80	1983-84
Intercept	.489	.519
	(.040)	(.031)
Mixed sectors	.050	-.062
	(.120)	(.080)
Nonprofit sector	-.113	-.117
	(.076)	(.057)
Labor	-.185	-.298
	(.026)	(.022)
Citizen	-.205	-.249
	(.044)	(.032)
Separate segregated fund	.125	.171
	(.040)	(.030)
Proportion of contributions in amounts > $500	.261	.233
	(.038)	(.027)
N	1,432	2,189
F-ratio	33.01	97.48
R^2	.12	.21

Source: Federal Election Commission/various sources for occupational codes (see app. B).

Note: Entries are ordinary least-squared regression estimates; dependent variable is the proportion of a committee's total disbursements devoted to express political purposes, including contributions to candidates or parties and independent expenditures.

nized in the profit sector? Business PACs not only enjoyed the advantages of mobilizing support around institutional and occupational roles; most of them also relied directly on institutional resources by means of SSFs. As table 3.9 demonstrates, 94.3 percent of profit sector PACs and virtually all labor committees were SSFs in 1984, but only 6.9 percent of citizen PACs were. Committees organized around citizen interests were less able to rely on institutional patrons than were other groups; their revenue sources were more restricted than for occupationally based PACs, which, by means of the SSF, may exploit a wide variety of revenue sources not subject to FECA restrictions; and a larger share of the individual contributions made to citizen PACs were absorbed by the organization's maintenance or administrative needs.

Because citizen PACs cannot or do not rely on institutional patronage to overcome their organizational problems, they place greater reliance on relatively large donors. Table 3.9 shows that citizen PACs got a larger share of their contributions in amounts greater than $500 than did any other type of PAC. Moderate-sized contributions accounted for a mean of 35 percent of their total support in 1984, over twice the percentage for profit sector PACs, which received an average of 16.2 percent of their contributions in these relatively large amounts. In fact, most business PACs relied even less on moderate-sized contributions than this figure suggests. The median business PAC got only 3.4 percent of its contributions in amounts greater than $500. For citizen PACs, the median value was still fairly high at 23 percent. Comparatively large

TABLE 3.9.   Incidence of Separate Segregated Funds and Reliance on Moderate-Sized Contributors among PACs, by Institutional Base, 1984 Election Cycle

	1983-84 Election Cycle; Only Including PACs with Receipts Greater Than $10,000		
Institutional Base	Percentage of PACs That Are Separate Segregated Funds	Mean Percentage of Contributions in Amounts Greater Than $500	Number of Cases
Profit sector	94.3	16.2	1,565
Mixed sectors	93.8	1.6	16
Nonprofit sector	81.3	.6	32
Labor	99.2	.5	244
Citizen	6.9	35.0	333
All PACs	81.4	17.0	2,190

Source: Federal Election Commission/various sources for occupational codes (see app. B).

individual contributors thus helped to *reduce* differences in effectiveness between citizen groups and business PACs, though there were obvious limits on their ability to use this organizational strategy to achieve parity. Truly large donors were excluded from the system by contribution limits to single committees as well as aggregate limits on individuals' contributions to all committees and candidates. These ceilings on individual contributions may have had little effect on business PACs, which can rely on institutional patrons, and which appeared to be adept at mobilizing small contributors. But the effects were different for citizen PACs, which were more likely to seek out large individual donors to help absorb or reduce the costs of mobilization because they typically had nowhere else to turn. To the extent, then, that the laws restrict the ability of interest groups to rely on large or moderate-sized contributors, citizen groups appear to be hurt the most by such limits. As we will see in chapter 5, this dependence of citizen PACs on moderate-sized contributors parallels a more general dependence of citizen groups on large individual donations, gifts, or bequests—an important asymmetry in the American interest group system that the campaign finance laws fail to recognize.

Comparison with Membership Associations

One might argue that the weakness of citizen PACs is largely inevitable, as are other differences in organizational effectiveness across the typology of occupational roles. Business interests may be assumed to dominate interest group politics regardless of organizational form (whether PACs, membership associations, or advocacy-type think tanks), political tactics (whether campaign financing, litigation, or legislative lobbying), or the institutional rules governing the interest groups' organization and activities (whether restrictive, subsidizing, or noninterventionist). Political organizations representing citizen interests may, according to this argument, be weak and ineffectual in all forms and contexts, except during occasional and brief periods of political stress or "creedal passion" (Huntington 1981, Edelman 1964). Rules and constraints regulating access to institutions, donors, or other sources of support are thus considered to be largely beside the point, since citizen groups—and many other interests outside the profit sector—are unlikely to be organized under any circumstances or, if organized, are unlikely to command significant political resources.

We can explore this objection by comparing the PAC system with its close but more established organizational kin, voluntary membership associations active in national policy-making processes. Like PACs,

these organizations are involved in national politics and claim to represent a base of members or contributors. Also like PACs, they are a form
of organization that is available to just about any type of interest group
as a means of advocating its interests. But there are several significant
and useful differences. Membership associations are, as such, not subject to the same restrictions on their sources of support that PACs must
deal with. Associations are not subject to any limits on the size of
individual contributions, donations, gifts, or bequests. They are not
prohibited from drawing support directly from the treasury funds or
budgets of corporations, labor unions, government agencies, or many
other institutions and using those funds to support political efforts (there
are certain exceptions, discussed in chapter 5). They are not restricted in
the class of persons they may appeal to, nor do they face the same strict
constraints on their ability to manipulate selective benefits in encouraging or even enforcing support for the organization's political aims. Finally, they generally do not have to maintain and file detailed reports
regarding individual contributions, except as required by tax and corporate regulations, and therefore they face fewer mandatory organizational costs. Membership associations thus confront weaker institutional
constraints in mobilizing resources and organizing for political action
and are useful as a comparison group for evaluating PACs and the rules
governing their formation and maintenance.

Fortunately, we also have good data on at least some of the membership associations involved in national policy-making processes. Jack
Walker's surveys of associations in 1980 and 1985 provided a wealth of
information on many of the largest, membership-based organizations
engaged in American national politics, including trade associations,
societies, national or international labor unions and federations, citizen
groups, and many others. The surveys included all membership organizations listed in the respective volumes of Congressional Quarterly's
Washington Information Directory, which indicated the major organizations involved in each of a fairly comprehensive range of policy areas.
There are, of course, important limitations regarding these data, limitations that qualify any direct comparisons with the PAC system. The
response rates were adequate for survey data—about 62 percent in
1980 and 55 percent in 1985—but they are probably much lower than
the registration and reporting rates of PACs. The PAC data are also
more inclusive than the Walker surveys with respect to their total popu-
lations. The Congressional Quarterly listing was generally restricted to
large organizations that had a permanent presence in Washington and
did not include state or local affiliates as separate organizations,
while the FEC registration and reporting data on nonparty committees

encompassed all such organizations whether they were small or large, located in D.C. or not, or national organizations and unions or their state or local affiliates. We should therefore be cautious when comparing PACs and membership associations.

Yet even with a strong dose of skepticism, the enormous differences in the typical size of these two types of organizations are hard to ignore. Consider table 3.10, which compares the average receipts and revenues of PACs and associations according to the typology of occupational roles. The mean of *annual* revenues for associations organized around citizen interests was $6,427,000, about 40 times the mean amount raised in the *two-year* election cycle by citizen PACs, that is, almost $161,000. A comparison of the medians showed an even greater contrast: the median citizen association in the Walker survey had annual revenues of $550,000, while the median citizen PAC reported biennial receipts of about $9,000. These contrasts are not limited to citizen groups. In all the occupational categories, the average PAC was an extremely small organization compared to associations representing similar occupational categories. Groups organized around nonprofit occupations showed an even greater difference: their associations had median annual revenues of $740,000, about 70 times the median biennial receipts of the few PACs

TABLE 3.10.   Comparison between PACs and Membership Associations Active in National Policy-Making, 1984–85: Mean Receipts and Revenues

Institutional Base	Mean Receipts/Revenues (in Thousands of Dollars)		Median Receipts/Revenues (in Thousands of Dollars)	
	PACs	Associations	PACs	Associations
Profit	$50.8	$4,461.5	$17.5	$1,000.0
Mixed	39.4	1,582.2	12.1	550.0
Nonprofit	67.3	34,463.7	10.6	740.0
Labor	146.6	33,674.7	22.6	5,723.0
Citizen	160.5	6,427.1	9.1	550.0
All organizations	$81.3	$5,325.8	$15.8	$850.0
Number of cases	3,624[a]	711	3,624[a]	711

Source: Federal Election Commission/various sources for occupational codes (see app. B); 1985 Walker survey.

[a] This case count refers to the number of organizations used to calculate the overall means and medians. Since some PACs could not be classified into one of the "institutional base" categories, the cases used to calculate the group-level means and medians were slightly fewer (i.e., 3,615).

that were organized around such occupations. Overall, the median PAC reported receipts of $15,800 in the 1983–84 election cycle, a rather paltry figure compared to the $850,000 in annual revenues reported by associations in the Walker study. If we assume that the associations' 1983 revenues were equal to 90 percent of the amount they raised and reported for 1984, it is fair to estimate that the median association had revenues equal to about 100 times the amount of the median PAC in the 1983–84 biennium.

One may question the reliability of the self-reported revenue data that the Walker study relied on, but data from other sources paint much the same picture. The *National Journal* conducted a survey in 1990 of major associations in Washington and got 1989 revenue data from Internal Revenue Service filings (*NJ*, 15 December 1990, 3010–22). Based on their data, the mean annual revenues of the 329 associations in the survey was $22.1 million, and the median annual revenues was $7.2 million. In contrast, the FEC reported that the mean biennial receipts of nonparty committees in the 1989–90 election cycle was $98,200, and the median was approximately $21,000 (both calculations only included the 3,917 committees reporting receipts). If we very conservatively assume that the 1990 association revenues were the same as their 1989 numbers, the mean biennial revenues of associations in the *National Journal* survey were about 450 times the biennial receipts of active PACs. In fact, only 1.7 percent of all active PACs in the 1989–90 election cycle reported biennial receipts of $1 million or more, a figure well below the *lowest decile* for *annual* revenues in the *National Journal* survey.

The contrasts are just as striking if we only look at associations representing citizen interests. The *National Journal* survey reported that the American Association of Retired Persons had annual revenues of $286 million in 1989; the Nature Conservancy, $168 million; Greenpeace USA, $43 million; the National Wildlife Federation, $69 million; the American Civil Liberties Union, $17 million; and so on. In another study, Shaiko (1991) analyzed data collected by the Foundation for Public Affairs in 1985 and found that nearly half of the 196 "public interest organizations" in their study had annual revenues greater than $1.25 million and that nearly one-third had revenues more than $2.5 million. Even though some of these organizations provided services to their members that yielded few if any political returns, one could discount most of their revenues as having little or no political value and still have enough left over to dwarf the typical PAC.

It is therefore not true that the weakness of citizen groups in the PAC system reflects gaps or biases in the American interest group system as a whole. An extraordinarily rich array of permanent political organizations—representing an elaborate distribution of disadvantaged, citizen, and diffuse interests—has been evolving for over a century in American national politics, particularly since the 1960s (Walker 1991; Gais, Peterson, and Walker 1984). Environmental lobbies are only the most obvious examples. They constitute major actors in national environmental politics that "command multimillion-dollar budgets" and "employ corps of full-time lobbyists, lawyers, and scientists" (Mitchell 1991, 81). Yet it is easy to find large, effective, and fairly stable organizations representing a wide variety of other interests, such as consumer groups, government reform groups, and taxpayer watchdog groups; groups representing the civil rights of racial minorities, women, handicapped people, homosexuals, and the elderly; organizations advocating standpoints on the Left and Right regarding national security, peace, nuclear weapons, and foreign policy; groups representing the rights and interests of children, mentally handicapped individuals, and other persons who cannot easily represent themselves; and general ideological groups advocating liberal and conservative views on a wide range of issues (Foundation for Public Affairs 1988).

In fact, the entire PAC system appears to be quite small. The total receipts of all nonparty committees in the 1983–84 election cycle were $294.4 million (see table 3.11). That may seem like a lot of money, but when we compare it with the reported revenues of membership associations in the 1985 Walker survey (which asked groups to report their total revenues in the previous year, i.e., 1984), it is minuscule. The 711 associations for which usable data were available reported $3,786,700,000 in *annual* revenues, nearly 13 times the total *biennial* receipts of all nonparty political committees. Since the 711 reporting associations represent only 47 percent of 1,501 organizations in the Congressional Quarterly directory, it would not be unreasonable to guess that the biennial revenues of all associations in the *Washington Information Directory* are between 40 to 60 times the total biennial PAC receipts. Of course, there are important qualifications to keep in mind. PAC receipts and association revenues are not strictly comparable, since associations have many nonpolitical functions and are usually more autonomous than SSFs, which spend more of their money on political activities and can rely on their connected organizations to absorb the costs of establishing and administering the PAC and raising funds from employees or members. But even if we try to discount the associations for their nonpolitical functions and factor in the extra income for SSFs from their connected organizations, those adjustments can hardly begin to outbalance the exclusion of smaller associations, those with no permanent D.C. presence, and all state and local chapters and union locals from the survey data. It is clear, then, that interest groups in the U.S. raise and spend a lot more political activity money outside the PAC system than within it. Regardless of whether or not we can characterize American politics as a "plutocracy" (Etzioni 1984), it is ridiculous to identify PACs as the center of "special interest" spending.

Despite their small size, PACs are not a widely or evenly distributed extension of the interest group system. They display unique patterns or biases in the kinds of interests they represent, as we can see in table 3.11, which compares the PAC system with the organizations in the Walker survey according to the typology of occupational roles. Business interests are much better represented in the PAC system than among membership associations, whether we look at the number of organizations or their total receipts/revenues. However, groups organized around occupations in the nonprofit sector constitute a major share of the associations active in national policy making, while they are almost entirely absent from the PAC system. Only 1.7 percent of the PACs are organized around administrative/professional/executive positions in the nonprofit sector,

TABLE 3.11. Comparison between PACs and Membership Associations Active in National Policy-Making, 1984–85: Overall Distributions.

Institutional Base	Percentage of Total Number of Organizations		Percentage of Total Organizational Receipts/Revenues	
	PACs	Associations	PACs	Associations
Profit	68.5	36.7	42.7	30.8
Mixed	0.8	5.6	0.4	1.7
Nonprofit	1.7	32.1	1.4	20.9
Labor	10.1	3.1	18.2	19.6
Citizen	18.9	22.5	37.3	27.2
Total	100.0	100.0	100.0	100.0
Total receipts/revenues (in millions of dollars)	—	—	$294.4	$3,786.7
Number of organizations	3,615	711[a]	3,615	711

Source: Federal Election Commission/various sources for occupational codes (see app. B); 1985 Walker survey.

[a] To ensure comparability *within* the table, this column excludes groups for which revenue data are not available. The distribution of all associations responding to the 1985 survey is, however, nearly identical. Of the 828 groups that responded and that were coded within these categories, 36.4 were based within the profit sector, 5.4 were mixed, 32 were within the nonprofit sector, 3.5 were labor, and 22.7 were citizen groups.

while 32.1 percent of the associations are classified in this category; and though 20.9 percent of all association revenues were raised by groups in the nonprofit sector, only 1.4 percent of PAC receipts were attributable to such interests. The contrast would be diminished somewhat if we took the teacher and nurses unions out of the labor category for associations and put them into the nonprofit or mixed categories, but the differences between the two systems would still be enormous.

PACs and associations organized around citizen interests reveal a more complex picture. Even in 1984, after the considerable growth of citizen PACs among conservative groups in the late 1970s and among liberal groups in the early 1980s, such groups constituted a smaller share of PACs (18.9 percent) than their share of membership associations (22.5 percent). However, the receipts of citizen PACs accounted for 37.3 percent of entire amount raised by the PAC system during the 1983–84 cycle, while the revenues of citizen groups accounted for 27.2 percent of the money received by all associations, suggesting that citizen interests might be reasonably well represented among PACs. But such a conclusion would not be true. Many citizen PACs do not represent distinct citizen interests, since over one out of four of them (in 1983–84) are organizations used by candidates or political leaders for personal career reasons rather than for the advocacy of specific issues. And as we have already seen, despite the large amount of money they may raise, citizen PACs are often weak. Typically about 81 percent of the receipts of citizen PACs go to fund-raising and other operating expenses, and many are rather short-lived. In contrast, membership associations organized around citizen interests not only are large in terms of receipts but rarely show the same inefficiencies that drain the political strength of citizen PACs. Major national associations representing citizen interests typically have substantial staffs, engage in a wide variety of political and public activities, and show considerable organizational stability (Shaiko 1991; Mitchell 1991; Foundation for Public Affairs 1988; Berry 1977).

Thus, despite the popular and journalistic preoccupation with PACs in Washington politics, the PAC system is really quite small. PACs are not a ubiquitous tool of political interest groups. They are generally dwarfed by other political organizations involved in national politics and policy making. Most important of all, they show large gaps in the types of interests they represent. With the exception of public sector unions and a few other interests, the PAC system excludes altogether the large number of Washington-based groups organized around occupations in the nonprofit sector or groups with members from both the profit and nonprofit sectors. Some of the PACs representing citizen interests raise significant sums of money, but such committees constitute only a small share of all citizen PACs, and many citizen PACs are extremely volatile and organizationally ineffective.

Why is the PAC system so small, and why does it display so little autonomy? Why are citizen interests so poorly organized for electoral action? Why is the nonprofit sector so narrowly represented in the PAC system? It may be possible that the small and truncated character of the PAC system is the result of tactical decisions by interest groups—maybe few groups find it to be in their political interests to engage in electioneering. Yet it is also possible that many interests may stand to gain from greater participation in campaign financing and elections but, because of the institutional constraints impinging on electoral activities, find themselves unable to participate more fully or effectively. To explore these questions and possible answers is the task of chapters 4 and 5.

CHAPTER 4

PAC Formation among Interest Groups: Incentives and Their Limits

The biases in the PAC system have important implications regardless of what produced those characteristics. PACs represent interests in different proportions than did the older system of membership associations. The near-absence of committees representing the nonprofit sector and the organizational weakness of citizen PACs imply that congressional candidates can build financial coalitions from only a limited range of interest groups active in national politics. The narrow scope of the system also suggests the possibility of upper limits on its potential expansion, since certain types of groups appear unlikely to participate. These upper limits, in turn, may help account for the slow growth of the PAC system since the mid-1980s, a trend that magnifies the importance of money by suppressing its supply (Sorauf 1992).

Yet a complete evaluation of these characteristics depends on an understanding of their causes. A small and biased system of PACs is of less concern if many groups shun participation because they have little or no interest in elections or legislative processes. Such groups might advocate small changes in long-settled, noncontroversial policies through meetings or hearings before administrative agencies. Or they might have such large and diverse memberships that political issues cut across the opinions of group members, and the groups might choose instead to embrace the safer function of reporting Washington developments without taking a position.

But more troubling questions arise if some groups with a significant interest in elections and legislative processes can establish large and effective PACs, while others with no less of an interest cannot. As long-term changes in elections and campaigns make campaign money an increasingly important resource in American politics, it is critical to understand why the PAC system remains so small, why it so poorly represents certain types of groups, and why PACs belonging to certain groups are so weak. I argue that the small size of the PAC system is partly the result of its biases and that those biases stem in part from the fact that many interest groups cannot mobilize significant resources under the constraints imposed by the campaign finance and tax laws.

Of course, other factors must be taken into account to explain the narrow scope of the PAC system. PAC formation is also related to political conditions that increase a group's need to use campaign contributions to get what it wants. Since campaign money is a relatively weak political resource—at least compared to constituency ties, large memberships, or institutionalized access—groups are most interested in forming PACs when they are forced to do so by a complex and conflictual political environment, that is, when they must compete vigorously for the attention of legislators. But these motivational factors lead groups to form PACs only if they can mobilize resources under the constraints imposed by the laws governing group involvement in elections. Neither motives nor institutional conditions, each operating alone, can cause a group to form a PAC. Both factors are critical in a group's decision to participate in elections. This chapter examines the effects and limitations of political incentives in explaining PAC formation; chapter 5 considers how these incentives interact with institutional constraints. Later chapters show that the resulting biases in the kinds of groups found in the PAC system are hardly neutral with respect to policy and partisan divisions.

The Narrow Scope of Interest Group Participation in Elections

I have argued that the system of PACs has little autonomy—little capacity to produce independent, self-sustaining organizations—because of the difficulty of mobilizing small contributors. Small, voluntary contributions are so hard to mobilize that a PAC must usually depend on the resources of a connected organization or institutional base to absorb the costs of mobilizing funds for its activities. This dependence obviously limits the scope of the PAC system. It is difficult for groups representing citizen interests to establish effective PACs, since citizen groups often do not have an institutional base to help mobilize contributors or to pay the costs of soliciting contributors and establishing and sustaining the committee. This lack of autonomy also magnifies the effect of any law regulating the ability of groups to rely on different institutions. Where the laws allow institutions (such as unions and corporations) relatively free rein to use their resources to support electoral activities, PACs can flourish. But where the laws restrict institutions even in small ways (as do the laws in the nonprofit sector), the groups that rely on them cannot develop effective electoral organizations.

So far, we have assessed these hypotheses by comparing aggregates—by comparing the size, organizational characteristics, and occupational base of PACs with those of membership associations. Aggregate comparisons are helpful in understanding the general characteristics of the PAC system as a form of interest representation, but such comparisons cannot be more than suggestive when we want to account for those characteristics. To evaluate explanations about why certain groups have PACs and others do not, we need microlevel data on political interest groups so that we can see where the PAC system has grown and where it has not, and we need fairly rich data to help us pinpoint these locations.

To conduct such analyses, I used the 1980 and 1985 Walker surveys of national associations, but I supplemented the surveys by merging them with data on PACs affiliated with the associations. This was done by searching for all PACs affiliated with the surveyed associations through FEC records, master lists of connected organizations, and privately published directories of PACs and their sponsors. For associations in the 1980 survey, I looked for PACs registered in the 1979–80 federal election cycle; for associations surveyed in 1985, I looked for affiliated committees in the 1983–84 biennium.[1] The resulting data sets have clear limits. They can only encompass PACs connected to national membership associations and unions that were deemed important enough in national policy-making processes to be included in Congressional Quarterly's *Washington Information Directory*. Nonconnected PACs, corporate PACs, and statewide or local PACs were almost completely excluded from the analysis, so any generalizations must be qualified or interpreted in that light.

Yet we should also emphasize the strength of these data. Because the *Directory* was designed as a listing of the major governmental and nongovernmental organizations active in important areas of national policy, the interest groups found in the *Directory* were generally the largest and most vigorous advocacy organizations in national politics. One of the worst problems in PAC studies has been their failure to place PACs within the context of the already highly developed American interest group system. This tunnel vision makes it easy for such analyses to make mistakes about the special qualities of the PAC system, including its size, spread, growth, and representational characteristics. However, if we analyze an important part of that larger interest group system, and if we look at where PACs grew out of that system, we can begin to understand how PACs have augmented parts of the interest group system while leaving other parts behind; how the choice to use PACs has differed from the choice to use other political tactics, such as administrative lobbying, litigation, and legislative lobbying without involvement in campaign financing; and whether the PAC system and other forms of electoral participation have now come to dominate interest group advocacy in Washington.

In fact, Walker's surveys reinforce the evidence presented in chapter 3 suggesting that, far from dominating the interest group system, PACs and other forms of electoral involvement are actually rather limited among interest groups. In both the 1980 and 1985 surveys, the questionnaires included several questions about the importance to the group of certain political activities, including legislative and administrative lobbying, litigation, protests and demonstrations, publicizing issues through the mass media, as well as working to elect sympathetic political leaders. Even though the questions differed somewhat between the two surveys, the results were similar and showed that electoral involvement was among the least common forms of political action. The first two columns of table 4.1 demonstrate this point by indicating the percentage of groups in each survey reporting they engaged in these activities. Administrative lobbying, legislative lobbying, and publicizing issues through the mass media were by far the most common activities among interest groups—engaging between about 83 and 89 percent of the associations—while significantly fewer groups employed litigation, electioneering, or protests and demonstrations. Electioneering was em-

TABLE 4.1. Percentage of National Membership Associations Reporting That They Used Various Political Tactics and That Those Tactics Were Important to Their Organization

Political Tactic	Percentage of Groups Reporting That They Use Tactic		Percentage of Groups Reporting That Tactic Is Important	
	1980	1985	1980	1985
Administrative lobbying	87.8	86.6	80.8	75.2
Legislative lobbying	84.8	84.7	79.0	74.8
Publicity—mass media	89.2	83.4	71.9	59.8
Litigation	53.1	54.3	33.2	27.9
Electioneering	33.6	33.0	26.4	20.2
Protests or demonstrations	18.5	19.0	8.2	7.2
Number of cases	572	811	572	811

Source: 1980 and 1985 Walker surveys.

ployed by only one-third of the groups in either survey, ranking below litigation (which was used by about half of the groups) and only above protests and demonstrations, which were carried out by less than one group out of five.[2]

Although it might have been possible that electoral activities were conducted by only a few groups yet were very important to those who deployed them, that does not appear to be the case in our data. The last two columns of table 4.1 show the percentage of groups reporting that a tactic is important to their organization, and the same general ranking of activities appears. In fact, the differences between the two most common activities—administrative and legislative lobbying—and the other political tactics, including electioneering, are even greater when we consider the relative importance that groups attach to these activities. In the 1985 survey, only about 20 percent of the associations reported that electoral activities were important to the work of their organizations, a response found among only about 26 percent of the groups in the 1980 survey.[3] In contrast, about 80 percent of the groups in the 1980 survey and about 75 percent of those in the 1984 survey reported that administrative and legislative lobbying were important tactics to their organizations. Only protests and demonstrations were considered by fewer groups to be important political tactics.

It may be argued that our data indicating low levels of electoral involvement by national political interest groups were really an artifact of the legal distinction between an association and its separate segregated funds—that data from the two surveys of national associations only showed that the associations' staff distinguished between their organization and its PAC. According to this criticism, if we looked at whether the groups had affiliated PACs, then we would find that group participation in campaigns and elections was much more widespread. In fact, if we were to examine the use of PACs by these associations, we would also be able to detect the involvement of groups that do not consider their campaign financing activities to be *electoral* activities. Groups might consider their PAC to be more of an adjunct to their lobbying activities rather than a form of electoral participation, since they might contribute only in the context of lobbying, without thought about their electoral effects.

Though it may be true that those who use and control PACs often consider them more a tool in a lobbying campaign than a way of influencing elections, there is no evidence that the survey responses underestimated the importance of electioneering. The use of PACs was even less common among national associations than responses by groups indicating that they were involved in elections. Only 19.1 percent of the 587 responding organizations in the 1980 survey had affiliated PACs that were registered anytime during the 1979–80 election cycle; and among the 828 groups surveyed in 1985, only 19 percent had affiliated PACs during the 1983–84 election cycle (see table 4.2). Thus, even among major national membership associations in Washington, only one out of five had adopted PACs by the mid-1980s.[4]

How can we reconcile the low incidence of PAC affiliation with the somewhat larger number of groups reporting that they worked "to aid the election of political leaders"? In the 1985 Walker survey, 15.8 percent of the responding organizations reported that, though they had no PAC, they had engaged in electoral advocacy (even if they did not consider it to be important). It is possible that some groups worked only on state and local elections—activities that do not require federal registration and reporting—but the national focus of the associations in the Walker surveys makes that prospect rather improbable. It is more likely that many of these organizations used electoral tactics that do not require a separate segregated fund. The laws are less strict about the funding of electoral activities when an organization is willing to restrict its audience. Membership associations may, like unions, engage in "partisan communications" with their members, just as corporations with capital stock may engage in such communications with their stockholders and administrative or executive personnel. Such communications may include express advocacy of the election or defeat of a "clearly identified candidate" (11 C.F.R. § 114.7(h)) and may be financed by general treasury funds—that is, they do not require a separate segregated fund.

TABLE 4.2.   Percentage of National Membership Associations with PACs, 1980 and 1985

Occupational Role	1980 Survey/1980 Elections		1985 Survey/1984 Elections	
	Percent with PACs	Number of Groups	Percent with PACs	Number of Groups
Profit sector	35.8	179	34.6	301
Mixed	12.3	65	4.4	45
Nonprofit sector	4.5	198	5.3	265
Labor	58.6	29	69.0	29
Citizen	12.1	116	9.0	188
All groups	19.1	587	19.0	828

Source: Federal Election Commission/Walker merged data (see app. A).

However, an organization may not stretch the concept of "member" to address the general public. Members may not simply be individuals who had given money during a fund drive or had shown an interest in the organization. They must display some "relatively enduring and independently significant financial or organizational attachment" to the organization, evidenced by concrete rights and obligations like the payment of dues at regular intervals or mandatory, periodic membership renewal (*FEC* v. *National Right to Work Committee* 1982; Bauer and Kafka 1984, chap. 10, 2–3). Associations and unions may also, like corporations, use their treasury funds to engage in a variety of "nonpartisan communications," such as the preparation of nonpartisan voting records and voter guides and the conduct of nonpartisan voter registration and get-out-the-vote programs (Bauer and Kafka 1984, chap. 10, 5), though it is doubtful that the respondents were referring to such activities when they reported working to "aid" specific candidates. It would be reasonable to assume that most of these "non-PAC" electoral activities involved endorsements in newsletters or other internal communications.

As chapter 3 suggests, the PAC system is also small in that it represents a narrow array of interests. PACs are much more likely to form among interest groups with strong ties to private economic institutions, such as labor unions or trade and professional associations in the profit sector. These large differences in the incidence of PACs among interest groups reappear in table 4.2, which compares the percentage of groups with PACs across the typology of occupational roles. In both 1980 and 1985, associations organized around profit sector occupations were, along with labor unions, much more likely to have PACs than were interest groups representing persons or organizations in the nonprofit, mixed, or citizen group categories. In 1985, 69 percent of the unions had at least one affiliated PAC during the 1983–84 election cycle, while about 35 percent of the business associations in the survey had separate segregated funds. In contrast, the nonprofit sector was almost entirely missing from the PAC system, as only one out of twenty groups had affiliated committees in each cycle. Citizen groups were more likely to have PACs than were associations in the nonprofit sector, but only about one out of ten citizen groups had PACs in the early and mid-1980s. Groups in the mixed category were also unlikely to have PACs.[5]

Even among groups that had PACs, the proportion of their resources devoted to campaign financing was typically small. Of the groups in the 1985 survey with affiliated PACs, a median of 1 percent of the total money raised by the association *and* all its affiliated PACs in the 1983–84 biennium were raised by the separate segregated funds; and the mean value was only a little higher at 4.9 percent, since a handful of groups devoted a large share of their total funds to electioneering.[6] Thus, not only were PACs fairly uncommon among these large, Washington-based, national associations; the funds raised by the few PACs that did exist constituted only a small share of all the money raised by their parent associations.

Political Motives and PAC Formation

The narrow distribution of groups in the PAC system may result from the lack of incentives among many interest groups to establish such organizations. Groups may be able to accomplish their political goals without making campaign contributions or otherwise participating in elections, and the costs of setting up and maintaining such an organization may not be worth the potential gains. For example, the limited size of the system might reflect the limited use of those activities that PACs support. Many political observers believe that PACs are used to serve the lobbying efforts of groups seeking to influence legislation. As former senator Gary Hart said, "interest groups now believe they have to pay to get in your office, and they believe they have to pay for you to listen to their arguments" (U.S. Senate Committee on Rules and Administration 1986, 6). If, however, a trade association, professional society, or other group is satisfied with the major federal programs affecting its members— programs that may have been enacted many years ago and that face no current opponents or political threats—it may choose to work to influence the interpretation of federal statutes by making appearances at administrative hearings, informal meetings with administrators, and litigation in behalf of its members. Unless something disrupts this situation, the organization has little need to build up additional support within the Congress by mobilizing and distributing campaign money.

This may explain why some major groups do not have PACs. In the 1985 Walker survey, 20 percent of the associations said they either did not work "with members of Congress or their staffs on the formulation or implementation of legislation" or, if they did, considered the activity to be unimportant. Of these associations, only 2 percent had affiliated PACs. But though a legislative agenda seemed to be a necessary condition for establishing a PAC, it was hardly sufficient. Even among associations reporting that working with Congress was "one of the most important" activities they engaged in, only 30 percent had PACs.[7] In other words, seven out of ten associations reported that they lobbied the Congress intensively without the aid of PACs.

Why aren't PACs used by more interest groups, especially those groups lobbying the Congress? I think that a major part of the explanation is found in the weakness of campaign contributions as a political resource; groups usually turn to them only when other resources can no longer ensure legislative success. In chapter 1, we reviewed several studies showing that contributions by a small number of PACs—such as those affiliated with a single industry, association, or labor union—typically had no significant impact on floor voting by members of Congress. This microlevel weakness can exist despite the fact that legislators need a lot of money. Unlike some things a group can offer, campaign money is *substitutable* from the perspective of a legislator. Members of Congress can usually compensate for a single group that refuses to provide campaign funds—or that makes unreasonable demands in exchange for contributions—by getting funds from another group that places fewer demands on the members' votes and activities.

In contrast, a group that provides strong resources that a legislator cannot get from other groups is in a better bargaining position. Ties to a member's constituency are surely a strong resource, especially if the constituency is large, since a legislator cannot easily substitute one large constituency group with another in his or her electoral coalition. Thus, groups can be very successful if they make a credible case to legislators that they know how a large constituency will respond to various policy decisions (Hansen 1991) or if they can communicate with legislators through members' constituents (Kingdon 1989). Control over important technical information can also be important. Some occupationally based groups enjoy access to legislators because they have unique expertise or information that government leaders need to develop policies affecting an industry (Brody 1978, 288–90; Schlozman and Tierney 1986, 298–99). Also, business groups are often granted special access because they control jobs and other critical economic resources in policymakers' districts (Lindblom 1977). And other groups enjoy significant access to certain legislators because they share values or ideological viewpoints and can provide credible and politically useful information on how to further these shared objectives. This control over important constituencies, scarce information, and economic institutions can therefore produce a sort of privileged access to legislators that campaign money cannot. Some groups have even succeeded in institutionalizing this access by getting the Congress to create committees, subcommittees, or special committees devoted to the needs of the constituencies they claim to represent, such as farmers or the elderly.

Thus, campaign contributions are a secondary or supplementary resource. They may be used by groups to strengthen relationships with legislators based on constituency ties or other resources, yet they cannot create exclusive, enduring relationships with candidates or legislators.

This point has implications for the goals of interest groups in establishing PACs. They are not likely to set up PACs with the expectation that they can use campaign contributions to "buy" support from legislators on floor votes. Even though that is theoretically possible, it would be a very costly thing to do, since there are so many legislators, and their votes are usually structured by ideology, constituency, personal history, party, and other factors. It is therefore not surprising—as we noted in chapter 1— that credible studies of the effects of a single PAC or of a small number of PACs generally find that their contributions do not directly affect floor votes. That is true even for low-visibility issues that do not evoke much constituency interest or elicit much ideological or partisan strife: because the intended beneficiaries of such votes are usually concentrated in a few constituencies—while their costs are spread among many—there are many institutional incentives for legislators to support these sorts of bills, so it is not clear why groups *need* to make contributions to encourage logrolling, credit claiming, or any other traditional forms of distributive politics.

However, contributions may be able to purchase greater access to a sympathetic member's time and energy—not just to convince the legislator that the group's demands are right, but even more so to secure the legislator's services in advocating the group's demands within the legislature (see Denzau and Munger 1986). This argument is not only compatible with the common observation that PACs usually contribute to those who already support them, a finding that would not make any sense if PACs were trying to switch members' votes. It is also compatible with the idea that legislators have greater discretion over the use of their time and energy than they do over the actual policy positions they take in legislative votes (Bauer, Pool, and Dexter 1963). And it dovetails with the frequent finding that PACs contribute to a small number of members of congressional committees with jurisdiction over issues important to the group—particularly in the House (Grier and Munger 1993)—since it is those legislators who are in the institutional position to serve as effective advocates or coalition builders in the group's behalf.

What kinds of services can sympathetic legislators provide to interest groups in return for contributions? Such services may include keeping a group representative informed—in a timely way—of legislative developments that might affect the group's interests, a service that conforms with what many scholars view as one of the most common activities of Washington representatives, namely, monitoring and alerting clients about what is happening in Washington (Salisbury 1992, 358–61). They may also include legislators' active participation in committee deliberations on issues important to the group, such as attending relevant committee or subcommittee meetings, speaking up on issues important to the group during those meetings, drafting or introducing amendments favored by the group, or working behind the scenes to build support for the group's demands (Hall and Wayman 1990). Policy services may also encompass activities on the floor of the Congress, including sponsoring or cosponsoring legislation, working with party leaders over scheduling and rule issues, and, of course, contacting other members to influence votes on the floor (Kingdon 1989).

The question of when groups have incentives to form PACs thus boils down to two more specific questions: When do interest groups need policy services beyond levels that legislators would provide in the absence of campaign contributions? And when are resources stronger than contributions no longer enough to attain the services needed? I think two situations are most important. One occurs when groups must deal with a lot of conflict and volatility in policy areas affecting their interests. If the group's relations with legislators are vulnerable to electoral or partisan shifts in national politics or if the group faces opponents or other kinds of conflict on issues important to it, it may need to strengthen its connections with legislators to ensure future success. Opposition creates obstacles in the way of the group's legislative aims, and the group needs active legislative supporters to overcome these barriers—to out-argue political enemies, to work out accommodations with moderate opponents, or to convince committee chairs to take up controversial issues. Conflict also makes it harder for groups to secure the coalition leaders they need, since it creates disincentives for even sympathetic legislators to take strong, active stands in support of the group's efforts. And conflict creates a more uncertain, volatile political situation, which groups seek to minimize by getting strong legislative supporters to help manage the legislative process.

Conflict can also facilitate electoral involvement. First, it may have the effect of removing disincentives to engage in electoral politics. Anytime a group decides to contribute to a candidate or party, its decision implies that some other candidate or party is *not* supported. If the group has any hope of creating the sense of political consensus—or at least noncontroversiality—that is critical in moving legislation along (Kingdon 1989), then even minimal involvement in campaigns and elections may undermine its efforts. But if conflict is already widespread, there are fewer reasons for a group to refrain from electoral intervention. Second, political conflict creates opportunities for some interest groups to use elections to publicize issues, especially when the conflict runs along party lines. Groups may try to increase an issue's salience by intervening in elections where the candidates are divided over the issue. They may try to demonstrate the importance of an issue and the costs of opposition by attacking well-known incumbents who have long opposed them; they may use contributions to encourage a sympathetic candidate to emphasize the group's concerns during the campaign; or the groups may raise those issues themselves through direct intervention, such as independent expenditures. In any case, a group can focus its efforts on a small number of highly visible, competitive races and use the results of those races (assuming they are successful) as "lessons" to enhance the group's access to other legislators or politicians. Not incidentally, the group's involvement in a highly divisive and salient campaign can also help to mobilize additional supporters and potential contributors to the PACs themselves. Thus, there are selective incentives for interest groups to intervene in elections and exploit them as "outside" strategies for greater access, but the tactic depends on the existence of a fairly high level of political conflict.

The second situation occurs when groups confront a highly *complex* legislative environment. A complex environment is one where a group must win the support of many committees, subcommittees, or legislators to achieve its ends. Interest groups may be able to nurture a small number of relationships with legislators in one or two subcommittees, especially if they work with the same subcommittees frequently and repeatedly. But if a group must deal with many legislators, it probably needs to strengthen at least some of those relationships, since the group is much more likely to need energetic legislator-advocates to shepherd bills or special provisions through the legislative process. In complex legislative contexts, the group may also need a way of encouraging the cooperation and aid of legislators whom they have rarely worked with before or whose committee assignments and constituencies do not predispose them to be active advocates of the group's interests.

The need for campaign contributions is therefore greatest where groups confront a complex, competitive, loosely coupled system of policy making in which allegiance and attention are up for grabs. An interest group's avoidance of electoral involvement may reflect its insulation from electoral change, as policy decisions affecting its members are made within a small policy subsystem where the group already enjoys considerable access and autonomy (Ripley and Franklin 1987; Lowi 1979). In such situations, there are already strong incentives for legislators to provide the services that groups need to advocate their demands effectively. Frequent interaction between legislators and groups—as well as the high number of legislators from districts that benefit from policies in their jurisdiction—often ensure a sympathetic audience for the group's demands. Note, for example, Wright's (1990) finding that while campaign contributions were not very important in providing access to members of the House Agriculture Committee, where relations with groups were already fairly intense and informal, they played an important role in structuring group access to members of the Ways and Means Committee, whose large jurisdiction meant that any one group was unlikely to work very often with any one legislator—and so access was more formalized and problematic. Establishing a PAC may therefore be a reaction to a widening scope or socialization of political conflict (see Schattschneider 1960)—a perception that conflict and participation is expanding beyond the confines of a stable, intimate subgovernment, and that additional political resources are needed to reinforce, construct, or recover good relations with government officials.

To say campaign money is a weak political resource is therefore not to say it is unimportant. It may be a significant factor in highly competitive situations where constituency ties and institutional structures fail to resolve and contain policy conflicts or where groups are forced to work with a large number of congressional subcommittees and members who are not predisposed to support the group and do not have the long-standing personal relationships that have characterized so many subgovernments. These sorts of open, complex, and competitive situations may be increasingly common in national politics (Gais, Peterson, and Walker 1984; Salisbury 1990), making it more important for more groups to add electoral activities to their tactical repertoire.

The relative weakness of campaign contributions also does not mean that it is unimportant to understand which groups form PACs and which ones do not. Even if campaign contributions have only a contingent or marginal impact at the level of individual groups, the aggregate distribution of money from large numbers of PACs is important. As we saw in chapter 1, contributions from large categories of PACs—such as business and labor, conservative or liberal—do seem to affect floor votes. And as we shall see in later chapters, different levels of PAC formation and effectiveness across the typology of occupational roles may have significant consequences for how money is distributed among candidates of different parties and policy views, and that aggregate distribution surely affects elections.

Estimating the Effects of Motivational Factors

It is possible that many of the representational characteristics of the PAC system reflect the distribution of incentives for groups to participate in elections. To see how far these motivational factors can lead us in accounting for the number and distribution of PACs, I estimated a linear model of PAC formation based on general political incentives. These

motivations included the reasons why any group, of whatever occupational role, would want a PAC.

Three types of motivations were assumed to be important to an
interest group's decision to form an affiliated PAC. One such factor was
the group's perception of issue conflict in its political environment. As a
group experiences more conflict in its environment, we expect that it
would use campaign contributions or other forms of electoral intervention to enhance its legislative access. Eight measures of issue conflict
were included from the 1985 survey, where the association was asked
whether certain statements were "poor" or "good" descriptions of the
association on a five-point scale. Specifically, the interest group was
asked whether it worked in a policy area marked by

> intense conflict or disagreement over fundamental policy goals;
> consensus on the appropriate means for achieving policy objectives;
> frequent conflict, that is, conflict that "erupts very often";
> stable opposition, that is, an atmosphere in which the association
>   faces the same opponents on different policy issues;
> opposition by important elected officials;
> opposition by other organized groups;
> opposition by important government agencies; and
> important differences between the two major political parties on
>   issues most relevant to the association's goals.

A second factor was the intensity and complexity of the group's
lobbying activities. We expect that PACs would be more common
among groups that have important legislative agendas and that face
complex legislative environments. A legislative agenda may be viewed
as a prerequisite for PAC activities, while a complex environment may
be a positive inducement to form a PAC. When a group faces a complex environment—that is, one requiring it to work with many legislators and subcommittees—it is probably in greater need of coalition
leaders and therefore must encourage their extra participation. Moreover, a complex environment means that the group must establish good
relations with many legislators outside of the one or two subcommittees predisposed to support its demands. To measure the general importance of legislative lobbying, I used a question in the survey that asked
whether "[w]orking with members of Congress or their staffs on the
formulation or implementation of legislation" was an activity that the
association engaged in; and, if it did, how important the organization
perceived lobbying to be for achieving its policy goals. Answers were
arrayed on a six-point scale. To measure the complexity of their lobby-

ing activities, I used a question that asked associations to indicate how many congressional subcommittees they communicated, consulted, or interacted with during the past year. The responses were arrayed on a five-point scale ranging from "none" to "more than six." And finally, the intensity of a group's interactions with Congress was measured by asking about the frequency of interaction between the group and the subcommittee that it works with the most. Those responses were placed on a five-point scale that ranged from "frequently interacts" (coded as one) to "almost never interacts" (coded as four) to no such interaction (coded as five).

A third factor was the group's emphasis on political representation and policy advocacy. For some groups, political representation and advocacy are not important functions, and we would not expect them to get involved in elections except in fairly extreme and unexpected circumstances. Certain professional societies, for example, exist primarily to publish journals, sponsor conferences, and provide other services to members of the profession. Trade associations in relatively unregulated segments of the economy may place little emphasis on political activities, as may some of the older groups that have evolved into largely social organizations. Much of their political work may be limited to monitoring Washington activities for their members. Even if these organizations were faced with sudden political threats, they may be hard to mobilize for electoral action, since their members did not join the organization because of their concern for or agreement on any political goals. We may not expect to find many apolitical organizations in the surveys, but some variation does exist, and any de-emphasis of political activities may inhibit the organizations' interest in or ability for mobilizing its members for electoral action. A group's emphasis on political representation and advocacy was measured by questions about the importance of two benefits to members: "[a]dvocacy of important values, ideas, or policies"; and "[r]epresentation of members' opinions before government agencies or legislative bodies."

These three factors and their underlying indicators were assumed to increase the probability that an interest group had one or more affiliated PACs according to a multivariate logistic model. Logistic regression was then used to estimate the relationship between these factors and a dichotomous variable indicating whether a group in the 1985 survey had one or more affiliated PACs in the 1983–84 election cycle. The motivational model and its estimated parameters are shown in table 4.3. Comparison of the coefficients with their standard errors suggests that four factors were particularly important in understanding whether a group was likely to have an affiliated PAC:

the complexity of the group's lobbying effort—groups that had lobbied several subcommittees in the last year were more likely to
have PACs than groups that had lobbied only one or two;

involvement in partisan issues—groups that perceived significant
differences between the two major parties on issues important to
their goals were more likely to have PACs than those that saw no
differences;

involvement in recurrent political conflicts—groups reporting that
they repeatedly faced the same opponents on significant policy
issues were more likely to have PACs than those that saw less
stable coalitional alignments; and

the group's emphasis on representing their members' opinions on
political issues—groups saying that the representation of members' opinions before government agencies or legislative bodies
was an important function were more likely to have PACs than
those that did not.

Thus, PACs were more likely to emerge where groups faced a stable,
partisan structure of conflict, and where they emphasized the representation of members' opinions. The importance and intensity of legislative
lobbying activities did not show a strong influence on whether groups
established and maintained PACs, though lobbying in a *complex* legislative environment did.

However, the overall model does not have a lot of explanatory
power. It correctly classifies only 81 percent of the groups with respect
to whether they had a PAC, a percentage that barely beats a simple
null model that none of the groups had affiliated committees, since 80
percent did not. Yet despite its limitations, the model is useful in
identifying certain *necessary* conditions for PAC formation. Groups
that did not face conflictual and partisan environments, that did not
stress the representation of members' opinions, and that did not lobby
multiple subcommittees rarely had separate segregated funds. That is
important because many groups did not face these circumstances. Most
groups did not, for example, see party difference on issues significant
to their organizations. As the top row of table 4.4 shows, the mean
value on the variable indicating whether a group perceived important
differences between the parties was quite low—2.5 on a five-point
scale, where 3.0 is the midpoint. Also, the means on two of the other
variables that showed the most impact were near the midpoint, suggesting that about half of the groups were not found at the higher end of
these scales: the mean value for whether a group faced the same opponents repeatedly was 3.0, and the mean for the question concerning the
number of subcommittees the group lobbied during the past year was

3.2—again, both on five-point scales. Only one variable that was rather strongly related to whether a group established a PAC was also fairly high for most groups in the survey: the mean value for whether a group emphasized representation of members' opinions was 4.8, a value considerably higher than the scale's midpoint of 3.5. Put more concretely, the small number of groups with PACs may in part be attributable to the fact that many national interest groups are not

TABLE 4.3. Logistic Regression of PAC Affiliation on Interest Groups' Emphasis on Political Benefits to Members, Perception of Political Conflict, and Legislative Lobbying, 1985

Variables	Beta Estimates	Standard Errors	Chi-Squared (Beta=0)
Intercept	-6.820		
1. Benefits provided to members (1=not provided - 6=one of most important):			
Advocacy of values/ideas/policies	-.142	.121	1.37
Representation of members' opinions	.560	.158	12.55[c]
2. Perceptions of political conflict or consensus (1=poor description - 5=good description):			
Intense conflict in policy area	-.079	.110	.51
Consensus in policy area	.004	.103	.00
Conflict erupts often	-.024	.117	.04
Same opponents faced repeatedly	.183	.094	3.82[c]
Some elected officials oppose aims	-.163	.102	2.55[a]
Some organized groups oppose aims	.065	.093	.49
Some government agencies oppose aims	-.060	.095	.39
Sees important party differences	.208	.080	6.70[c]
3. Lobbying activities:			
Importance of legislative lobbying (1=not engaged in - 6=one of most important)	.141	.131	1.14
Number of subcommittees worked with in year (1=0, 2=1-2, 3=3-4, 4=5-6, 5=7+)	.569	.119	23.04[c]
Frequency of interaction with top subcommittee (reverse scoring; 1-5)	-.048	.188	.07
Number of cases = 777 Percent correctly classified = 81 Model Chi-squared (13 df) = 145.35			

Source: FEC/Walker merged data (see app. A).
[a]Probability (Beta = 0) < .15.
[b]Probability (Beta = 0) < .10.
[c]Probability (Beta = 0) < .05.

involved in recurrent, partisan conflicts, nor do many of them face a complex legislative environment.

The equation also helps us to understand at least some of the differences in the rate of PAC formation across the typology of occupational roles. We can see this in the lower rows of table 4.4, which show the average values of these four main factors across the typology. Although the actual differences between the means are small, the differences that do exist regarding the importance of representing members' opinions parallel their rates of PAC formation. Labor and business groups place the most emphasis on representing member viewpoints, groups in the nonprofit and mixed categories stress it the least, and citizen groups fall in between—a ranking that is identical to their affiliation rates in the merged 1985/1984 data set (see table 4.2). Close linkages and responsiveness to members facilitate the formation of affiliated PACs—because PACs depend on their voluntary actions—and business and labor may dominate the PAC system in part because they have succeeded in creating these connections.

Other data extend this point to suggest that some of the differences in PAC formation grow out of differences in the way in which a group conceives of its representational role. If we look back at the equation in

TABLE 4.4.   Average Values of Factors Related to the Establishment of Affiliated PACs by Associations, by the Typology of Occupational Roles, 1985

	Mean Values of Factors Related to the Establishment of PACs			
Occupational Role	Political Representation as Member Benefit	Nature of Conflict: Same Opponents Faced Frequently	Nature of Conflict: Sees Important Party Differences	Interaction with Congress: Numerous Subcommittees Lobbied
All groups	4.8	3.0	2.5	3.2
Range of values	1-6	1-5	1-5	1-5
Profit	5.1	3.0	2.3	3.3
Mixed	4.2	2.6	2.2	2.8
Nonprofit	4.5	2.7	2.3	3.0
Labor	5.2	4.1	4.5	3.7
Citizen	4.8	3.5	2.9	3.4
Number of cases	823	817	814	813

Source: Federal Election Commission/Walker merged data (see app. A).

table 4.3, we see that there is a slight *negative* relationship between a group's emphasis on the "advocacy of important values, ideas, or policies" and its probability of having an affiliated PAC. In contrast to the representation of members' opinions, many citizen groups place particular emphasis on this representational role. Their mean score on this variable is 5.5 on a six-point scale, higher than any other category of group, while labor groups place relatively little stress on this "member benefit," with an average of 4.9. PACs seem, in other words, to fit a representational style that is delegate-like, in the sense of representing actual opinions within the group's membership or constituency. They are less common among, and not as well suited to, caucus organizations that view themselves as trustees for the advocacy of certain values, ideas, or policies, a role that puts members into a somewhat subsidiary role of providing support.[8] As we will see in chapter 5, this distinction with respect to the roles of members, and its consequences for PAC formation, appears in another guise when we consider where groups get their financial support—whether from member dues or from a variety of patrons in the form of grants, contracts, gifts, or donations.

But if these representational roles help us understand the different rates of PAC formation across the typology of occupational roles, the other factors in table 4.4 create certain anomalies. Consider, for example, the two conflict variables: whether a group faces the same opponents repeatedly, and whether it sees important differences between the major parties. Although it is true that labor groups rank high on these factors—just as they show the highest rates of PAC affiliation—citizen groups also score high on these measures, though only a few of them have PACs. Business groups are also anomalous. As a category, they tend not to see significant party differences, nor are they especially likely to see the same opponents repeatedly. Yet they show comparatively high rates of PAC formation. Finally, when we examine which groups face complex legislative environments by having to lobby numerous subcommittees, we see that profit sector and labor organizations are both high on this measure and thus seem to parallel their high rates of PAC affiliation. But we also see that many citizen groups lobby several subcommittees, though they tend *not* to form PACs.

This motivation-based model thus leaves certain patterns of PAC formation unexplained. Representational style, political conflict, and legislative complexity may help us understand some of the differences in PAC formation—such as the high rates found among labor unions or the low rates among groups in the mixed category—but they make the small number of PACs among citizen groups even more mystifying, since these groups tend to face stable, partisan alignments and to lobby multiple subcommittees. These deficiencies in the motivation-based model are particularly striking when we note how it fails to predict the large, observed differences in the incidence of PACs across the typology of occupational roles. Using the model reported in table 4.3, we can compare the predicted number of PACs for each type of interest group with the actual number. Since the predictions are based on a motivational model of PAC formation, we can see precisely where such explanations fail. This comparison is shown in table 4.5. The top row indicates the number of groups that actually had one or more PACs in the 1983–84 election cycle. Most of these groups (100 out of 152) were in the profit sector; labor unions had the next largest number of organizations with PACs with 19.

But the predictions tell a different story. Based on the group's emphasis on political representation, its perception of conflict, the number of subcommittees with which it works, and other motivational factors, we would expect roughly twice the number of nonprofit and citizen interest groups to have affiliated PACs. These predictions suggest that, based on these motivational factors alone, business and labor organizations should constitute only about 49 percent, not 78 percent, of all groups with PACs. The motivational model thus grossly overpredicts the

TABLE 4.5. Comparison of Predicted and Actual Numbers of Interest Groups with Affiliated PACs, by the Typology of Occupational Roles, 1985 Survey

	Occupational Role—1985 Survey					
	Profit Sector	Mixed Sectors	Nonprofit Sector	Labor	Citizen	All Groups
Actual number of groups with PACs	100	2	14	19	17	152
Predicted number of groups with PACs[a]	65	3	36	10	38	152
Difference between actual and predicted	**35**	**-1**	**-22**	**9**	**-21**	0[a]
Total number of groups	283	43	253	27	171	777

Source: Federal Election Commission/Walker merged data (see app. A).

[a] The predicted number of PACs was derived from probability values generated by the equation reported in table 4.4. However, I changed the probability value "cut," or classification midpoint, used to predict whether a group had a PAC. The cut was shifted downward from 0.5 (where values above that amount were predicted to have a PAC) to 0.363 in order that the predicted marginal distribution of groups with PACs equaled the actual marginal distribution (i.e., where type I and type II errors were equal). This was done to make comparison easier and to ensure that the classification bias in the model was not just due to the possibility that business and labor groups were disproportionately found at the "high" end of the probability curve.

number of groups with PACs in the nonprofit and citizen categories and underpredicts the number of groups with PACs in the business and labor categories. The lack of PACs among nonprofit and citizen interest groups is not a consequence of their facing quiescent and relatively simple political circumstances with little partisan division. Many groups in those categories face just as much political conflict and legislative complexity as do labor and business groups. Other factors either inhibit the formation of PACs in these two categories or encourage their establishment among business and labor organizations. We will consider those factors in chapter 5.

CHAPTER 5

PAC Formation among Interest Groups: Institutional Constraints

What prevents organizations representing citizen interests or the non-profit sector from establishing PACs, even when they have the political motives to do so? The causes, I believe, are found in legal constraints. The basic problem is that the ways in which certain types of interest groups have traditionally mobilized resources for political action are impeded or closed off altogether by the laws regulating interest group involvement in elections. The small, private contributor model of electoral participation that underlies these laws bears little resemblance to the complex, ad hoc, and heterogeneous coalitions of supporters—which often combine public and private patrons—that many groups have constructed to support their lobbying efforts, litigation activities, and other nonelectoral activities. The result of this mismatch between the laws regulating campaign finance and the ways in which certain groups mobilize resources is a small, weak, and highly biased system of interest group involvement in national elections.

Patrons and Group Mobilization

This mismatch becomes clear when we examine the ways in which organizations representing citizen interests and the nonprofit sector raise the money they need to form and sustain their political efforts. In his analyses of the 1980 and 1985 surveys of membership associations, Jack Walker found that these two types of groups raised a relatively small share of their annual revenues from contributions by members, whether in the form of dues, conferences, or publication sales and subscriptions. In contrast to business associations, which raised a mean of 76 percent of their annual revenues from members through dues and conferences, citizen groups in the 1985 survey got only 36 percent of their revenues from members, and nonprofit sector groups received only 58 percent (Walker 1991, 82). These findings paralleled Walker's earlier estimates from the 1980 survey, where he found that dues and conferences composed an average of 84 percent of the annual revenues for profit sector groups, 55 percent for groups in the nonprofit sector, and 39 percent for citizen groups (1983, 400).

Citizen groups compensated for this lack of financial support from members by securing funds from a variety of political patrons, especially from foundations and from individuals contributing large gifts, though they also received significant amounts of support in the form of corporate and business gifts, government grants and contracts, and various types of aid from other associations. Taken together, these five sources accounted for an average of 43 percent of the annual revenues of citizen groups in the 1980 survey and 38 percent in 1985. Groups organized around occupational roles in the nonprofit sector also relied on patrons but depended on a somewhat different mix. They got little support in the form of individual gifts yet received significant amounts from government contracts and grants, which averaged 15 percent of their revenues in 1980 and 10 percent in 1985. When these government sources were added to the amounts they received from foundations, corporate and individual gifts, and other associations, nonprofit sector groups reported in 1980 that they raised over 24 percent of their revenues from these various individual and institutional patrons, though these sources declined to 21 percent by 1985 after the Reagan Administration reduced the discretionary funds available to nonprofit and citizen groups (Peterson and Walker 1986). Given these findings, it is fair to conclude that a broadly representative system of interest groups—that is, one that extends beyond private economic institutions—depends on the availability of a wide variety of public and private patrons for political action, and Walker illustrates this point by arguing that the expansion of the interest group system during the 1960s and 1970s depended greatly on the actions of government agencies, private foundations, and large benefactors.

If individual and institutional patrons are important in maintaining citizen and nonprofit sector associations, they are critical in the early, formative stages of these organizations. Nearly all citizen groups and most groups in the nonprofit sector reported that they received financial aid from one or more political patrons, aid that may have taken the form of large gifts from individuals; grants from foundations, government agencies, or business corporations; or start-up support from other associations (Walker 1983, 398; 1991, 78–79). Nonprofit sector groups placed greater reliance on government grants, while citizen groups depended more on foundations and on individual and corporate gifts; but quite often groups secured support from more than one type of patron, especially among groups founded since the early 1960s. Based on the 1985 survey, citizen groups founded since 1960 relied on an average of

2.1 ($N = 108$) different types of patrons—with a maximum of six types, including foundations, other associations, corporations, religious institutions, government, and large individual gifts. Nonprofit sector groups established since 1960 used an average of 1.3 ($N = 93$) different types, also much higher than the mean for profit sector groups—that is, 0.8 ($N = 96$), whose patrons were mostly corporations. Many of the groups that depended on institutional and individual patrons in their early histories eventually developed a base of individual members and reduced their reliance on patrons, which suggests that an organizational structure resembling a "grassroots" model of small individual contributors may sometimes *depend on* the availability of early patrons to invest in the organization and its leadership.

We can even see such patterns among PACs—at least insofar as the laws permit—such that certain PACs in their earliest stages of growth rely on institutional sources and relatively large contributors. In addition to the support provided to separate segregated funds by their parent organizations, PACs were able to use two sources of financial support in lieu of small contributors: (1) relatively large or "moderate-sized" individual contributors, that is, contributors who gave more than $500 to the committee in a single election cycle; and (2) nonindividual sources of support, such as loans and transfers or contributions from political parties and other PACs. Table 5.1 displays the percentage of PAC receipts from these two sources during the 1983–84 election cycle and shows how these percentages were related to the typology of occupational roles and the PAC's age.

Table 5.1 shows that newly formed citizen PACs were very dependent on moderately large contributors, loans, and institutional transfers—which is another way of saying that such PACs did not rely much on small individual contributors. Note that new PACs were those that were first registered in the current election cycle or the one just before it—in our data, the 1983–84 or 1981–82 cycles. Old PACs had existed for at least four years, that is, they were registered in both the 1983–84 *and* 1979–80 cycles. When we compare PACs according to this distinction and the typology of occupational roles, we find that newly formed citizen PACs received an average of over 18 percent of their receipts from organizational transfers, loans, and other sources of support outside individual contributions, a percentage greater than that found for committees of any other type. Labor and nonprofit sector PACs also showed greater dependence on sources of support outside individual contributions, while profit and the few mixed sector PACs placed very little reliance on these sources of revenue.

Citizen PACs further reduced their dependence on small contributors by getting many of their contributions in relatively large amounts (i.e., more than $500), a tendency we noted in chapter 3. But what we did not note was that this reliance on moderate-sized contributions was especially pronounced among new PACs. Recently formed citizen PACs got 31 percent of their receipts from moderate-sized contributors, while more-established citizen PACs received 25 percent of their receipts in such amounts.[1] Newly formed profit sector PACs also depended more on moderate-sized contributions than did older business PACs, but their reliance on these larger contributions still did not reach the level of citizen PACs, old or new.

When we combine PACs' reliance on relatively large contributors and their receipts from sources of support outside individual contributions, we find some striking differences among PACs. Newly formed citizen PACs get, on average, nearly half their receipts from sources other than small contributions from individuals. Older citizen PACs also showed relatively little reliance on small individual contributors (though

TABLE 5.1.   Reliance of PACs on Sources of Support Other Than Small Contributions by Individuals, by the Typology of Occupational Roles and the Age of the PAC, 1983–84 Election Cycle (Only Includes Committees with Aggregate Receipts Greater Than or Equal to $10,000)

	Mean Percentage of PAC Receipts from					
	Sources Other Than Individual Contributions[a]		Larger Individual Contributions[a]		All Sources Other Than Small Individual Contributions[a]	
Occupational Role	Older PACs[b]	New PACs[b]	Older PACs	New PACs	Older PACs	New PACs
Profit	7.5	7.2	12.2	23.5	19.7	30.7
Mixed	4.7	3.8	2.5	0.3	7.2	4.1
Nonprofit	17.3	8.4	0.2	0.9	17.5	9.3
Labor	13.7	10.7	0.5	0.3	14.2	11.6
Citizen	16.7	18.3	24.8	30.9	41.5	49.2
All PACs	9.7		15.3		25.0	
Number of PACs	2,190		2,190		2,190	

Source: Federal Election Commission.

[a]"Sources other than individual contributions" include contributions and transfers from political party committees or other nonparty committees, including affiliated committees; loans and loan repayments received; and offsets to operating expenditures, such as refunds or rebates. Most of the money under this category comes from contributions or transfers from other, often affiliated nonparty committees. "Larger contributions" include contributions from individuals that equal or exceed $500 when summed over the entire election cycle.

[b]"Older PACs" are those that were registered in the 1979–80 election cycle. "New PACs" were first registered in either the 1981–82 election cycle or in the 1983–84 cycle.

not to the same degree as recently formed committees), as did newly established business PACs. Our data on PACs thus parallel Walker's findings that group formation raises especially difficult problems of collective action, and that many groups—especially those without an occupational or institutional base—are disproportionately helped by relatively large donors and institutional forms of support while getting established.

Legal Constraints in Campaign and Electoral Activities

But although citizen and other PACs can find limited ways of reducing their reliance on small individual contributors, the campaign finance and tax laws governing PACs limit their ability to do so. The central problem stems from the fact that many of the institutions, public subsidies, and patrons that have traditionally been critical in establishing and maintaining citizen and nonprofit sector groups are either prohibited or curtailed in the PAC system. The most obvious constraint is perhaps the most important. The "hard money" that PACs use to make contributions and political expenditures must come from individual contributors, and small ones at that. We have already reviewed the restrictions that prevent individual contributors from making truly large donations to PACs. Other restrictions limit the ability of PACs to raise money from other organizations. Annual contribution limits of $5,000 apply to party or nonparty committees when they give to PACs, support that committees must raise in small or moderate amounts from individual contributors. And though ceilings are not placed on the total amount of loans that PACs can take out, loans are treated as contributions and are subject to contribution limits unless they are made by banks or other depository institutions in the "ordinary course of business," which means that written arrangements must have been made to repay the loan according to a specific schedule and bearing a "usual and customary" rate of interest (Bauer and Kafka 1984, chap. 3, 36). Thus, eventually, the loan must be paid out of funds raised from individual contributors. All these constraints prohibit citizen and nonprofit sector groups from getting money for their electoral expenditures and contributions from the individual and institutional patrons they have traditionally used to support their activities. The rules enforce a grassroots model of political mobilization at which American interest groups, outside of business and labor, have not been particularly adept.

Not only do the laws prevent groups from drawing directly on political patrons for campaign contributions and expenditures, but they also inhibit the ability of citizen and nonprofit sector groups even to establish and maintain PACs. These latter constraints grow largely out of the tax treatment of nonprofit organizations under the Internal Revenue Code, especially organizations that enjoy tax-exempt status under Section 501(c)(3), which not only exempts charitable, educational, and religious organizations ("C-3" organizations) from taxation but also permits them to receive tax-deductible contributions (IRC § 170(c)(2); Goedert 1989, 145). These C-3 organizations constitute the largest single category of nonprofit organizations in the United States (U.S. General Accounting Office 1987, 8), and they include private foundations, religious institutions, schools, museums, research institutes, public and private charities, and any other entities "organized and operated exclusively" for religious, charitable, scientific, public safety, or educational purposes (IRC § 501(c)(3)).

C-3 organizations include many citizen groups, such as environmental groups, public interest law firms, and civil rights organizations. Berry, for example, found that 60 percent of the public interest groups in his sample had C-3 status or were affiliated with C-3 organizations (1977, 51; also see Shaiko 1991). If a citizen association were to lose this status, it would no longer be able to receive tax-exempt contributions and would thus lose one of the subsidies critical for raising large donations from individual and corporate patrons. Nearly as important, the association could not obtain support from private foundations, which, "because of their own tax-exemption requirements, cannot contribute to 'political or propagandistic activity' " (Berry 1977, 48).

The electoral problem arises from the fact that the Internal Revenue Code prohibits C-3 organizations from engaging in any "political activity," which has been interpreted by the Internal Revenue Service (IRS) in its regulations as "all direct or indirect participation or intervention in any political campaign on behalf of or in opposition to any candidate for public office, including publication or distribution of written statements on behalf of or in opposition to such a candidate." This prohibition was enacted by Congress in 1954, apparently at the insistence of Senator Lyndon Johnson, who was angered by the rumors that a private foundation (some say the H. L. Hunt Foundation) had provided indirect financial support to a campaign opponent in Texas (Hopkins 1987, 281). This ban was much stronger than the older restriction on the lobbying activities of charitable organizations. That provision, which was enacted in 1934, only prevented C-3 entities from "carrying on propaganda or otherwise attempting . . . to influence legislation" to the point where they became a "substantial part of the [organization's] activities." Indeed, in 1976, the Congress admitted the widespread lobbying of C-3 organizations by enacting safe harbor provisions that allowed "public charities"—a subset of C-3 organizations—to elect to be governed by specific dollar limits on their lobbying activities, which may run as high as 20 percent of their expenditures. However, the IRS has long interpreted the ban on "political"—that is, electoral or campaign— activities to be "an absolute prohibition," regardless of whether the activities were "substantial" (Hopkins 1987, 281).

What is interesting about this interpretation is that business corporations and unions also confront statutory language that seems to prohibit electoral intervention absolutely, but those provisions have never been interpreted that way. The Federal Corrupt Practices Act makes it "unlawful for . . . any corporation . . . to make a contribution or expenditure in connection with" any federal election (2 U.S.C. § 441(b)). Yet "the courts have read a substantiality test into the absolute proscription of the statutes" (Hopkins 1987, 281)—usually to protect First Amendment liberties—while neither the IRS nor the courts have shown much interest in applying such a test to nonprofit groups. Presumably the different treatments of these statutory bans are based on the belief that the withholding of public subsidies does not constitute a selective burden on the rights of speech and assembly—which is contrary, of course, to our argument and interpretation of the theory of collective action. Thus, while the courts and the FECA qualified this "absolute" ban by allowing corporations and unions to form separate segregated funds, there is no such qualification for C-3 organizations, which may *not* use their treasury money to establish, maintain, or solicit funds for a PAC. Many citizen groups cannot set up a separate segregated fund without forgoing private foundation money and tax-exempt contributions from individuals and corporations—sources typically critical to their formation and maintenance.

These tax laws also inhibit the mobilization of occupational interests in the nonprofit sector. Many of the institutions in that sector are themselves C-3 organizations, including such private institutions as religious organizations, foundations, private schools and colleges, day-care centers and preschools, charitable hospitals and clinics, homes for the elderly, public interest law firms, and scientific organizations, as well as such "public charities" (which typically draw at least one-third of their support from government or the general public) as public schools and universities, public hospitals or medical research organizations, libraries, zoos, community centers, blood banks, dance and repertory theater organizations, and symphony orchestras. Thus, unlike the case in the profit sector, many of the basic service-delivery institutions in the nonprofit sector are prohibited from directly or indirectly participating in election campaigns, including establishing a separate segregated fund, or authorizing and facilitating a trade association that wants to solicit the institution's employees to contribute to the association's PAC. Indeed, many of the membership associations that represent nonprofit institutions are themselves C-3 organizations—such as church associations and conventions, medical societies, and associations of colleges and universities—and, as such, are banned categorically from partisan political activities.

Not all nonprofit institutions are C-3 organizations and subject to the ban on electioneering. Civic leagues, social welfare organizations, business leagues, credit unions, social clubs, mutual insurance companies, veterans organizations, labor organizations, political organizations, and many others are exempt from taxation under other provisions of Section 501(c) or elsewhere in the tax code, and they are not prevented from engaging in electoral activities except as provided by the campaign finance laws. But these organizations cannot receive tax-deductible contributions, so they tend to be more dependent on service fees or other selective incentives to generate revenues in the absence of subsidies and large donations. Also, many of these organizations do not represent or form a part of the "nonprofit sector," as I have used that term. Business trade associations or local chambers of commerce represent occupational roles in the profit sector, and labor organizations may represent public employees, employees in the profit sector, or a mix of the two. The unique core of the nonprofit sector—that which offers services and organizes interests that are often not provided for elsewhere in the economy—is generally found among the more restricted Section 501(c)(3) organizations. Thus, although associations representing the profit sector enjoy unrestricted access to their patrons (i.e., corporations) *and* have all the authority they need to form a PAC, many associations representing citizen interests and occupational interests in the nonprofit sector are forced to choose *between* access to their traditional patrons and participation in elections.

Still other asymmetries exist between corporations, unions, and nonprofit organizations with respect to their ability to engage in electoral activities. Corporations and unions may make partisan political communications to a "restricted class" of corporate stockholders, administrators, and executives, or union employees and officers. They may also use their facilities to allow candidates or party representatives to address these people, and they may establish and operate phone banks to urge members of the restricted class to register or vote for specific candidates (11 C.F.R. § 114.3). However, C-3 organizations are not free to engage in partisan "internal communications," since the ban on electioneering by nonprofit organizations concerns "participation" or "intervention" in campaigns, regardless of the size or nature of the audience. A federal court found, for example, that a C-3 medical society had violated the ban just by naming in its own newsletter certain candidates who were members of the society and by stating that they supported the fight against "socialized medicine" (*Hammerstein* v. *Kelly* 1964, 64).

Also, though the IRS has said that "voter education activities" directed at the general public do not constitute electioneering, it has interpreted those activities more narrowly than the FEC's interpretation of exempt, nonpartisan activities by unions and corporations. The IRS views "voter education" as encompassing the situation where an organization "annually publishes the voting records of members of Congress on legislative issues on a wide range of subjects" or where an organization "solicits answers to a questionnaire from all candidates for an office, and publishes the responses without comment or bias" (Goedert 1989, 148). However, if "the questions reflect a bias" or if "distribution by the C-3 of information about candidates' views . . . is limited to issues with respect to which the C-3 has a particular interest," or if the information is distributed in a way that might affect any campaign outcome (such as heavier distributions in particular states or congressional districts), the activity is prohibited. However, a corporation or union may distribute "voting records" of members of Congress to the general public, even including the publication of indexes or scores, which, though constituting a "factual recital" of the member's position, might be construed as evaluative, so long as the preparation and distribution is not for the purpose of influencing a federal election (11 C.F.R. § 114.4(b)(4)). In fact, in a 1991 decision (*Faucher* v. *FEC* 1991), a circuit court held that the federal statute prohibiting corporations from using treasury funds to make contributions or expenditures in connection with federal elections applies only to those "voter guides" that constitute "express advocacy," that is, statements advocating the election or defeat of a clearly identified candidate in "express terms." According to the decision, they *do not* include a guide distributed by an incorporated pro-life organization that explicitly referred to the 1988 congressional elections, that indicated candidate and party positions on pro-life issues, and that pointed out whether the candidates agreed or disagreed with the organization's pro-life positions. The court ruled that the federal regulations requiring that such voter guides be nonpartisan and devoid of any issue advocacy (11 C.F.R. § 114.4(b)(5)) were beyond the FEC's statutory authority to promulgate. The decision implies that corporate treasury funds may be used for all kinds of issue advocacy, partisan communications, and evaluations of candidates, so long as the communications do not include express language urging the defeat or election of a specific candidate. In contrast, the tax code's prohibitions on the electoral activities of C-3 organizations cover many forms of issue advocacy and candidate assessments, and they apply to all campaigns for public office (whether federal, state, or local), while the ban on corporate and union activities concerns only federal contests.

Some political observers have argued that the Supreme Court weakened the restrictions on the electoral activities of nonprofit organizations in its 1986 decision *FEC* v. *Massachusetts Citizens for Life*. In that case, the Supreme Court decided that the federal election law's prohibition against corporate independent expenditures—where the money was drawn from treasury funds rather than a separate segregated fund—was unconstitutional when applied to a small nonprofit corporation that was established to promote political ideas rather than engage in business activities, that did not have shareholders or other persons with claims on its assets or earnings, and that was neither set up by another corporation nor received contributions from corporations. But the exemption was actually a narrow one that did little to change the fact that citizen groups and associations representing the nonprofit sector cannot get support for their electoral activities from their traditional patrons. Although the antiabortion group involved in the case was exempt from federal taxes as a political organization, it was not a C-3 organization that could collect tax-deductible contributions. Large contributors could underwrite the organization's activities, but it did not enjoy the competitive advantage for individual patronage that like-minded C-3's had, nor was it able to secure any funding from corporate patrons or private foundations. Finally, the exemption only extended to independent expenditures, not contributions to candidates or parties, and most groups consider such expenditures as ineffective or likely to backfire. What is left unregulated are nonprofit organizations with exclusively political purposes, engaged in independent expenditures, and with no support from corporations, foundations, or tax-deductible contributions—that is, organizations that have no institutional patronage and are unable to mobilize support through by-product (nonpolitical) methods of political mobilization. It is not difficult to see why the Court thought that such organizations did not "present the spectar of corruption" (*FEC* v. *Massachusetts for Life* 1986, 263). It is a wonder they even exist.

Finally, an important asymmetry exists between institutions in the profit sector and the governmental segment of the nonprofit sector with respect to the ability of individuals to take part in elections and campaigns. Until the Hatch Act was changed in 1993, most employees of the federal government were prohibited from taking "an active part in political management or in political campaigns," including partisan fundraising activity and soliciting votes for or against any candidate (Bauer and Kafka 1984, chap. 7, 29).[2] The restrictions on soliciting contributions or interfering in elections also applied to "employees of private, nonprofit organizations which plan, develop and coordinate federal Head Start, Community Services Block Grant or Economic Opportunity Programs" (U.S. Merit Systems Protection Board 1988, 3). State and local government employees working on programs financed in whole or in part by federal loans or grants were allowed to contribute money and attend fund-raisers, but they were not permitted to "directly or indirectly coerce, attempt to coerce, command, or *advise* a State or local officer or employee *to pay, lend, or contribute anything of value* to a party, committee, organization, agency, or person for political purposes" (5 U.S.C. § 1502(a)(2); italics added). Finally, similar bans on solicitations by government employees may be found in the laws of many states, such as Florida, Indiana, Massachusetts, and Wisconsin (U.S. Federal Election Commission 1986, chart 2-B).

There are ways of evading the electoral prohibitions on nonprofit organizations, but they are costly and often infeasible for many organizations. A Section 501(c)(3) organization may, for example, establish a separate Section 501(c)(4) organization to carry out political activities. Section 501(c)(4) organizations—often called "social welfare organizations," which include many membership associations—are exempt from taxes but cannot usually receive tax-deductible contributions (unless the contribution is deductible as a business expense). The gain from setting up a C-4 organization comes from its ability to engage in lobbying activities without limit and to use its funds to establish, maintain, and solicit contributions for a separate segregated fund, so long as the electoral activities do not constitute the organization's primary purpose (U.S. General Accounting Office 1987, 12–13). For example, a citizen group may establish a three-part structure, with tax-deductible contributions and private foundation grants routed to a C-3 organization involved in research and education activities; membership dues and nondeductible contributions going to a C-4 organization, which carries out the group's lobbying activities and absorbs the costs of setting up a PAC; and political contributions, regulated by the FECA, going to a separate segregated fund. This sort of arrangement may help the PAC in several ways. The C-3 foundation may conduct issue research on contract with the group's lobbying arm (the C-4 organization), which can then use that information in guiding the PAC; the foundation may train volunteers in grassroots organizing, whom the PAC may deploy in specific races; or the C-3 may generate a list of sympathetic contributors that can be used by the C-4 and PAC in soliciting small contributions (Latus 1984, 140, 144–46). In one of the more elaborate networks, Senator Jesse Helms presided over a number of C-3 think tanks (the Institute of Family

Relations, the Center for a Free Society, the American Family Institute, and the Coalition for Freedom), a couple of C-4 lobbying organizations (the IAR Foreign Affairs Council and the Congressional Club Foundation), and a PAC (the National Congressional Club).

But though these networks afford citizen and nonprofit sector groups some flexibility in mobilizing for electoral action, they hardly overcome the legal restrictions. The law does not permit a C-3 organization to transfer funds raised from tax-deductible contributions to an affiliated C-4 lobbying organization, much less to a separate segregated fund. Effective transfers may nonetheless occur as organizations share facilities, staff, and equipment and underestimate the allocations to the C-4 organization or the PAC, a tactic made easier by unclear definitions in the law and relatively weak enforcement by the IRS (U.S. House Committee on Ways and Means 1987, 88–89). Still, flagrant violations are not hard to detect, and the costs of setting up and maintaining a separate C-4 organization to act as a connected organization for a separate segregated fund may be high enough to keep groups from creating such a network. In any case, networks do not eliminate the fundamental discrepancy between the campaign finance regulations and ways in which these types of groups have traditionally mobilized support. The money that the PAC raises to make contributions and expenditures must still be "hard money," that is, money that is subject to all the contribution limits, reporting requirements, and prohibitions against the use of institutional sources found in the federal campaign finance laws.

Finally, the campaign finance laws make it very hard for citizen groups to use selective incentives to elicit contributions from small contributors in order to compensate for their inability to tap individual or institutional patrons for electoral support. If the association (such as a C-4 organization) establishes a separate segregated fund, the SSF may only solicit members, and it may not withhold any benefits of membership from individuals who refuse to contribute to the PAC (11 C.F.R. § 114.7(g)). Of course, the group may simply decide to establish a nonconnected PAC, which may supply or withhold various selective benefits to mobilize small contributors. But it is unclear how the group will get the resources to create such benefits, since a nonconnected PAC must get its revenues exclusively from small contributors. This dilemma may not exist for groups with an institutional base, since such groups can often rely on implicit selective incentives, such as organizational hierarchies and peer pressures. Yet it is a severe constraint on citizen groups, which must usually "manufacture" selective benefits themselves. The consequence is that groups with an institutional—and usually occupational—base may be able to deploy by-product methods of mobilizing small contributors, while groups without such a base cannot.

The Effects of Institutional Constraints on PAC Formation

To examine how these various institutional constraints affect PAC formation, we can estimate a model of PAC adoption that includes factors related to these constraints as well as variables measuring the political motivations predisposing a group to electoral activities. The model assumes that interest groups want to form PACs if their political environment is complex and conflictual enough that campaign contributions are needed to smooth relations with legislators or to engage in the party struggle. However, legal constraints and other institutional conditions inhibit some groups from forming committees despite their strong incentives to do so, while such factors make it easier for others.

These constraints and linkages affect groups through the composition of their membership and their typical sources of revenue. One institutional factor affecting PAC formation is the group's occupational base—specifically, whether group members work in profit or the nonprofit sector. We expect that groups representing persons or institutions in the profit sector are more likely to form PACs than groups representing the nonprofit sector. That is particularly true when the group is organized around a *single* profit sector occupation or industry—first, because the narrow occupational and institutional base reduces the costs of communications and makes it easier for the group to develop an effective package of selective incentives; and second, because trade associations that organize around a single industry in the profit sector may, if authorized by their corporations, use many of the institutional resources that are available to corporate or union PACs but are not available to other associations. In contrast, legal constraints inhibit groups representing the nonprofit sector from drawing on the resources of the institutions where *their* members work. Tax laws prevent many private nonprofit organizations from engaging in electoral activities. Also, civil servants may not set up PACs—and in some instances they are prohibited from taking an active role in soliciting contributions (though these restrictions have been relaxed at the federal level since the Hatch Act was revised in 1993).

The other institutional factor affecting PAC formation is the group's sources of revenue. There are several ways in which an interest group's sources of revenues may inhibit its ability to establish a PAC.

First, the tax laws prevent associations or other organizations that receive tax-deductible contributions from engaging in electoral activities or setting up a PAC. Second, the laws also prevent certain private foundations, churches, or other nonprofit institutions from funding "action organizations," which include all organizations that engage or affiliate with organizations involved in electoral activities. Groups that rely on private foundation grants could thus lose revenues if they formed political committees. Finally, by relying on patrons who cannot be used to fund a PAC, the group does not develop the organizational capacity to mobilize small individual contributors that is needed to build a contribution pool.

The effects of these two factors were tested by estimating a logistic regression model of PAC formation among associations in the 1985 survey. The model assumes that a group is more likely to have a PAC when it faces a complex and conflictual political environment and has an institutional base that facilitates rather than inhibits electoral mobilization. To keep the model as simple as possible and to reduce multicollinearity among the independent variables, I used only the three most important variables in the equation reported in table 4.3 to measure a group's motivation to form a PAC—namely, a group's perception of party differences, the number of congressional subcommittees with which it works, and the importance to the group of representing members' opinions before government. The specific variables and their estimated coefficients are shown in table 5.2.

The estimated equation is consistent with our discussion of the effects of institutional variables on PAC formation. Motivational variables are still strongly and positively related to PAC formation. But other factors can inhibit even a highly politicized group with a partisan and complex issue environment from establishing a PAC. Associations with a membership base in the nonprofit sector are less likely to form PACs, even after controlling for motivational factors. The same is true for associations that raise revenues from corporate gifts, private foundation grants, and gifts or bequests from individuals. Associations that rely on these various patrons are less likely to form PACs than are those that depend on other sources of revenue, such as member dues. But associations organized around a single industry or occupation—and who probably have better access to the mobilizing powers of the industry's corporations, firms, or agencies—are much more likely to form PACs than are broader-based occupational groups. In some ways, this parallels our finding in chapter 3, where we saw that corporate PACs were organizationally stronger than business PACs based on wider interests within the profit sector. As group interests span more and more economic institutions, the problems of establishing and maintaining an effective PAC become more acute. Theoretically, both these tendencies may be caused by problems of collective action as well as by the legal advantages enjoyed by corporations or single-industry associations in forming and maintaining PACs. But general collective action problems cannot account for much of the difference, since we are using as our baseline only those groups that have already overcome the problems of collective action, as evidenced by the fact that they do have major membership

TABLE 5.2. Logistic Regression of PAC Adoption on Interest Groups' Motivations and Institutional Constraints, 1985

Variables	Beta Estimate	Standard Error	Chi-squared (Beta = 0)
Intercept	-6.786		
Group perceives important party differences on issues relevant to its goals (1=poor description - 5=good description)	.237	.082	8.40[c]
Group consults with many congressional subcommittees (1=none, 2=one to two, 3=three to four, 4=five to six, 5=more than six)	.726	.110	43.72[c]
Representing members' opinions before government is an important member benefit (1=not provided - 6=one of the most important)	.346	.143	5.89[c]
Members are affiliated with a single profit-making industry or occupation (1=poor description - 5=good description)	.294	.073	16.25[c]
Membership base is in the nonprofit sector (1=yes, 0=no)	-1.578	.372	18.01[c]
Percentage of revenues received from government grants or contracts (0-100)	-.004	.010	.14
Percentage of revenues received as gifts from private foundations (0-100)	-.082	.039	4.50[c]
Percentage of revenues received as gifts or bequests from individuals (0-100)	-.020	.013	2.13[a]
Percentage of revenues received as gifts from firms (0-100)	-.024	.015	2.67[b]
Percentage of revenues received from churches (0-100)	-2.585	4.176	0.38
Number of cases = 744 Percent correctly classified = 86 Model Chi-squared (10 df) = 244.93			

Source: Federal Election Commission/Walker merged data (see app. A).
[a]Probability (Beta = 0) < .15.
[b]Probability (Beta = 0) < .10.
[c]Probability (Beta = 0) < .05.

associations. From this perspective, the biases we find among PACs must be attributed to constraints or problems unique to the PAC system, such as relevant campaign finance laws and tax regulations.

However, though the model in table 5.2 is compatible with our belief that motivations and institutional factors are both important for PAC formation, it is still not completely satisfactory. Although the model's explanatory power is greater than that of the motivation-only equation reported in table 4.3, it is still not very high; and though most of the estimated coefficients for the institutional variables are significant, they do not show as much strength as we might have expected. These weaknesses in the model may result from incorrect model specification. Rather than assuming that motivational and institutional factors operate independently, as our current model does, we might consider how these factors interact with each other.[3] For example, if institutional constraints are strong, they ought to prevent even highly motivated groups from establishing PACs, not just reduce their probability of forming a committee. And simply because a group faces very weak institutional constraints, we should not expect it to have a PAC; some political motivation is necessary. It does not, in short, make sense to assume that motivational and institutional factors each have an independent impact on PAC formation. It is more reasonable to assume that *both* these conditions are necessary for PAC adoption, that neither is sufficient— which is another way of saying that they have an *interactive* relationship with PAC formation. We would expect a relationship between PAC adoption and motivational factors *if and only if* institutional constraints are weak, as they are for business groups, unions, and a few other occupationally based organizations.

We can test this hypothesis by developing and estimating an interactive model. To do this, we can regress PAC formation on motivational factors, but rather than requiring the relation between motivations and PAC formation to be the same for all associations, we can allow the slopes and intercepts to vary for different categories of associations. These categories, in turn, may be defined according to the strength or weakness of institutional constraints regarding PAC formation. If both motivational factors and institutional conditions are necessary conditions for PAC formation, we would expect that the relationship between motivations and PAC adoption would be strong only among groups that face few institutional constraints; that the relationship would be nonexistent among groups that face the strongest constraints; and that the relation would be weak for groups that confront intermediate levels of constraint. We would also expect that those groups that have the weakest motivations would not establish PACs, even if they faced an unconstrained institutional environment.

To keep the model simple, I used only a few variables to measure motivations and constraints. To measure the strength of a group's motivation to establish a PAC, I used the predicted values from the equation reported in table 4.3—values that depended on a group's perception of partisan and stable conflict in its political environment, its emphasis on legislative lobbying and especially the number of subcommittees it worked with, and the group's stress on representing members' opinions before government. A dichotomous variable indicating whether or not a group had an affiliated PAC in the 1983–84 election cycle was then regressed onto this motivation variable, but the slopes and intercepts characterizing the relationship were allowed to vary across four categories. These four categories, in turn, were defined by the three institutional conditions that I thought would be most closely related to the ability of groups to establish and maintain PACs:

> the association has little or no connection with the nonprofit sector—that is, less than 5 percent of a group's membership worked in nonprofit institutions;
>
> the association has little or no support from patrons—the group did not receive significant funding from foundations, large individual gifts, corporate donations, or religious institutions; and
>
> the association is organized around a single profit-making industry or occupation—the group reported that the statement "Members of this association are affiliated with single profit-making industry or occupation" was a good description of their association.

These three conditions were each dichotomized; and I created a four-point scale, ranging from zero to three, indicating the number of institutional conditions a group faced that would facilitate electoral mobilization. The model was estimated using ordinary least squares regression, and the results are displayed in figure 5.1. Details about the model and the estimated coefficients may be found in appendix C. A single equation was estimated for all associations, but since the slopes and intercepts were allowed to vary for each of the four levels of institutional conditions, the estimated coefficients were the same as if four separate regressions were estimated.

Figure 5.1 clearly shows that the relationship between motivational factors and PAC formation depends on institutional conditions. Among associations that satisfied two or three of the institutional conditions

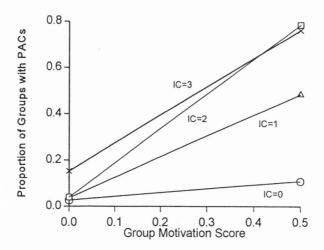

Fig. 5.1. Relationship between PAC affiliation and motivational factors, by number of facilitating institutional conditions, 1985. IC refers to the number of institutional conditions that the group satisfies. The three institutional conditions include (1) dependence on private patrons (individual and corporate gifts, foundations, and churches), (2) an insignificant number of members working in the nonprofit sector, and (3) members drawn from a single industry or occupation in the profit sector. For a description of the equation used to construct this figure, see appendix C. (From Federal Election Commission/Walker merged data [see app. A].)

facilitating mobilization, motivational factors were strongly related to the probability that an association had a PAC. Where only one condition was met, the relationship was much weaker; and among groups that satisfied none of the conditions, only a slight and insignificant relationship existed between motivational factors and PAC formation. More specifically, groups representing citizen interests or the nonprofit sector—and that relied on private patrons for support—failed to establish PACs regardless of how much partisan conflict they experienced, how much stress they placed on legislative lobbying, how many subcommittees they worked with, and how important they deemed representing members' opinions before government institutions. However, business groups and many unions—which did not rely on private patrons and often drew members from a single industry or occupation in the profit sector—were very sensitive to these motivational factors in forming PACs. This interactive model certainly fits the data more closely than a simple model relating motivational factors and PAC formation. When motivational factors are as-

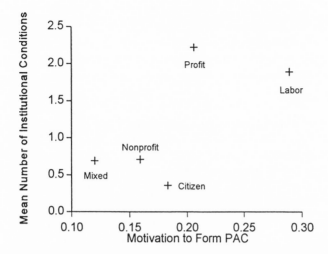

Fig. 5.2. Mean values of summary motivational score and the number of facilitating institutional conditions, by occupational role of association, 1985. (From Federal Election Commission/Walker merged data [see app. A].)

sumed to have the same impact for all associations, we can account for only 17 percent of the variance in PAC formation. But when we allow for interactions based on institutional conditions, the percent of variance explained nearly doubles to 31 percent, an increase large enough to justify rejecting the simpler, more restricted model, and thus rejecting its assumption of a homogenous relationship (see app. C).

Both appropriate motives and accommodating institutional conditions are therefore necessary for PAC formation, and both motives and conditions must be taken into account in explaining differences in PAC formation across the typology of occupational roles. We can see this in figure 5.2, which shows the mean values of the two factors used in the previous model—the summary motivational score and the number of institutional conditions a group satisfies—for each of the five occupational types of associations. By examining the average scores of each of these types, we can use the results of our model to address the original question of why such biases exist in the PAC system. Labor unions show very high rates of PAC formation because they have strong motives to engage in electoral activities—they perceive large differences between the parties on issues, and they have complex and wide-ranging agendas and connections with Congress—and because they are not inhibited by institutional constraints from responding to these situations through electoral activities. Business groups show relatively high rates of PAC formation but for somewhat different reasons: they enjoy the most accommodating institutional conditions, which allow them to respond electorally to whatever conflict and complexity they may confront; and the level of this conflict and complexity tends to be moderate.

Citizen groups and groups representing the nonprofit sector show low rates of PAC formation. Citizen groups perceive, on average, moderately divisive and complex political environments—only slightly lower than business groups—but they also face the greatest barriers to effective electoral action. Associations organized around occupations in the nonprofit sector have few PACs not only because the institutions they rely on for support are not easily employed for electoral activities, but also because their political environments reveal low levels of conflict and complexity. Finally, groups that draw members from both the profit and nonprofit sectors have the weakest motives to form PACs, and they face institutional conditions nearly as constraining as those impinging on groups in the nonprofit sector.

Are Biases in the PAC System Unique?

The legal constraints imposed on the electoral activities of interest groups are much stronger than those placed on other forms of political advocacy. As we have already noted, federal tax laws restricting the legislative lobbying activities of certain nonprofit organizations are nowhere near as strong as the outright ban on their electoral activities. Nonprofit groups may engage in legislative lobbying so long as it does not constitute either a "substantial" activity of the organization or its primary purpose. Citizen groups or groups representing nonprofit interests may therefore rely on tax-deductible contributions from large corporate or individual donors while engaging in some lobbying. Moreover, the funds used in carrying out these activities may come from any source and in any amount: groups are not limited to using contributions from small individual contributors.

Groups involved in administrative lobbying have even greater flexibility. Restrictions on lobbying by tax-exempt organizations only apply to "legislation," which "does not include action by the executive branch, such as the promulgation of rules and regulations, nor does it include action by the independent regulatory agencies" (Hopkins 1987, 266). There are no restrictions on how groups that lobby administrative agencies may fund or maintain themselves. And they are not required to register anywhere or disclose information about their officers, finances, or other aspects of their organization. It is true that making administrative rules is a complex process involving many regulations relating to agencies' contacts with interest groups. But unlike the campaign finance laws, these regulations mostly concern the *procedures* by which groups participate in the rule-making process—such as notice and comment requirements—not the internal organization of the groups themselves.

The same point applies to groups using litigation as a political strategy. The IRS does not consider litigation to be a political or legislative activity that is restricted under the laws governing charitable organizations, nor are there any other significant restrictions on the funding or organization of groups using the courts to press their political demands. Again, most of the regulations are procedural. Some of the regulations prevent particular groups from playing particular roles—thus, if groups want to be plaintiffs, they must satisfy the requirements of jurisdiction and justiciability (Olson 1990). Yet even if they cannot be direct parties in an action, groups still have many options for involvement—they can file amicus curiae briefs, provide counsel, or contribute technical expertise or money to legal efforts they support (Olson 1990, 860)—and they can fund their activities anyway they want.

If electoral activities are more strictly regulated than other forms of political advocacy, and if these constraints have sharply different effects across the typology of occupational roles, we would expect the use of PACs and other electoral tactics to vary across the typology of occupational roles more than do other political activities. And that is exactly what we find. Figure 5.3 demonstrates this point by showing the average (mean) scores of interest group responses to questions—in the 1985 Walker survey—regarding the importance that organizations placed on four political tactics: administrative lobbying, or "working with government agencies in policy formulation and administration"; legislative lobbying, or "working with members of Congress or their staffs on the formulation or implementation of legislation"; litigation, that is, "pursuing issues through litigation in courts"; and electioneering, or "working to aid the election of political leaders." The survey permitted groups to indicate their responses on a six-point scale, ranging from "one of the most important" activities for the association (coded as six) to an activity that the association was "not engaged in" (coded as one). The measures thus indicate the subjective importance of a tactic as well as whether groups use it at all. The mean scores on these four variables were calculated for each of the five categories in the typology of occupational roles, and the means are shown by separate bar graphs for each tactic.

When we compare the use of these tactics across the typology of occupational roles, we find important differences between electoral and other political activities. There is little variation between different types

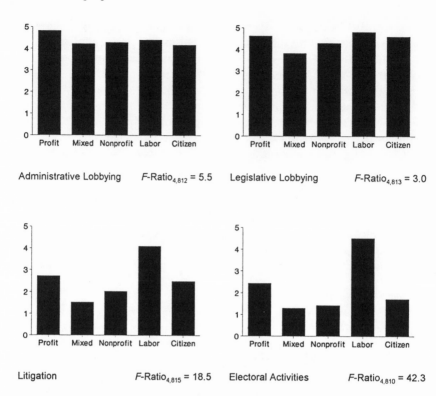

Fig. 5.3. Differences in interest group assessments of the importance of various political tactics, across the typology of occupational roles, 1985. Bars show the mean of scores indicating the importance of different political tactic variables for interest groups in the 1985 Walker survey. (From Walker 1985 survey; Federal Election Commission/Walker merged data [see app. A].)

of interest groups for the two most common political tactics, legislative lobbying and administrative lobbying. This is not because *all* groups consider these tactics to be important. There is still a lot of variation among interest groups in the importance they assigned to lobbying—yet most of the variance is found *within* each category of groups, not *between* different types. For example, the average citizen group places just as much emphasis on legislative lobbying as the average business group. But some citizen and business groups fall well above or below these averages, as evidenced by the fact that the estimated standard deviations are nearly two points in each of these two categories. Underneath each graph in figure 5.3 is a simple measure of the degree to which the typology accounts for the variance in the importance that associations attach to various political tactics—namely, the F-ratio in a one-way analysis of variance. This ratio tests whether we can reject the hypothesis of *no* systematic differences among the five categories of our typology, and the ratio is bigger when the differences among the categories are large relative to the sample variance. All the ratios are statistically significant by traditional standards, but they are only marginally so for the importance groups assign to administrative and legislative lobbying. Whatever factors influence the use of administrative or legislative lobbying, those factors are not closely related to the typology of occupational roles.

In contrast, our typology does capture important differences in groups' use of litigation. Most unions place a lot of emphasis on court-centered strategies, most groups in the nonprofit and mixed sector categories do not, and business associations and citizen groups are pretty close to each other and fall somewhere in between. What accounts for these differences? I think the single most important factor is found in the incentives for litigation strategies—in particular, the incidence of political conflict (Olson 1990; Scheppele and Walker 1991). Olson described litigation as being "inherently adversarial" and found that the "presence and nature of opposition loom large in recent examinations of interest-group litigation" (1990, 861, 862). As we noted in chapter 4, nearly all unions confront a great deal of opposition; citizen and business groups also see a lot of conflict, though not as consistently; and nonprofit and mixed sector groups face relatively little conflict. This pattern closely parallels the use of litigational tactics, and the importance of conflict has been borne out in multivariate analyses of court-related tactics (Scheppele and Walker 1991).

Electoral activities clearly show the greatest variation across the typology of occupational roles, as suggested by the large F-ratio as well as by the graph itself. The importance of electoral activities is greatest for unions, followed by associations in the profit sector. Election-related activities are less important or widespread among citizen groups—and are even less so among groups in the nonprofit and mixed sector categories. This pattern resembles—though it is not nearly as striking as—the distribution of the most formal method of electoral participation, the PAC (see table 4.2).

When compared to other political tactics, PACs and general electoral activities thus show much larger differences across the typology of occupational roles. I have already argued that these differences cannot be attributed solely to political circumstances, such as a group's interest in lobbying or its perceptions of partisan conflict and legislative complexity—circumstances that make electoral activities a more appropriate or valuable tactic for a group. Nor can we attribute these differences to general collective action problems or a simple lack of money for electoral efforts. By examining which associations form PACs and which do not, we have used as our baseline a sample of organizations that are large, well funded, and clearly interested in national policy processes—groups that have demonstrated that they *can* overcome collective action problems in other situations and raise considerable sums of money in support of other political activities. We have not even considered how PACs also reflect general biases pervading all forms of interest group organization, such as the lack of organizations representing the unemployed or nonunionized labor.

To account for the special biases of the PAC system, we must therefore look to causes that are unique to that system and that exacerbate the problems of collective action for certain groups. I have argued that a primary cause lies in the legal restrictions imposed on their formation and maintenance—restrictions that limit the ability of some groups to rely on their traditional sources of funding. We have found evidence that many membership associations—especially those representing citizen interests and occupational roles in the nonprofit sector—rely on large contributors in the form of individual and institutional patrons, sources of revenue that are largely prevented by law from supporting campaign finance and other electoral activities. We have seen this dependence on large contributors even within the PAC system—to the extent that the laws allow—such that PACs representing citizen interests rely the most on larger contributors, especially during their formative stages. We have found that institutional conditions strongly affect a group's ability to respond to its political environment and establish a PAC to deal with partisan conflict and manage a complex legislative environment. And we have seen that the use of PACs is much more biased with respect to the typology of occupational roles than are other, less-regulated political tactics.

All these findings suggest that the restrictions on large contributors and certain institutional patrons have a highly selective impact on PAC formation: they generally inhibit the spread of PACs among groups representing citizen interests and occupational interests in the nonprofit sector, and they enhance rather than diminish the role of private economic institutions like business corporations and unions in financing federal campaigns. It is therefore *not* coincidental that the tactic least used by groups and exhibiting the greatest differences across our typology is also the most strictly regulated. Because the typology delineates important differences in how groups raise money to support their activities, regulatory strategies that focus on funding sources—like the campaign finance and tax laws—*cannot* be neutral with respect to different interests.

What are the political consequences of these properties? Does the small and selective character of the PAC system have any definite effects on what issues and issue positions are represented? Does it have any impact on the party or electoral system? It is to these questions we now turn.

CHAPTER 6

PACs, Groups, and Public Policies

Differences in the rate of PAC formation across the typology of occupational roles would be of little interest if the typology were unrelated to distinct views and preferences regarding national policies. But that is hardly the case. These different types of groups take contrasting stands across a broad array of public issues, and the selective impediments confronting certain occupational categories of groups mean that the PAC system will show a distinctive bias in the policy views and interests it represents. A major aspect of this bias is the weak representation of liberal standpoints among PACs, since two of the sectors that have historically played strong roles in advocating liberal policies—namely, the nonprofit sector and citizen groups—are precisely the ones that are least well represented in the PAC system.

However, the findings of this chapter require some qualifications. Although my argument up to this point has been well grounded in the interaction between collective action theory and current law, the discussion in this and the next chapter depend on empirical and not necessarily robust relationships between a group's occupational type, its policy preferences and concerns, and its relations with the national parties. Indeed, the arguments in chapters four and five suggest considerable room for change in these relationships. For example, groups that are caught up in partisan conflicts are more likely to form PACs than others, but where those party divisions occur and how they divide up the interest group system surely change from time to time and depend on many factors. Relationships and alignments found during Reagan's presidency may still persist in the 1990s, but we cannot be sure unless we have comparable survey and PAC data—which, for the moment, we have not. Yet even if these findings prove to be time-bound, they are useful in understanding the dynamic relationships between organized interest groups, policy subsystems, and political parties during one important period of American political history, and they can provide us a benchmark for examining how and why the dynamics themselves might have shifted over time.

PACs in Different Policy Arenas

One of the most critical sources of political power is control over the agenda of governmental institutions (Schattschneider 1960; Crenson 1971; Cobb and Elder 1972; Kingdon 1984). Decisions about what issues to pay attention to not only precede decisions regarding what to do about those issues but also involve more discretion on the part of politicians and more opportunities for influence by persons outside of government. In fact, if we may draw any conclusions from the scholarly literature on the effects of lobbying and campaign contributions on the behavior of members of Congress, it is that interest group activities exert the most impact, not on their policy positions or votes, but rather on the amount of attention and personal involvement legislators invest in issues. Hall and Wayman (1990) found that campaign contributions were related to legislators' participation in committee markup sessions and their willingness to negotiate with other members of Congress behind the scenes (also see Denzau and Munger 1986). Contributions may thus help groups to express their intensity on an issue, enhance its salience, and encourage sympathetic members of Congress to initiate legislation or use their influence on their colleagues to build coalitions—all critical functions in an increasingly complex legislative environment with more and more competition for space on the agenda. To the extent, then, that PACs and campaign financing provide certain interest groups with a way of building support that is not available to others, it is important to understand whether groups with PACs are advocating attention to different issues than is the interest group system as a whole. Certain issues might enjoy a privileged position on the legislative agenda because members of Congress find that they are good in activating the kinds of groups that contribute the most money, while other issues struggle for attention and coalition leaders.

Indeed, our evidence suggests that significant differences do exist. Since the 1985 Walker survey included several questions about the public policy interests of membership associations, we can compare the policy concerns of groups that have affiliated PACs with the interests of groups that do not. Table 6.1 presents these data for nine policy areas: agriculture; civil rights and liberties; education; housing and urban affairs; transportation; health and other human services; energy and natural resources; management of the economy; and defense, national security, and foreign policy. The first column shows the percentage of associations with affiliated PACs reporting that they were "very interested" in each of these policy areas. Management of the economy was clearly the most common policy concern of associations with PACs, with over 57 percent of such groups reporting a strong interest in related issues. Energy and natural resource issues, policies regarding health or other social services, and transportation issues were also common concerns among interest groups with affiliated committees. However, only a small number of groups with PACs reported a strong interest in education or housing and urban affairs, while agriculture, civil rights, and foreign policy issues were slightly more popular. In general, groups with PACs were most interested in policies that directly involved private economic interests, if we can assume that health issues were the dominant concern in the "health and other social services" domain.

A very different set of priorities, however, emerges when we look at associations without affiliated PACs. Rather than economic management, the most common interest is health and social services, closely followed by education issues, with both policy domains commanding the attention of about one-third of the groups without election committees. At the other end of the distribution, transportation, agriculture, and housing and urban affairs issues were of interest to only a few of the groups without PACs, numbers that contrast sharply with the relatively large proportions of groups with PACs interested in transportation and agriculture issues.

TABLE 6.1. Comparison of Policy Interests of Interest Groups with and without Affiliated Political Action Committees, 1985

		Percent of Groups That Are "Very Interested" in Policy Area		
Policy Area	*N*	Groups with PACs	Groups without PACs	Difference between Groups with and without PACs
Management of the economy	802	57	27	30
Energy and natural resources	808	36	25	11
Health and social services	809	32	35	-3
Transportation	807	29	16	13
Agriculture	810	22	12	10
Civil rights and liberties	807	21	24	-3
National security and foreign affairs	808	21	20	1
Education	811	15	33	-18
Housing and urban affairs	803	14	12	2

Source: Federal Election Commission/Walker merged data (see app. A).

We can get a clearer sense of how the priorities of these two subsets of groups differ when we compare the percentages of each subset interested in these nine policy areas. The last column of table 6.1 makes this comparison by subtracting the percentage of groups without PACs that are interested in a policy from the percentage of groups with PACs that report a concern in the policy. By far, the largest difference was found in the policy area called "management of the economy"—57 percent of the groups with PACs said they were strongly interested in such issues, in contrast to 27 percent of the groups without election committees, for a difference of 30 points. But large differences were also found on other economic policies, such as transportation, energy and natural resources, and agricultural issues. In contrast, education issues were much more important to groups without PACs than among groups with affiliated committees. Relatively small differences in priorities existed on other issues, including health and social services, civil rights and liberties, national security and foreign affairs, and housing and urban affairs.

These differences in priorities grow out of differences across issue areas in the rate of PAC affiliation among interest groups. These rates—measured by the percentage of associations with affiliated election committees—are displayed in table 6.2. The four economic policy domains that showed the largest differences in table 6.1 were also the ones that were clearly above the sample average in the rate of PAC affiliation, which was 19 percent in the 1985 survey. Groups that were very interested in management of the economy showed the highest rate of PAC affiliation, with almost 34 percent of such groups having PACs. Just below this rate, about 30 percent of the associations interested in transportation and agriculture issues had PACs, while affiliated committees were established by one out of every four groups interested in policies affecting energy and natural resources. PACs were found among fewer groups—between one out of five and one out of six—in housing and urban affairs, national security and foreign affairs, health and social services, and civil rights and liberties. Groups interested in education issues showed the lowest rates of PAC formation, with fewer than one out of ten groups having affiliated committees in 1985.

These differences suggest that the PAC system highlights certain policy domains and underrepresents others, but though I think these conclusions are essentially correct, they need to be qualified. The number and size of PACs affiliated with each interest group vary, so policy areas with the lowest rates of PAC formation do not necessarily have the least money to offer candidates. We can see examples of potentially offsetting inequalities in the right-most column of table 6.2, which shows the 1984 average contributions to candidates by all PACs affiliated with groups in each policy domain. Not many of the groups concerned with issues of education or civil rights and liberties had PACs, but the few groups that did tended to have fairly large ones. The National Education Association PAC, for example, was the largest of all labor committees during the 1984 elections in terms of contributions ($1,574,000) and the fourth largest contributor among all PACs; and the civil rights and liberties domain included such large committees as NARAL-PAC, established by the National Abortion Rights Action League ($212,000 in 1984 contributions); NOW/PAC, created by the National Organization for Women ($217,000); and the National Rifle Association's Political Victory Fund ($700,000). Some of these group-level differences in average contributions are related to the number of PACs established by a single group: interest groups interested in education issues and questions of civil rights and liberties had more PACs than groups involved in other policy areas. Typically these additional committees were affiliated with state chapters. Education groups with PACs had an average of 4.2 committees, and groups interested in civil rights and liberties had a mean of 3.4 affiliated PACs, compared to averages ranging from 2.4 to 2.9 PACs in the other categories.

TABLE 6.2.   Rates of PAC Affiliation by the Policy Interests of Interest Groups, 1985

Policy Area	Number of Groups "Very Interested" in Policy	Number of Groups with PACs	Percentage of Groups with PACs	Mean Contributions per Group, 1984 (in Thousands of Dollars)
High rates of PAC affiliation				
Management of the economy	264	89	33.7	192.0
Transportation	148	45	30.4	187.5
Agriculture	117	35	29.9	153.3
Energy and natural resources	217	56	25.8	178.9
Moderate to low rates of PAC affiliation				
Housing and urban affairs	96	21	21.9	250.3
National security and foreign affairs	165	32	19.4	228.2
Health and social services	278	50	18.0	233.7
Civil rights and liberties	188	32	17.0	330.3
Education	242	23	9.5	328.1

Source: Federal Election Commission/Walker merged data (see app. A).

But these differences in the size and number of affiliated PACs probably do not threaten our basic conclusions, especially if we consider the PAC system as a whole and not just PACs affiliated with membership associations. Many of the groups interested in economic policies are business associations that only control a small part of the electoral resources provided by the industries they represent. For example, in addition to the PACs affiliated with the National Association of Life Underwriters and the American Council of Life Insurance (which are the kinds of organizations that were surveyed in the Walker study), there are a large number of corporate committees established by individual life insurance firms (which were not in the survey); and, of course, trade association PACs seek contributors from the same pool as corporate committees within their industry. Thus, the smaller size of PACs affiliated with business associations—which constitute many of the groups interested in economic issues—may be attributable to the partial and more competitive role such committees perform in mobilizing electoral resources within their industry or "group." Still, definite conclusions would require survey data from all the organizations involved in a policy domain—corporations as well as voluntary associations and unions—which we unfortunately do not have.

However, there are also important differences between a policy area dominated by a few large PACs and one in which PACs are common among many of the groups interested in the policies. Large yet narrowly distributed PACs in a policy subsystem may produce a highly skewed distribution of policy views within that domain. Education issues may in some sense be well represented in the PAC system due to the enormity of PACs affiliated with the teachers' unions. But because PACs do not represent over 90 percent of the groups interested in education policies, they only highlight a narrow band of views regarding such issues. Many of these other groups—for example, administrators, parents, researchers, churches, and citizen advocates for various educational reforms—may lobby legislators with reasonable effectiveness, but candidates interested in education issues can really only turn to teachers for financial support.

Another qualification is really more of a clarification. Table 6.2 does not primarily describe the distribution of policy interests among PACs. Rather, it relies on the national interest group system as a baseline in order to understand where the PAC system augments organized political advocacy in national politics and where it does not. Thus, even though the health and social services category is low in terms of PAC formation, while the agriculture category is high, their relative placement does not mean that there are more PACs interested in agriculture issues than PACs concerned with health and social services. Indeed, the opposite is true in our sample, since there are many more interest groups concerned with health and social services (278) than with agriculture (117). That difference is, in fact, a major strength of our study and distinguishes it from simple listings of PACs according to their policy "interests," since such listings do not present any baseline for comparison that indicates how and where PACs have changed the representation of organized interests in national politics.

But to return to our argument, why is there so much variation in the use of PACs across different policy areas? Most scholars who have discussed the formation of PACs have stressed motivational explanations. In his analyses of corporate PACs, for example, Epstein argued that large nonindustrial companies—such as commercial banks, diversified financial companies, utilities, and transportation companies—were more likely to establish PACs than large industrial companies because of "the extent to which federal decisions [bore] on the operations of any given industry or firm" (1980, 133; also see Sabato 1984, 30). Some also argue that PACs spread within a policy domain through processes of diffusion, emulation, and social learning. Rival associations may compete with one another by adding more services, including PACs; opponents may imitate each other, as do labor organizations and unionized industries or pro-life and pro-choice groups; or peer pressures among association leaders and CEOs might be enough to spread the use of PACs within an industry or policy area (Sabato 1984, 31; Epstein 1980, 146)

As I argued in chapter 4, motivational factors are no doubt important in understanding variation in PAC formation rates within the profit sector, but a general model of PAC formation—that is, one that applies to all types of interest groups—must also incorporate the effects of institutional constraints. I estimated such a model in chapter 5, and we can now see how well it works in accounting for differences among policy areas in the adoption of PACs based on the characteristics of groups involved in a policy area. To the extent, then, that the model predicts the proportion of groups with PACs, it would be reasonable to conclude that the differences in the formation of PACs across issue domains grow out of the relationships assumed by the model—specifically, the interaction between institutional conditions affecting PAC formation for the groups involved in a policy area and such motivational factors as the degree of partisan conflict and legislative complexity that the groups perceive.

To make these predictions, I calculated the probability of PAC formation for each group and then took the mean of these predicted probabilities

136   Improper Influence

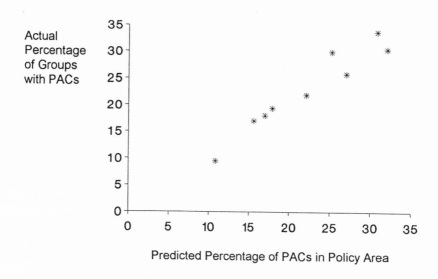

Fig. 6.1. Relation between actual and predicted percentages of associations with PACs in nine policy areas. Predictions are based on the model of PAC formation reported in fig. 5.1. An association is included in a policy area if it reported that it was "very interested" in that issue. (From Federal Election Commission/Walker merged data [see app. A].)

for all groups interested in a policy domain. I calculated these averages for all nine policy areas, and I then compared the averages or expected proportions of PACs with the actual or observed proportions. The comparison is found in figure 6.1, which plots the actual percentages of PACs against the predicted percentages, based on the group-level model of PAC formation displayed in figure 5.1.

The scatter plot shows a fairly close fit between the actual and predicted percentages of PACs in each of the nine policy areas. The fit suggests that we do not need to turn to sui generis explanations of the use of PACs in particular policy domains. Rather, most of the variation may be explained by a model, applicable to all interest groups, based on the importance of institutional constraints and their interaction with a group's political environment. Groups establish PACs because they have the political incentives to do so and because their memberships and revenue sources fit within the regulations imposed on groups involved in financing campaigns.

We can see more clearly how specific factors affect the adoption of PACs by comparing, across different issue domains, the mean values of the variables used in our institutional model of PAC formation. Such comparisons help us see *why* the model works in predicting the percentage of groups with PACs in different policy areas. The mean values on the variables used in the equation were thus calculated for each policy area—that is, for each subset of groups reporting that they were "very interested" in a particular class of issues. To make comparisons easier, I subtracted the sample mean from each entry. The resulting entries are thus deviations from the sample mean of that variable. These values are found in table 6.3, with the sample means and variable ranges listed in the last two rows.

By comparing these averages across different levels of PAC formation, we can see *how* policy areas with many PACs differ from those with relatively few; and when we do, we find that institutional conditions appear to be more important than a group's political context in

TABLE 6.3. Differences in Political Context and General Characteristics of Members in Different Policy Domains, Ranked according to their Rates of PAC Affiliation

Policy Area	Political Context			Organizational and Institutional Characteristics		
	Parties Differ on Important Issues	Number of Subcommittees Lobbied	Represents Members' Opinions	Percent of Revenues from Patrons	Members Drawn from Single Industry	Percent of Membership Base in Nonprofit Sector
High rates of PAC affiliation						
Management of the economy	.3	.5	.6	-2	.5	-10
Transportation	.1	.4	.5	-7	.6	-16
Agriculture	.1	.2	.3	-1	.3	-10
Energy and natural resources	.2	.5	.3	1	.1	-12
Moderate to low rates of PAC affiliation						
Housing and urban affairs	.6	.4	.3	7	-.2	-3
National security and foreign affairs	.2	.3	.1	12	-.5	-2
Health and social services	.2	.2	.1	5	-.3	7
Civil rights and liberties	.7	.2	.1	12	-.5	4
Education	.0	-.1	-.2	7	-.6	24
Sample mean	2.5	3.2	4.8	20	2.4	32
Variable range	1-5	1-5	1-6	0-100	1-5	0-100

Source: Federal Election Commission/Walker merged data (see app. A).

determining which policies have lots of PACs. Note, for example, that groups are less likely to see important party differences on transportation and agriculture issues than on housing and urban affairs and civil rights and liberties; nonetheless, the former show a higher rate of PAC formation. This does not undermine our finding that partisan conflict is a critical variable in understanding which interest groups form PACs. But it does suggest that other factors counteract the role of party conflict in determining the rate of PAC formation *across* different policy areas, or that perceptions of partisan conflict are more important in explaining variation *within* policy domains than *between* them. In contrast, legislative complexity does appear to have its expected impact on PAC formation across policies. Three out of the top four issue areas with respect to PAC formation are also high on the number of legislative subcommittees they work with, while groups interested in education issues, which show the lowest use of PACs, report working with relatively few subcommittees. PACs thus appear to be important in helping interest groups in complex policy arenas to develop and maintain relationships.

Institutional and organizational factors show more consistent differences between policy areas. Groups in policy domains that are high in PAC formation tend *not* to get revenues from government grants and contracts, gifts from firms or individuals, grants from private foundations, or support from religious institutions. But groups in policy domains that have moderate or low levels of PAC formation get substantial sums from these sources, typically totaling between one-fourth and one-third of their reported revenues. Groups in the latter domains are also more likely to emphasize representing members' opinions rather than advocating policy views or causes. Thus, policy areas with many PACs include many groups with a strong membership orientation and dependence, while areas where PACs are infrequently found tend to include more caucus-style groups.

Finally, the institutional bases of groups in a domain are very important in distinguishing policies and their rates of PAC formation. Policy areas are more likely to have a lot of PACs when the interest groups involved draw their members from a single industry or occupation in the profit sector, and they are less likely to have PACs when many of the groups have a membership base in the nonprofit sector. Both these relationships reinforce the basic findings of the analysis of group-level decisions to establish PACs—namely, PACs flourish only where they can draw on the resources of social or economic institutions; that capability is particularly strong only for businesses connected to narrow segments of the profit sector, such as single corporations or industries; and groups in the nonprofit sector generally cannot apply their institutional resources to electoral activities. PAC formation seems, in short, to depend on how different policies draw interest from different sectors of the political economy: where the policies excite the interest of business institutions, PACs are plentiful, but where nonprofit institutions and occupations make up a greater proportion of the political constituency, PACs are relatively scarce. In sum, institutional and organizational factors exert a very large influence over the rate of PAC formation in different policy areas, even to the point of inhibiting widespread PAC formation in policy areas characterized by considerable political conflict, as we can see, for example, in the area of civil rights and liberties.

Biases in the Policy Preferences of PACs

The growing importance of PACs and campaign contributions may not only have the effect of increasing the salience of certain types of economic issues; these changes may also enhance the strength of certain policy positions with respect to those issues. If the PAC system diminishes the political voice of citizen groups and organizations representing institutions in the governmental and private nonprofit sectors, we should expect that it reduces the relative amount of support for an expansion in the role of government in the nation's economy and society, since interest groups representing citizen and nonprofit interests have been important pillars of support for progressive and expansive domestic policies. The mobilization of PACs may, in other words, strengthen opposition to further growth in governmental functions.

We can evaluate this hypothesis by comparing the policy preferences of interest groups with PACs and those without PACs in both the 1980 and 1985 surveys. The 1985 survey was especially useful because it asked the groups to report their positions in several general policy areas. These policy or issue areas were the same ones discussed in the previous section of this chapter, but two additional questions were asked with respect to each policy area: whether the group's policy positions generally favored or opposed government provision of services and whether its positions generally favored or opposed government regulation. The survey had seventeen questions on each group's policy positions: questions about the group's position on service provision and regulation by government were included for eight policy areas, and one question was included regarding "service provision" in the area of defense, national security, and foreign affairs. However, I deleted the question concerning "service provision" of civil rights and liberties, since this policy seems to me to serve an exclusively regulatory role.

I estimated the biases produced by the PAC system by comparing the responses of groups with PACs and those without PACs on these fourteen questions regarding the government's role in providing services or regulating the economy. There were five possible responses to each question. A group was asked to indicate which of several statements reflected "most accurately the policy of this association *concerning expenditures or the provision of services* [or *concerning the level of federal regulation*]: There should be *much more provision of federal services* [or *federal regulation*], somewhat more, the present level, somewhat less, much less, or this association has no position on that issue" (italics not in original). These responses were then coded: a two was assigned to groups that supported much more provision of services or regulation, a one was assigned to groups that said they supported more service provision or regulation, a zero was given to groups that supported the present level, and a negative one and two were assigned respectively to groups that wanted less or much less in the way of service provision or regulation. Only those groups reporting that they were "very interested" in the policy area were included in the calculations.

The data on the mean scores and differences between PAC and non-PAC groups are presented in table 6.4. The right-most column shows the difference in policy preferences. A negative difference means that interest groups with PACs show less support for an expansion in government services or regulation (or greater support for contraction) than interest groups without PACs; a positive difference means that groups with PACs are on average more supportive of government responsibilities with respect to this policy area than are groups with no affiliated committees.

We expect that interest groups with PACs are more conservative than those without because we think that the groups that are prevented by institutional constraints from using their resources in campaigns and elections—namely, citizen groups and groups representing the nonprofit sector—also tend to be fairly liberal. The data in table 6.4 bear out that expectation. Of the sixteen different policy areas, twelve of them show negative differences, meaning that groups with PACs are less supportive of government responsibilities than are groups without PACs. Only four policy areas show the opposite pattern of greater support for government intervention among groups with election committees, including both transportation categories as well as the regulation of education and agriculture. The highly selective development of PACs with respect to different institutional affiliations thus appears to produce a conservative bias in most policy areas, such that groups with campaign contributions generally favor less expansive government responsibilities or even a reduction in the government's role.

But despite this overall pattern of conservative bias, there is considerable variation among different policy areas in the degree and direction of bias. The pattern of conservative bias is found most often among social services, such as housing and urban affairs, health and other social services, and educational services. However, differences are less negative or even positive on economic policies like energy and natural resources, management of the economy, and transportation. In sum, although many of the differences in policy preferences between groups with PACs and those without are not very big, PACs clearly do not always balance off against each other within particular areas of public policy.

What accounts for these different patterns of bias? The simplest explanation assumes an interaction between the policy preferences of groups based on different occupational roles and their proportion within

TABLE 6.4. Differences between Groups with and without PACs in Their Policy Preferences Regarding Government's Role in Selected Policy Areas; Including Only Groups Reporting That They Were Very Interested in a Policy Area, 1985

Policy Area (Services or Regulation)	Number of Groups	Groups with PACs	Groups without PACs	Difference
		Mean Score on Preferences Regarding Expansion of Government Role in Policy Area		
Housing and urban affairs (regulation)	79	-.53	.22	-0.75
Health and social services (services)	133	.90	1.37	-0.47
Housing and urban affairs (services)	85	.78	1.10	-0.32
Agriculture (services)	91	.17	.43	-0.26
Civil rights and liberties (regulation)	150	.41	.66	-0.25
Education (services)	212	1.10	1.32	-0.22
Energy and natural resources (services)	180	.55	.77	-0.22
Management of the economy (services)	195	.23	.43	-0.20
Health and social services (regulation)	206	.00	.13	-0.13
Management of the economy (regulation)	176	-.26	-.16	-0.10
Energy and natural resources (regulation)	169	-.13	-.07	-0.06
Transportation (regulation)	127	-.02	-.20	0.18
Transportation (services)	125	.79	.56	0.23
Agriculture (regulation)	86	-.30	-.60	0.30

Sources: Federal Election Commission/Walker merged data (see app. A).

different policy areas. In most policy areas, interest groups based on profit sector occupations or institutions are much less supportive of expanded government responsibilities than are groups representing the nonprofit sector, citizen interests, or labor. Data demonstrating this point are presented in table 6.5, which shows, for each of the sixteen policy areas, the preferences regarding government involvement for the four largest occupational types of groups: profit sector, nonprofit sector,

TABLE 6.5. Mean Scores on Interest Groups' Preferences for Expansion or Contraction of the National Government's Role in Various Policy Areas, by Occupational Role

Policy Area	Profit	Nonprofit	Labor	Citizen
		Occupational Role		

1. Support for expanded government role by nonprofit, labor, and citizen groups; weak or no opposition to status quo from profit sector

Strong patterns

Health and social services (service)	-.01	1.18	1.28	1.14
Housing and urban affairs (service)	-.27	.85	.70	.78
Education (service)	.20	1.27	1.16	.81

Weak patterns

Management of the economy (service)	-.10	.62	1.12	.47
Energy and natural resources (service)	.06	.75	.74	.78
Transportation (service)	.11	.59	.96	.45

2. Support for expanded government role by labor, with weak or no support from citizen or nonprofit groups; support for contraction by profit sector

Energy and natural resources (regulation)	-.75	.31	.57	.32
Civil rights and liberties (regulation)	-.68	.23	.84	.58
Health and social services (regulation)	-.71	.00	.84	.48
Agriculture (service)	-.55	.45	.60	-.04
Transportation (regulation)	-.56	.17	.71	.20
Management of the economy (regulation)	-.63	.10	.96	.08
Housing and urban affairs (regulation)	-.69	-.04	1.00	.79
Agriculture (regulation)	-.78	-.50	—	.26

Source: 1985 Walker survey.

Note: A positive score indicates support for an expanded role of government in the policy area, while a negative score means a preference for contraction. Scores equal to zero indicate that the group supports the status quo.

labor, and citizen groups.[1] Each of the cells in the table represents the mean score regarding the groups' preferences on whether the federal government's role should be expanded (indicated by positive scores), should be reduced (indicated by negative scores), or should remain the same (indicated by scores equal to zero).

In all but one of the fourteen policy areas, profit sector groups are less supportive of federal government responsibilities than are citizen groups, groups representing the nonprofit sector, and labor unions. The only exception is national security and foreign affairs issues, which comprise an area that appears to cut across the typology of occupational roles, though citizen groups are somewhat distinctive in favoring a reduced role. The strongest patterns of contrast between profit sector groups and the other three are found among three social services: health and other social services, housing, and education; while somewhat weaker contrasts are found among such economic issues as management of the economy, energy and natural resources, and transportation. The table also shows that for many of the regulatory issues, a bipolar pattern of opposition exists between profit sector groups and labor, with nonprofit sector and citizen groups providing mixed or moderate support to an expanded governmental role.

These patterns of conflict suggest that the inability of citizen and nonprofit sector groups to form PACs may, under certain circumstances, help account for the biases we see in PACs' representation of policy preferences. Since these two types of groups are likely to be liberal in their views and opposed to the preferences of business groups, and since they are also unlikely to have PACs, their involvement in a particular policy area is likely to create a contrast between the interests represented by groups with PACs and the views or preferences represented by groups not involved in campaigns or elections. We can examine this hypothesis in a rough sort of way by examining the relationship between the amount of bias in each of the fourteen policy areas and the percentage of citizen or nonprofit sector groups interested in the policy. This relationship is shown for citizen and nonprofit sector groups in the scatter plot in figure 6.2. The pattern suggests that the degree of conservative bias increases (shown as the line slopes downward) as the proportion of citizen and nonprofit sector groups active in a policy grows. A large proportion of citizen and nonprofit sector groups in a policy domain means that liberal views are likely to be well represented but that few of the liberal groups are likely to have PACs. However, when there are few such groups active in a policy area, the policies are more likely to be dominated by profit sector and labor unions (putting aside the other two categories for a moment), and PACs are more likely to be involved

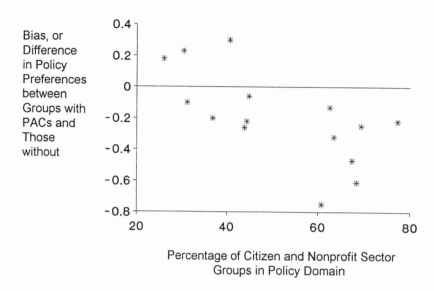

Fig. 6.2. Relation between bias in PAC formation and the percentage of citizen and nonprofit sector groups in policy domains. Positive numbers mean that groups with PACs support greater governmental intervention in a policy area than do groups without PACs. Negative numbers mean that groups with PACs are less supportive of governmental intervention. (From Federal Election Commission/Walker merged data [see app. A].)

on both sides. The greater the proportion of citizen and nonprofit sector groups in a policy area, the greater the discrepancy between a conservative PAC system and a more liberal system of membership associations.

We can see then that the growth of PACs is likely not only to highlight certain economic issues but also to create new imbalances of power within certain types of policy areas with respect to the federal government's proper role. These imbalances are especially likely to be found among certain social service issues, where the major sources of support for an expanded role of government have encompassed groups in the nonprofit sector and citizen groups. However, to the extent that the primary polarity in a policy domain is between business and labor—or between certain types of businesses or labor unions—the growth of PACs is less likely to create a new imbalance of power.

The policy interests and positions of groups in the PAC system thus differ significantly from those represented by membership associations. PACs represent more conservative standpoints and are generally more interested in economic policies than in civil rights and liberties, education, and other social policies. This difference is due in part to the occupational base of the PAC system, which largely excludes groups representing the nonprofit sector as well as many groups representing citizen interests in other political arenas. The effects of these differences for legislative and electoral institutions deserve their own study—and we cannot properly assess those effects with the data we have been using—but the findings are suggestive. Has the growth of PACs, coupled with the increasing difficulty of fund-raising, created a greater tension between legislators' campaign-finance coalitions and the legislative coalitions they attempt to put together, especially among liberal members of Congress? And if there are systematic biases in the kinds of policy positions and concerns represented in the PAC system, does that mean that the PAC system also shows a tilt in favor of one major party or the other, since the party system is obviously related to some of these policy cleavages? If so, how are those biases expressed in terms of contributions or other actions? Finally, how do PACs respond to partisan or electoral change? Though many of these questions are beyond the scope of this study, I address some of these issues in chapter 7.

CHAPTER 7

PACs, Groups, and the Political Parties

Even though little systematic research has been done on the subject, a conventional wisdom has evolved among many political observers regarding the effects of PACs on the political parties. According to this view, PACs fracture the party system and diminish its capacity to structure conflict in American politics. They are said to create a new politics based on pragmatic interests rather than partisan principles, and as such they give a critical advantage to the national Democratic Party, which until recently has controlled the House of Representatives, where most PAC money is spent.

As is the case with most conventional wisdom, there is some truth to these claims. PACs obviously represent a wide variety of interests whose demands do not always coincide with either party's platform. Sometimes PACs raise issues that cut across party cleavages and that party leaders want to avoid because of the danger of alienating parts of their traditional coalitions; and sometimes PACs raise particularistic issues that interest only a handful of citizens and institutions and thus fail to penetrate the national partisan debate. And it is true that PACs have favored Democratic candidates, who received 64 percent of all PAC contributions in the 1992 congressional elections.

These conclusions make a lot of sense if we only look at PACs from the perspective of the parties and their candidates. Obviously PACs are more complex and less structured in their relations to one another and to candidates than are the national parties. But though this perspective is not unreasonable, it is hardly complete. Political parties are not simply competing teams of candidates seeking to win elections (Downs 1957, 25, 28). They are also coalitions of groups (Axelrod 1972; Eldersveld 1964; Petrocik 1981) and institutions that develop, sustain, and enact specific policies and ideas (Sundquist 1968). From this viewpoint, it is important not just *who* gets the money but also *where it comes from*. It matters whether a party's candidates have succeeded because groups that traditionally supported the party have adapted well to the new forms of political action; because candidates have found a new coalitional base, representing different interests and policies, after the old coalition failed to handle the new rules and the need to raise campaign money; or because opposing groups have supported certain members of the majority party only because they have been forced to work with that party to get what they want. It is thus important to examine the relations between parties and PACs from the perspective of the interest group system as well as from that of the candidates.

Indeed, when we look at PACs in the context of the interest group system, the groups that form PACs are generally *not* raising issues that cut across or undermine the party system. Instead, they are *more* likely than others to have been buffeted by partisan change and conflict, and they seem to have fairly strong party preferences. These preferences and alignments may not always be evident in PAC contributions, but contributions reflect many factors, including temporary ones like a party's current control of the Congress. Such short-term influences are important, but they should not be confused with long-term commitments. When we try to discern these more basic relationships between groups and parties, we find that the burdens and advantages of the PAC system and its rules have not fallen evenly on the groups aligned with each party; that organized groups that have supported Democratic policies and administrations have been less successful in forming effective PACs than groups that have sided with Republican presidents and policies; and that this asymmetry has had important implications for the dynamics of the party and interest group systems.

The Institutional Bases of Groups and Relations with the Parties-in-Government

As we saw in Chapter 6, a group's occupational base is not only related to its ability to establish effective PACs; it is also correlated with significant differences among groups in the kinds of issues they are concerned with and the policy positions they espouse. Given these differences, we would expect the typology of occupational roles to articulate different relationships with the political parties. Just as organized groups representing the nonprofit sector, labor, and certain citizen interests are more supportive of liberal policies and press different agendas than business groups, we might expect them to show stronger ties to the Democratic Party and its candidates—and that is generally what we find.

We can begin to sort out these relationships by noting how interest group experiences with the political parties have varied across the typology of occupational roles. Of course, interest groups relate to the parties in a host of ways—from attending fund-raisers to recruiting candidates and convention delegates—but the center of those relationships lies in the ability of groups to work with and secure cooperation from the parties-in-government. Each party is disposed to respond to the interests of some groups while paying relatively little attention to the demands of others. These basic predispositions—based on bonds of ideology and constituency—can be extremely important in structuring interest group relations with government. Groups that find important differences in their treatment by the parties not only have stronger incentives to form PACs and engage in electoral activities; they are also restricted in their search for legislative allies and so are likely to respond to this partisan environment by giving most of their money to candidates of one party in the hope of nurturing vigorous advocates for the groups' political demands.

These basic ties of sympathy and cooperation between groups and parties are obviously complex and hard to summarize, but the Walker surveys tried to discern their outlines by asking groups to describe how changes in party control of the presidency and the Congress affected their relations with the federal government. The 1985 survey contained two relevant questions: (1) "How did the change in 1981 from Democratic to Republican control of the Presidency affect the amount of cooperation and consultation between the association and federal agencies?" and (2) "How did the change in 1981 from Democratic to Republican control of the United States Senate affect the amount of consultation and cooperation between this association and the Congress?" Answers to these questions were arrayed on a five-point scale, from an "important increase in cooperation" to an "important decrease in cooperation."[1]

Table 7.1 shows that associations' experiences with the national parties varied a lot in the early 1980s and that the typology of occupational roles captured many of these differences. Part A of the table shows that four out of ten business groups experienced an increase in cooperation under federal agencies as a result of the 1981 transition from Democratic to Republican control of the presidency; almost half the business groups saw no change in their relations with the executive branch; and only one out of seven profit sector associations reported a *decrease* in cooperation. In contrast, nearly all labor groups saw a decline in cooperation, as did most citizen groups—which, as we saw in chapter 6, were typically liberal in their policy views. Groups with members from both the profit and nonprofit sectors (i.e., the "mixed" category) showed the least sensitivity to the 1981 presidential transition, while groups representing the nonprofit sector were evenly split between those who were affected by the presidential switch and those who were not.

The vulnerability of over half the groups in the nonprofit sector to partisan change was probably a novel experience for many of them. Not

many of these groups were affected by the 1977 switch in party control
(Gais, Peterson, and Walker 1984), but the Reagan Administration was
different. As Alan Abramson observed, "Particularly in the 1980s . . .
you saw nonprofits [becoming] much more active" when their government support was threatened, since "[i]n the social services area, 50 per
cent of the budgets of these [nonprofit] organizations come from government" (*NJ* 26 January 1991, 221). The Reagan Administration and its
budget cuts (or threats thereof) were clearly polarizing forces with re-

TABLE 7.1.   Effects of Party Shifts of 1977 and 1981 in Control of the Presidency on
Interest Groups' Relations with the National Executive Branch, by Occupational Role

Part A. Effects of 1980 Presidential Election (from 1985 Survey Data)

| Occupational Role | N | Change in Cooperation between Group and National Administration as Result of 1981 Shift from Democratic to Republican Control | | | |
		Increase (Favors Republican Party)	No change	Decrease (favors Democratic Party)	Total
Profit	273	39%	47%	14%	100%
Mixed	39	18%	59%	23%	100%
Nonprofit	238	15%	48%	37%	100%
Labor	29	0%	7%	93%	100%
Citizen	157	13%	33%	54%	100%
All groups	736	23%	44%	33%	100%

Part B. Effects of 1981 Senate Swing to Republican Control (from 1985 Survey Data)

| Occupational Role | N | Change in Cooperation between Group and Congress as Result of 1981 Shift from Democratic to Republican Control | | | |
		Increase (Favors Republican Party)	No change	Decrease (Favors Democratic Party)	Total
Profit	267	32%	61%	7%	100%
Mixed	35	20%	57%	23%	100%
Nonprofit	222	14%	68%	18%	100%
Labor	27	0%	33%	67%	100%
Citizen	160	16%	49%	36%	100%
All groups	711	21%	59%	20%	100%

Source: 1980 and 1985 Walker surveys.

spect to the major institutions in the U.S. economy, drawing many new groups in the partisan fray and forcing a wider political split between the profit and nonprofit sectors (Peterson and Walker 1986).

Similar differences in party relations across the typology of occupational roles were found when groups were asked about the ascendancy of the Senate Republican party in 1981 (see table 7.1, part B). Of the groups that perceived change in their relations with national political institutions, profit sector groups strongly favored the Republican Party, labor and citizen groups strongly favored the Democratic Party, and groups in the nonprofit and mixed categories showed little preference either way. All types of groups were less affected by partisan changes in the Senate than by changes in the executive branch.

The levels of cooperation between interest groups and parties are surely affected by specific administrations and political circumstances, but they also reflect long-standing connections between groups and parties based on policy preferences, ideological affinities, and shared constituencies. In the most complete analysis of these data, Peterson and Walker (1986) found that changes in cooperation between different interest groups and parties were strongly related to groups' policy preferences. And as we saw in chapter 6, the same typology that helps to distinguish groups with respect to their relations with the parties also articulates significant and reinforcing differences regarding their general policy agendas and preferences. These connections between a group's membership base, its policy views, and its relations with the parties-in-government provide an important and relatively stable context for understanding how interest groups and PACs relate to the party system: which party PACs turn to when they want to enhance their access to governmental decision making, what different barriers groups aligned with each party face in establishing and maintaining effective PACs, and the consequences of group partisanship and asymmetric constraints for the distribution of campaign money and candidate strategies for raising it.

Partisanship in PAC Contributions

If interest groups use campaign donations to enhance their access to sympathetic legislators, PAC contributions to candidates of different parties ought to reflect the basic level of cooperation or sympathy that interest groups can expect from the parties-in-government. As I have already argued, contributions are not strong resources: they do not create allies from scratch as much as they build on existing predispositions to create vigorous advocates out of passive supporters. Thus, a conservative business group will give most of its money to Republicans, an agriculture group may find potentially active legislative allies in both political parties if they represent districts with substantial numbers of farmers, and an environmental group will work most closely with, and give most of its contributions to, liberal Democrats. Differences in PAC contributions across the typology of occupational roles should therefore reflect differences in where interest groups find a basic predisposition of cooperation and sympathy among current or potential legislators.

Indeed, PAC partisanship seems to track the degree of cooperation that different groups have experienced at the hands of the national parties. Table 7.2 reveals this connection between a group's occupational base and its party orientation by showing the average percentage of contributions by PACs to Democratic candidates for each occupational category. Just as business associations found greater cooperation in a Republican presidency and a Republican Senate in the early 1980s, most business PACs favored GOP candidates. Corporate PACs were especially likely to support Republicans, giving three out of five dollars to GOP candidates, while committees affiliated with trade associations and other multifirm interests split their contributions between the par-

TABLE 7.2. Mean Percentage of Contributions Given to Democratic Candidates by PACs, by Occupational Role

Occupational Role	Subcategory	Mean Percentage of Contributions Made to Democratic Candidates; Includes all PACs Making Contributions	
		1979-80	1983-84
Profit sector	Corporate	39	41
	Multifirm, industry	49	49
Mixed sector	None	70	67
Nonprofit sector	None	62	72
Labor	Profit sector	93	95
	Mixed sector	97	96
	Nonprofit sector	93	95
Citizen interests	Party, candidate	41	48
	Issue	45	60
Number of PACs		2,170	3,035

Source: Federal Election Commission/various sources for occupational codes (see app. B).

ties, perhaps because many of these latter groups had extensive lobbying operations that forced them to work with Democrats in the House. When we only look at Senate contributions (not shown) and thus remove the influence of Democratic control of the House—whose structures and procedures made House Republicans largely unimportant to lobbying groups during this period—we find that corporate PACs gave only 31 percent of their Senate contributions to Democrats in 1984, while multifirm committees gave 36 percent. Labor unions gave nearly all their money to Democrats—regardless of the chamber—which is consistent with the fact that they saw big differences in their treatment by the national parties. Business and union PACs showed very little aggregate change between 1980 and 1984 in how they distributed their money to each party's candidates, although the appearance of stability among profit sector committees was somewhat misleading, since business PACs dropped their support for Senate Democrats (from 41 percent of Senate contributions to 32 percent) while they increased their support for House Democrats (from 45 percent to 51 percent).

Groups representing the nonprofit sector, and those with members from both the profit and nonprofit sectors, typically preferred Democrats to Republicans by about a two to one margin. For the small number of PACs in the nonprofit sector, that preference became even stronger between the 1980 and 1984 elections, as these committees increased their average support for Democrats from 62 to 72 percent. PACs representing citizen interests also showed increased support for Democratic candidates. Citizen PACs generally supported Republicans in the 1980 elections—but by 1984, they were as a whole much more supportive of Democrats, especially citizen PACs organized around issues rather than candidates or parties.

The averages in table 7.2 may suggest that, except for those connected to labor unions, most PACs gave substantial contributions to both parties. But that is not true. These averages actually conceal a lot of partisanship in PAC contributions. Table 7.3 corrects this impression by showing the average partisanship scores for PACs by occupational roles. The score for each PAC is simply the percentage of its total contributions made to candidates of the party favored by the PAC. Thus, a PAC that gave exactly half its contributions to Democratic candidates and half to Republican candidates would have a score of 50, a committee that contributed three out of every four dollars to Republicans would receive a score of 75, and a PAC that gave all its money to Democratic candidates would have a score of 100. The average partisanship scores for all PACs were 79 in 1980 and 80 in 1984. Most PACs strongly favored one party.

However, as table 7.3 demonstrates, the degree of partisanship varied a lot from one occupational type to another. Business PACs were the least partisan, though even they typically gave three-fourths of their contribution to one party. Citizen groups and labor PACs were extremely partisan; they generally gave over 90 percent of their contributions to a single party. The high partisanship scores of citizen PACs—combined with the fairly even split between Democratic and Republican candidates—meant that these groups were divided between highly partisan camps of the Right and the Left.

We can examine directly the connection between PAC contributions and how their parent interest groups are treated by the parties if we view that connection at the level of individual groups. Do groups that find one party to be more cooperative in the course of their lobbying activities tend to give more of their money to that party's candidates? Quite simply, yes. The relevant data are displayed in table 7.4, which shows the relationship between interest groups' treatment by the national parties and the contribution patterns of their affiliated PACs. Interest group

TABLE 7.3.   Mean Partisanship Scores of PACs, by Occupational Role

Occupational Role	Subcategory	Mean Percentage of Contributions Made to Candidates of Favored Party; Scores Range from 50 to 100; Includes all PACs Making Contributions	
		1979-80	1983-84
Profit sector	Corporate	75	76
	Multifirm, industry	77	75
Mixed sector	None	86	74
Nonprofit sector	None	78	79
Labor	Profit sector	96	97
	Mixed sector	96	96
	Nonprofit sector	93	97
Citizen interests	Party, candidate	99	99
	Issue	90	91
Number of PACs		2,170	3,035

Source: Federal Election Commission/various sources for occupational codes (see app. B).

relations with the parties are measured by the survey questions regarding changes in cooperation after the Republican victories in 1980. The partisanship of PACs affiliated with these groups is measured by the percentage of each PAC's contributions going to Democratic candidates for House and Senate seats in the 1984 elections; the means of these percentages are displayed in the table.

Table 7.4 shows a strong relationship between the cooperation groups received from the national parties and the partisan split of their PACs' contributions in the 1984 elections. On the whole, PACs seemed to support candidates of the party with which they worked best, which was what we expected if groups used contributions to transform passive

TABLE 7.4. The Partisan Preferences of PACs with Respect to Their Contributions as Related to the Level of Cooperation They Have Received from the National Parties-in-Government

| Change in Relationship between Interest Group and Government Institution as Result of Party Shift in Control | Percentage of Contributions Given to Democrats by PACs Affiliated with Survey Groups, 1984 Elections | | | |
| | 1981 Shift in Control of the Presidency from Democratic to Republican Party | | 1981 Shift in Control of the Senate from the Democratic to the Republican Party | |
	Percent Democratic	N	Percent Democratic	N
Contributions to Senate candidates				
Important increase in cooperation	32.6	16	35.2	13
Moderate increase in cooperation	36.9	28	30.5	26
No change in the relationship	44.5	50	52.0	65
Moderate decrease in cooperation	69.9	20	75.7	24
Important decrease in cooperation	92.3	22	95.6	8
Contributions to House candidates				
Important increase in cooperation	49.7	18	52.0	15
Moderate increase in cooperation	53.3	29	54.7	27
No change in the relationship	65.2	51	68.0	67
Moderate decrease in cooperation	81.5	21	82.0	24
Important decrease in cooperation	93.3	22	93.8	8

Source: Federal Election Commission/Walker survey merged data (see app. A).

supporters into active legislative advocates. PACs affiliated with groups that saw a large decline in cooperation with the federal government after the GOP won control of the presidency—mostly unions and liberal citizen groups—responded by giving nearly all their contributions to the Democrats. On the other end of the scale, PACs affiliated with groups that witnessed a large increase in cooperation under the Republicans—generally business associations and conservative citizen groups—typically gave most of their contributions to Republicans. This was especially the case in the more individualistic and Republican-controlled Senate, where conservative business PACs were not forced by the institution's structure and procedures to nurture allies within the Democratic Party. Finally, groups that reported no change in the level of cooperation under different parties contributed substantial amounts to both parties, though the balance was greater in the Senate than in the House. Note that both measures of cooperation between groups and parties show roughly the same correlation with PAC partisanship, which suggests that they reflect an orientation to the parties that is common across different representative institutions.

This relationship between a group's experiences under partisan change and how its PAC makes contributions helps us explain the fairly high levels of partisanship we noted in table 7.3. As table 7.4 demonstrates, PACs are more partisan when the interests they represent are strongly affected by party shifts in the control of government. And as we noted in chapter 4, PACs are more likely to be established by interest groups when they confront partisan conflict. Groups whose relations with government institutions are such that they have insulated themselves from electoral and partisan change—for example, groups within an autonomous "subgovernment" or "iron triangle"—are more likely to be bipartisan in their contributions, but they are also less likely to form a PAC in the first place. Thus, the incentives leading groups to establish PACs imply that the PAC system will be predominantly made up of the kinds of groups that are likely to give a large share of their PAC contributions to a single party.

PAC Formation and Party Differences

We therefore find a close connection between an interest group's experiences with the national governing parties and the partisan split of its contributions; and both these factors are related to its occupational or institutional base. These connections have important implications for the political parties. That the two parties are aligned with very different types of interest groups—groups that face different burdens and opportunities for mobilizing resources for electoral action—suggests important asymmetries in the capacity that the groups supporting each party have to form effective PACs. These asymmetries, in turn, may mean that the rules governing PACs and interest group involvement in elections are not—and perhaps cannot—be neutral with respect to the parties and their candidates.

We can begin to see these implications if we examine the rate of PAC formation among groups according to their experiences with party shifts in the control of the presidency after the 1976 and 1980 elections. These data are displayed in table 7.5, which shows the percentage of interest groups with affiliated PACs for each level of change in cooperation as a result of the 1977 and 1981 transitions. PACs were least common among groups that saw no change in their relations with the executive branch. Only one out of six groups had PACs in these stable political environments; but among groups that had failed to insulate themselves from partisan conflict, about one out of four had affiliated PACs. Thus, although many political observers view PACs as undermining the party system, the PAC system actually owes much of its structure to the parties. PACs are usually found among interest groups that perceive important differences between the political parties, presumably because PACs are useful to interest groups in struggling to manage complex and conflictual political environments—conditions often produced by partisan conflict.

TABLE 7.5. Evidence that Interest Groups Are More Likely to Have PACs When Their Relations with the National Government Are Affected by Partisan Shifts, and that the Tendency Is Particularly Strong for Groups Favoring Republican Administrations

Change in Relationship with Institution as Result of Party Shift in Control	Percentage of Interest Groups with PACs in 1980 and 1984	
	1977 Shift in Control of the Presidency to the Democrats	1981 Shift in Control of the Presidency to the Republicans
Important increase in cooperation	20%	31%
Moderate increase in cooperation	23%	29%
No change in the relationship	16%	17%
Moderate decrease in cooperation	38%	17%
Important decrease in cooperation	28%	21%
$N =$	546	736

Source: Federal Election Commission/Walker survey merged data (see app. A).

Yet there is also an interesting asymmetry in these patterns. In both columns, PACs were particularly abundant among groups that favored Republican administrations. PACs were more common among groups that had seen a decline in the level of cooperation with the executive branch after the Ford–Carter transition and among groups that had experienced an increase in the cooperation after Reagan took office in 1981. Almost one-third of the groups that found Republican administrations to be more congenial had PACs, while only about one-fifth of the groups that saw greater cooperation under Democratic administrations had PACs. There seems to have been an asymmetric effect in the formation of PACs with respect to partisan swings: the groups alienated by the Democratic administration formed PACs at relatively high rates, while the groups hurt by the Republican administration did not.

This partisan asymmetry also emerges from an examination of the dynamics of PAC formation at the level of individual groups. We can see these dynamics by tracing the behavior of associations in the Walker panel study, which includes all groups that responded to both the 1980 and 1985 surveys. By comparing the PAC affiliations of the *same* groups in 1980 and 1984, we can see precisely which groups established new PACs. These data are shown in figure 7.1, which shows that PACs were most commonly found—and expanded most rapidly—among groups that perceived the Reagan Administration to be much more cooperative than the Carter Administration. Groups that saw a decline in cooperation—that is, those that favored Democrats—added PACs at a rate no higher than that for groups in quiescent policy areas that experienced *no change* in their relations with the government. At least among large membership associations, PACs spread much more widely and quickly among groups friendly to the Reagan Administration.

A different asymmetry appears when we examine changes in the average size or receipts of PACs. Here, we find a shift in favor of groups preferring Democratic administrations. We can see this in figure 7.2, which shows the average receipts in 1980 and 1984 of PACs affiliated with interest groups in the Walker panel study. The growth of PAC receipts was, like PAC formation, a process that was closely keyed to group vulnerability to the party system: PACs had greater receipts and saw greater increases in receipts when their relations with the executive branch depended on national party swings. But rather than seeing the largest expansion among groups that experienced greater cooperation with the Reagan Administration—as we did when we looked at PAC formation—the growth of receipts was stronger among groups that had found greater cooperation under Carter's presidency. These panel data

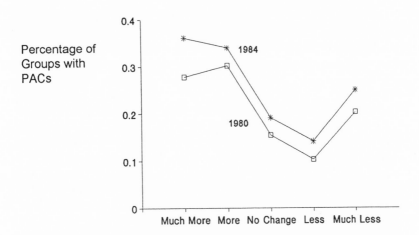

Fig. 7.1. Changes in the percentage of associations with affiliated PACs, by changes in cooperation with the federal government after the 1981 shift in control of the presidency, 1980–84. (From Federal Election Commission/Walker panel survey merged data [see app. A].)

suggest that groups on the Right and Left responded to partisan change in different ways. While the Right expanded its organizational base by adding new PACs, the Left intensified its mobilization efforts among existing PACs.

What gives rise to these different responses? I think they are best understood in light of the uneven impact of institutional constraints on electoral action. The kinds of interest groups that were aligned with Republican administrations—and presumably supporting their policies—faced few constraints in extending their institutional base and greatly increasing the total number of PACs serving those interests and supporting Republican candidates. In contrast, the kinds of interest groups aligned with Democratic administrations had a very narrow occupational or institutional base on which to build, so they reacted to the aggressive conservatism of President Reagan's first term by mobilizing more resources from *within* a more or less fixed institutional base and by expanding the number of mostly nonconnected citizen PACs, that is, PACs *without* direct occupational or institutional ties. Thus, important differences emerge in the dynamic patterns of electoral mobilization when we compare the kinds of groups that support Democratic candidates and Democratic-controlled governments with the kinds of groups that support Republican candidates

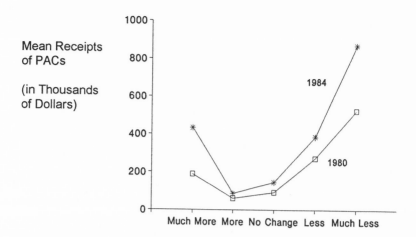

Change in Cooperation with Federal Government

Figure 7.2. Changes in the average receipts of PACs affiliated with national associations, by changes in cooperation with the federal government after the 1981 shift in control of the presidency, 1980–84. (From Federal Election Commission/Walker panel survey merged data [see app. A].)

and Republican-controlled governments—differences influenced by the rules governing the PAC system.

We can see these contrasting patterns of electoral mobilization in table 7.6, which shows changes in the number of PACs and their average receipts between the 1980 and 1984 elections, within the typology of occupational roles. For convenience, the typology is divided into the categories of PACs that typically favor Republican governments and support Republican candidates and those that favor Democratic governments and contribute to their candidates (based on tables 7.1 and 7.2). As the resources mobilized by groups in each of these categories shift, we should therefore see a corresponding shift in the amount of money available to candidates of each party. Since citizen PACs include strong supporters of *both* parties, I divided them into two categories: pro-Democratic PACs that gave more money to Democrats than to Republicans (a mean of 92 percent in both 1980 and 1984), and PACs that favored Republicans (contributing an average of only 7 percent to Democrats in 1980 and 4 percent in 1984). The left-hand side of table 7.6 shows the number of committees per category making contributions in each election cycle and the changes in those numbers between 1980 and 1984. The right-hand side of the table indicates the average receipts provided by PACs in each of these categories, as well as changes in these averages between the 1980 and 1984 elections. Only PACs making contributions to candidates are included in the calculations.

Table 7.6 suggests that the kinds of groups that generally favored the Republican Party—and often supported its candidates—mobilized considerable electoral resources but in a way that was quite different from that of groups that typically sided with the Democrats. Pro-Republican categories *extended* their institutional base by adding 645 new committees between 1980 and 1984 (only including those that actually made contributions). Many of these new committees were corporate PACs in various financial industries (Eismeier and Pollock 1988, 48), perhaps organized in response to the 1984 tug-of-war between the Democratic-controlled House Banking Committee and the Republican-majority Senate Banking Committee over banking reform and deregulation. Some of the largest of these new committees were Salomon Brothers Inc. PAC ($356,000 in receipts during 1983–84), MBank PAC ($314,000), and Amsouth PAC

TABLE 7.6.   Differences in the Number and Average Receipts of PACs, by Occupational Role, 1980 and 1984 (Only Including PACs Making Contributions to Candidates)

Occupational Role	Number of PACs Making Contributions			Mean Receipts per PAC (in Thousands of Dollars)		
	1980	1984	Difference, 1980-84	1980	1984	Difference, 1980-84
Categories of groups favoring Republican candidates						
Profit sector—corporate	1,162	1,646	**484**	29.5	42.0	**12.5**
Profit sector— multifirm	531	636	**105**	62.8	83.6	**20.8**
Citizen—pro-GOP	105	161	**56**	328.9	418.5	**89.6**
Categories of groups favoring Democratic candidates						
Mixed sector	13	20	**7**	23.3	53.3	**30.0**
Nonprofit sector	33	48	**15**	34.7	85.7	**51.0**
Labor—profit	183	221	**38**	104.6	162.5	**57.9**
Labor—mixed	21	13	**-8**	131.4	265.7	**134.3**
Labor—nonprofit	41	53	**12**	109.0	224.6	**115.6**
Citizen—pro-Democrat	79	238	**159**	86.3	158.9	**72.6**

Sources: Federal Election Commission/various sources for occupational codes (see app. B).

(affiliated with Amsouth Bancorporation: $158,000).[2] However, many other industries also gave rise to major new corporate committees, such as Shoney's PAC ($270,000 in receipts during 1983–84), Boeing Company PAC ($190,000), and Joseph E. Seagram and Sons, Inc. PAC ($174,000). Multifirm PACs also increased substantially in number between 1980 and 1984—adding 105 new PACs—with one of the most successful being the Auto Dealers and Drivers for Free Trade PAC, a nonconnected committee that organized auto and truck dealers with franchises from Japanese manufacturers and that raised $1,182,436 in the 1983–84 election cycle. Pro-Republican citizen PACs also grew in number, adding 56 new PACs, such as Representative Bob Dornan's American Space Frontier Committee ($417,000 in 1984 receipts).

In contrast, pro-Democratic categories added only 223 new PACs. Although administrative and professional groups in the nonprofit and mixed categories increased their numbers significantly between 1980 and 1984, their numbers had been so small to begin with that their growth had little overall impact. Labor PACs fared even worse: their total numbers inched up only slightly between 1980 and 1984. Most of the growth in the number of pro-Democratic committees occurred among citizen PACs, which tripled in number from 79 to 238. The largest of these new committees were antiwar or antinuclear organizations—such as Freeze Voter ($1,491,000 in 1983–84 receipts), U.S. Committee against Nuclear War ($927,000), and Peace PAC (affiliated with the Council for a Livable World; $374,000)—mobilizing against the Reagan Administration's defense policies. Yet such PACs also included pro-Israel PACs, such as National PAC ($2,103,000) and Joint Action Committee for Political Affairs ($395,000), and candidate-centered committees, such as Representative Morris Udall's Independent Action, Inc. ($918,000). Thus, the increase in pro-Democratic PACs came largely among groups without an occupational base.

Pro-Democratic interests mobilized additional resources to counter the Reagan Administration's aggressive brand of conservatism less by expanding their institutional base than by intensifying their mobilization efforts among existing PACs. We can see this in the far right-hand column, which shows changes in the average receipts of PACs within each category. PACs in the Democratic-leaning categories greatly increased their receipts between 1980 and 1984. This was especially true for PACs with at least some members in the nonprofit sector. Overall, union PACs in the mixed and nonprofit categories more than *doubled* their receipts. The National Education Political Action Committee increased its receipts from $629,000 in 1980 to $2,498,000 in 1984; the American Federation of State, County, and Municipal Employees' PAC grew in receipts from $527,000 to $1,463,000; and the Committee on Letter Carriers Political Education swelled from $36,000 to $1,341,000.

An even higher rate of growth occurred among the small number of PACs representing professional or administrative interests in the non-profit sector, as well as among committees organized around occupations in both the profit and nonprofit sectors. The committee called Political Action for Candidate Election for Human Services—the PAC affiliated with the National Association of Social Workers—increased its receipts from $31,000 in the 1980 elections to $205,000 in 1984; the receipts of the National Association of Retired Federal Employees Legislative and Public Relations Committee grew from $19,000 to $1,635,000; and the main PAC affiliated with the National Electric Cooperative Association increased its already substantial receipts from $467,000 in 1980 to $775,000 in 1984. Finally, pro-Democratic citizen PACs grew at only a slightly lower rate, as their receipts increased by 84 percent; and labor PACs with members in the profit sector raised 55 percent more money in 1984 than they had just four years before.

These contrasting reactions to the contentious issues raised during the first Reagan Administration were consistent with the ways in which various institutional constraints placed different organizational burdens on different types of groups. The constraints were strongest for interest groups representing the nonprofit sector, many of which had long been a major source of political support for Democratic programs. With few exceptions, the social workers, educators, health care workers, librarians and curators, religious institutions, academicians, and state and local officials involved in developing, administering, and overseeing social programs obviously could not deploy for direct electoral purposes the institutional resources of the government agencies, libraries, homes for the elderly, universities, churches, schools, and nonprofit hospitals in which they worked. Instead, the few groups that could establish viable PACs—such as the one affiliated with the National Association of Social Workers—reacted by intensifying their mobilization efforts.

That does not mean that groups in the nonprofit sector had no political resources to draw on. Many of these groups had large lobbying staffs and commanded a lot of expertise in their own policy areas. A few others, like the National Governor's association, enjoyed considerable access to legislative processes based on their nonpartisan stance as well as the status and power of their individual members. Still, many groups in the nonprofit sector—public or private—have felt a disadvantage in bidding for the time and energy of lawmakers who might prefer to serve as coalition leaders on legislation that also makes their fund-raising easier. As the executive director of the National Conference of State Legislatures observed, " 'We don't have PACs. . . . we don't grease things in the way that I guess has become the standard in this town today' " (*NJ*, 25 April 1989, 1042). Many of the groups in the nonprofit sector have responded to these limitations by fashioning coalitions with private groups, such as coalitions between retail merchants and state officials on attempts to collect sales taxes on mail-order and other out-of-state purchases. Some of the groups that were hurt by cutbacks in block grants and other discretionary spending in the 1980s banded together in large coalitions to pool their lobbying resources and often established aggressive public education programs (Wolman and Teitelbaum 1985, 312). But even if groups in the nonprofit sector succeeded in their lobbying activities, their countermobilization against the conservative governments of the 1980s yielded little in the way of resources that their allies in the Democratic Party could use to win back electoral support.

The Democrats' other institutional base—labor unions—also had little room for expansion. PACs have been used by labor unions since the late 1930s, and nearly all the national or international unions had PACs by 1980. Although many locals did not have their own PACs, the campaign finance laws treat PACs connected to locals as "affiliated" with one another as well as with the union's national committees. As such, the limits on candidate contribution apply to all as if they were a single committee, thereby making the proliferation of such committees less important. Again, the only way to mobilize additional resources in the 1980s was to intensify fund-raising among existing labor PACs, which, as we saw, was an especially common practice among unions in the public sector.

Liberal citizen associations might have served as fertile organizational ground for expanding the number of pro-Democratic PACs, yet their longtime reliance on patrons and the laws inhibiting the use of that patronage for electoral purposes prevented many of these groups from forming effective committees. As early as 1980, many of the public interest groups and other liberal citizen associations that were potentially able or willing to form separate segregated funds had already done so. Thus, much of the growth among citizen PACs after 1980 was in the form of nonconnected committees. Only 4.7 percent of the pro-Democratic citizen-issue PACs formed between 1980 and 1984 were separate segregated funds, compared to 20.6 percent of older PACs of the same type, that is, pro-Democratic citizen-issue committees active in the 1984 elections that had been established on or before 1980. Nonconnected citizen committees certainly proliferated in the early 1980s, but because they had no parent organizations to help absorb their substantial solicitation and administrative costs, they also tended to be marginal or ineffective organizations unable to fashion durable solutions to their problems of collective action.

The Implications of Partisan Asymmetry

These contrasting patterns of electoral mobilization have important repercussions. That interest groups aligned with the Democratic Party could not extend their organizational base—and therefore had to mobilize resources more intensively among existing committees—meant that such groups were more likely to run up against contribution limits *to* candidates, thereby constraining their decisions about how to allocate their money. PACs cannot give more than $5,000 per candidate in each election and therefore "max out" after giving $10,000 to a candidate in most election cycles (where $5,000 is given during the primary election and another $5,000 is provided for the general election contest). Thus, the greatest tactical flexibility is afforded a coalition of many moderate-sized, like-minded PACs—a coalition that business PACs may have developed but that differs significantly from the relatively few large labor and citizen organizations that constitute the core of pro-Democratic PACs.

We can see this asymmetry in table 7.7, which shows how committees supporting Democratic candidates are more likely than others to be

TABLE 7.7.   The Average Percentage of PAC Contributions Made in Amounts of $5,000 or More, by the PAC's Support for Democratic Candidates, 1983–84 Election Cycle (Only Includes PACs Making Contributions of at Least $25,000 during the Election Cycle)

Contribution Patterns, Based on Percentage of PAC's Contributions Given to Democratic Candidates	Mean Percentage of PAC Contributions Made in Amounts Greater Than or Equal to $5,000	Number of PACs Making Contributions
Strongly pro-Republican (0 - 20 percent Democrats)	17.7	160
Pro-Republican (21 - 40 percent Democrats)	12.2	157
Bipartisan (41 - 60 percent Democrats)	8.2	219
Pro-Democrat (61 - 80 percent Democrats)	16.1	125
Strongly pro-Democrat (81 - 100 percent Democrats)	31.3	140
All PACs	16.1	801

Source: Federal Election Commission.

affected by laws restricting the size of contributions. The table was constructed by calculating, for each PAC, the percentage of contributions made to candidates in amounts equal to or greater than $5,000 in the 1984 elections. Note that this number is an upper bound for the percentage of contributions where a PAC is constrained by the legal ceiling. A PAC can give up to $10,000 to a candidate in an election cycle if it gives during both the primary and general campaigns. But many committees either do not give during primary campaigns or do not give very much, so their effective limits are often closer to $5,000. To assess the relative impact of these constraints on the two parties, I then divided PACs into five categories according to the amount of support they gave to Democratic candidates, ranging from PACs that gave less than 20 percent of their contributions to such candidates to committees that contributed more than 80 percent of their money to Democrats. Finally, in each of these categories, I calculated the average percent of contributions made in amounts grater than or equal to $5,000. In table 7.7, we only consider PACs that made at least $25,000 in total contributions during the 1983–84 election cycle—committees that accounted for 88 percent of all PAC contributions in the 1984 elections—since small PACs were obviously unlikely to be affected by contribution ceilings.

Table 7.7 demonstrates that PACs supporting Democratic candidates were the most likely to be affected by contribution ceilings. On average, almost one-third of the contributions made by strongly pro-Democratic committees were in amounts greater than $5,000. This percentage was much higher than that for any other category of PACs, including strongly pro-Republican PACs, which typically neared the maximum amount in only about 18 percent of their contributions. The PACs least affected by the ceilings were also the least partisan in their contributions: PACs that contributed at least 40 percent of their money to both parties only gave an average of eight percent of their contributions in large amounts. Contribution ceilings were clearly not neutral with respect to the parties or even to partisanship in general. The PACs that were most closely aligned with the parties were also the ones most constrained by the ceilings, and that was especially so among PACs that sided with the Democratic Party.

The campaign finance laws thus had a highly selective effect across different kinds of groups. The contribution ceilings were the least restrictive for business groups—which ranged from strongly to moderately pro-Republican in their contributions—since they could rely on a large elaborate institutional base to launch and sustain many new PACs. On average, only 11 percent of 1984 contributions by business PACs were large, that is, $5,000 or more.[3] The ceilings were more restrictive for unions and citizen groups, which had a much narrower institutional base, depended on intensive mobilization among a small number of organizations to build up electoral support, or may have relied on economies of scale to overcome the high costs of raising money from a large number of small independent contributors. Labor PACs gave an average of 31 percent of their money in large sums during the 1984 elections, while citizen PACs gave a mean of 39 percent. The selective effects of these ceilings may inhibit the tactical decisions of the kinds of groups supporting Democratic candidates, making it harder for them to bring together as much money into a few highly competitive races. These asymmetric effects also help explain the unwillingness of House Democrats to go along with even a moderate reduction in legal ceilings on PAC contributions—an unwillingness that, among many other things, helped to doom campaign finance reform in the 103d Congress.

Another consequence of the different group coalitions aligned with each of the parties concerns the relative effectiveness of their PACs. Because the expansion of pro-Democratic PACs in the early 1980s depended a lot on nonconnected citizen PACs—and because such PACs have difficulties organizing effectively—many of the receipts mobilized by pro-Democratic PACs were never transformed into direct electoral support. PACs that strongly supported Democrats—that is, those that gave 80 percent or more of their contributions to Democratic candidates in the 1983–84 election cycle—only spent 53 percent of their total disbursements on direct political support, such as contributions to candidates, contributions to parties, in-kind contributions, or independent expenditures. In contrast, PACs that strongly supported Republicans spent 67 percent of their total disbursements on direct support, and PACs that gave at least 20 percent of their contributions to each party spent 76 percent of their money on direct political support. Other measures of organizational effectiveness displayed a similar pattern. For example, 15 percent of PACs that strongly supported Democrats in the 1980 elections did not survive to 1984, compared to 11 percent of PACs that strongly supported Republicans and only 5 percent of PACs that gave significant amounts to both parties. Thus, PACs that were the least partisan were the most efficient in translating contributions from individuals into direct political support as well as the most likely to survive, those that sided strongly with Republican candidates were somewhat less effective organizationally, and committees that were strongly aligned with Democratic candidates were the least effective of all.

When we take into account all these asymmetries, it becomes clear that Democratic candidates may have been forced to reach out for other sources of financial support to raise all the money they needed—or wanted. This problem was not yet evident in the 1984 elections, since the growth in the size of labor PACs and the entry of many liberal citizen PACs dramatically pushed up the contributions available to Democratic candidates. PAC contributions to Democrats more than doubled between 1980 and 1984, from $31.8 billion to $64.1 billion, while PAC contributions to Republicans only increased by one-fifth, from $40.5 billion in 1980 to $48.9 billion in 1984. But after this burst of activity in response to President Reagan's first term, the growth on the Left slowed considerably, and Democratic candidates had to look for other sources of funding. They turned more and more to business PACs, which not only had a lot of money to give out but were also less likely to have "maxed out" in the latter stages of a campaign. For example, Democratic candidates received 28 percent of their PAC contributions from corporate committees in the 1992 elections, up from 23 percent in 1984. Democrats also increased their reliance on PACs in the FEC's "Trade/Membership/Health" category, which is mostly composed of business groups. They got only 22 percent of their PAC contributions from this category in 1984, but that share grew to 26 percent by 1992. At the same time, Democrats received only 32 percent of their PAC contributions from labor unions in 1992, down from 38 percent in 1984; and they got only 10 percent of their 1992 contributions from the "nonconnected" category, where many citizen PACs are classified—down from 13 percent in the 1984 elections. Democrats have come to rely more on business PACs and less on labor and citizen committees since the 1984 elections, perhaps in response to the limited ability of groups outside the profit sector to expand and even maintain their presence within the PAC system.

What are the implications of Democrats' growing dependence on business PACs? One possible consequence is that Democrats have had to manage and balance an increasingly diverse set of constituencies. While Republicans have been able to raise money from many of the groups that lobby them and agree with them on a wide range of policies, many of the groups that lobby Democrats and support their views either do not make contributions or cannot be counted on as effective and enduring electoral supporters. Although Kingdon (1989; originally published in 1973) found two decades ago that liberal Democrats faced fairly homogenous political environments when compared to other members of Congress, that situation may have changed due in part to the asymmetry in the capacity of liberal and conservative groups to mobilize electoral resources.

Increasing reliance on business PACs may have also put Democratic candidates in a precarious position. Whether Democrats were raising more from business committees by demanding it, backed by a more or less implicit threat that failure to cough up the money will have adverse consequences for the businesses involved (see, for example, Jackson 1988, 70), or whether they were just beneficiaries of an increasingly pragmatic and obsequious community of business PACs—or even whether Democrats have become more responsive to a wider variety of business interests—the loss of institutional power in the Congress after the 1994 elections will eliminate the incentives for most business PACs to continue their support for Democratic incumbents. We might expect that the 1996 elections would show an overall drop in business support for Democratic candidates at least as large as the 9 percent decline in business contributions to Senate Democrats between the 1980 and 1984 elections—and perhaps a much larger drop in the House.

Concluding Comments

While many political observers have argued that the rise of PACs implies the decline of political parties and the emergence of an unstructured jumble of special interests, we have seen that the PAC system owes much of its structure to the party system. PACs are not drawn from autonomous "subgovernments" that have succeeded in insulating policy decisions from the effects of partisan change. Instead, they are formed by groups that are sensitive to electoral shifts and partisan conflict, apparently because campaign contributions are used as a means of overcoming political volatility and complexity. This sensitivity or vulnerability to the party system also implies that most PACs are likely to favor one party or the other and that their contributions will be distributed in a fairly partisan manner to sympathetic legislators or candidates who might become active and useful supporters.

But its grounding in partisan conflict does not mean that PACs simply reproduce the two-party system within the population of organized interest groups. There are important asymmetries between the groups allied with the two major parties regarding their ability to mobilize electoral resources, and these asymmetries grow in part from the selective access to institutions and patrons that the laws permit. Specifically, the mobilization of electoral resources against the Reagan Administration was limited in several ways by the lack of an accessible and expandable institutional base sympathetic to the Democratic Party: PACs affiliated with unions and the nonprofit sector were unable to expand their numbers greatly, while pro-Democratic citizen groups were able to grow in number but unable to produce a large increase in effective and enduring campaign support. Thus, pro-Democratic groups were forced to intensify their resource mobilization efforts within a more-or-less fixed pool of institutions. In contrast, business groups were able to expand their institutional base as well as exploit their current base and increase their average contributions, even while their political interests were not immediately threatened. These differences suggest that the rules governing the PAC system are not neutral with respect to the parties—not just the rules that affect PAC formation and resource mobilization but also those that affect contributions to candidates, since pro-Democratic PACs are more likely to be constrained by contribution limits. A possible consequence of these asymmetries may have been the growing dependence of Democratic candidates on business PACs since the early 1980s, despite the fact that their sponsoring groups have generally sided with Republican administrations and more conservative policies. What these and other findings about the PAC system imply about the role of interest groups in our political processes and about our capacity to use institutional reforms to control their behavior are the subjects of chapter 8.

CHAPTER 8

Conclusions

The electoral reforms of the 1970s were intended by many of their supporters to eliminate the corrupting influence of large donors and replace it with a system dominated by small, individual contributors. Underlying these intentions was a "grassroots," or Progressive, conception of politics, which assumed that a broader base of small contributors would produce a more representative and public-regarding system of electoral advocacy. Yet my analysis of the PAC system—a large component of the new regime of campaign financing—shows that it has several limitations as a system of interest representation. First, the PAC system is small, as measured by the total resources available for electoral activities compared to other interest group tactics. Second, it lacks organizational autonomy, in the sense that it has little capacity to develop stable, independent, and self-sustaining organizations that truly extend the institutional base of politics. And third, it displays important biases, or significant differences between the memberships, policy preferences, issue concerns, and partisan leanings of groups within the PAC system and groups otherwise involved in American national politics. However, these representational deficiencies are not the result of incomplete reform or of reforms not fully enforced. Instead, they seem to be a direct, though perhaps unintended, consequence of the reforms themselves. The limited scope of the PAC system appears to grow out of a fundamental tension in American politics between reformists' ideals about how interests *ought* to be organized, represented, and involved in elections and the ways in which interests actually *do* get represented in American politics. While reformers seek to restrain the involvement of "special interests" in campaigns and elections—often in the service of egalitarian ideals—the requirements of a broader based, more inclusive political system are quite different and are even harmed by such efforts.

Implications for Reform

One of the many ironies of the history of campaign financing in the United States is the failure of the basic debate about institutional reforms to improve or even undergo much change in recent decades, despite the wealth of data and experience generated by the reforms (Malbin 1993). Many of the assumptions in legislative and judicial discussions are not much more sophisticated now than they were almost two decades ago, when *Buckley* v. *Valeo* struck down several provisions of the Federal Election Campaign Act and forced free speech considerations into the debate. Yet this study undermines several premises found in discussions of reform.

First, my findings contradict the common assumption that greater equality with respect to individual contributions is likely to produce greater equality in the representation of political interests. This assumption underlies the attempt by reformers to create a campaign financing system based on a "grassroots" ideal of a large base of small contributors. This viewpoint is captured rather cogently in the equation of campaign contributions with "weighted voting." As Alexander Heard put it over three decades ago:

> A deeply cherished slogan of American democracy is "one man—one vote." . . . Concern over the private financing of political campaigns stems in significant measure from the belief that a gift is an especially important kind of vote. It is grounded in the thought that persons who give in larger sums or to more candidates than their fellow citizens are in effect voting more than once. (1960, 48–49)

Adamany and Agree went even further with this assumption by arguing that strict limits on the size of individual contributions are virtually required by the Constitution:

> Congress may have authority under the Fourteenth Amendment to preserve for citizens the equal protection of the laws by reducing the disparity between the size of campaign contributions, and hence the amount of political influence, of different citizens of varying financial means. The goal is to maintain the one-man, one-vote principle against the vastly unequal electoral influence that some can attain through large campaign contributions. (1975, 207)

The same assumption that unequal contributions produce unequal representation—or conversely, that greater equality in the size of individual contributions will produce greater equality in the representation of interests—runs through court decisions, law journal articles, legislative debates, and works of political theory, and it is a fundamental tenet among advocates for reform (Nicholson 1974; Wright 1976; McFarland

1984, 154–55; Cole 1991, 244; Rawls 1993, 358; Raskin and Bonifaz 1994; Foley 1994).

But the premise is simply not true. Strict ceilings on contributions obviously limit inequality with respect to individuals' participation in politics, but they also suppress the articulation or representation of many interests, especially those that encompass large groups of persons without an institutional base, such as widespread "citizen" interests. These large groups are likely to remain latent or at least highly unstable unless patrons or "large members" are able to provide large contributions or unless laws or other institutional incentives are applied in a way that encourages small contributors. The latency of such groups means that many political opinions will not be organized for political action and that only those opinions that enjoy an institutional base, and one that may be legally exploited in elections, will be effectively represented in elections and campaigns. This inequality in the representation of interests may be of a more subtle sort than the inequality of participation that evokes so much fear among reformers, but it is, I believe, a more important type of inequality in large and complex democracies. An electoral system that causes many shared-interest groups to remain latent is essentially a system that handicaps or even shuts out certain ideas people might have regarding their self-interest. Giving people an equal "weight" while restricting the scope of the opinions they may organize around, and thus effectively advocate, violates a core element of most conceptions of democratic or polyarchal systems, whereby citizens exercise control over the public agenda (Dahl 1989).

Although this point is valid if citizens have complete knowledge of their political interests—the assumption Olson made in his analysis (1965)—the problems produced by constraints on contributions are even greater if we consider the more realistic situation where people are uncertain about their interests, that is, the relationship between their private needs and public issues (Downs 1957, 79–80). When we allow for this sort of uncertainty, we need to be particularly careful not to construct any barriers to the entry of different conceptions of political interest or, what is nearly equivalent, political groups. Yet political patrons are even more important in this formative stage, when it is impossible to mobilize many small contributors precisely because few citizens yet know or believe that their interests are linked to the group's demands. Walker (1991), for example, found that patrons were even more important in the formation of interest groups than in their maintenance. Large contributions to an electoral organization do not represent overly "weighted" votes; they are essential conditions for the building of new coalitions around new values, ideas, or demands. As such, they would permit a measure of flexibility and innovation in the development of new groups or interests that does not exist in a political system that prevents the early involvement of supportive patrons, wherever they might be found.[1]

This perspective on the role of large contributors is at odds with recent arguments employed by the U.S. Supreme Court to justify limits on campaign expenditures and contributions. As the Court stated in *Austin* v. *Michigan Chamber of Commerce* (1990):

> Michigan's regulation [prohibiting corporations from using treasury funds for independent expenditures in state elections] aims at a different type of corruption in the political arena: the corrosive and distorting effects of immense aggregations of wealth that are accumulated with the help of the corporate form and that have little or no correlation to the public's support for the corporation's political ideas. . . . The Act . . . ensures that expenditures reflect actual public support for the political ideas espoused by corporations. (664–65)

The Court's argument misses the essential point. To require that campaign expenditures reflect existing public support is really to deny their primary function: to persuade citizens to support a cause, party, or candidate—that is, to build coalitions or even establish new political groupings. The expenditures—and for the same reason, the contributions—cannot be viewed as exerting "unfair influence" because they are poorly correlated with existing popular support, since there would be little reason to spend money if citizens were already certain about whom or what they supported. Restrictions on contributions—even if intended to ensure greater equality in participation or "voice"—may prevent the mobilization of new or latent ideas regarding citizens' needs and thus exacerbate inequality in the development, understanding, articulation, and representation of citizens' political interests. The potential effects of these constraints are especially important in the highly public forum of national elections. These campaigns receive so much media attention that many groups make contributions to candidates or spend money on elections to encourage or even force candidates to address certain issues so that large numbers of citizens are exposed to the groups' concerns. However the Supreme Court and the political branches eventually resolve the question of whether it is constitutional to restrict political participation in order to bring about greater political equality or fairness, it should be clear that limits on contributions do not bring about greater political equality and therefore can not be justified on those grounds.

The problems produced by contribution limits undermine a second assumption found in major court decisions and legislative debates on campaign financing laws: that there is a meaningful distinction between "contributions" and "expenditures" regarding the effects of legal restrictions on the free flow of information. The distinction was drawn with special boldness in *Buckley* v. *Valeo* (1976). In that case, the Supreme Court found that limits on the expenditures of candidates and committees were unconstitutional because they directly restricted the scope and level of political speech, which the First Amendment forbids the Congress from doing:

> A restriction on the amount of money a person or group can spend on political communication during a campaign necessarily reduces the quantity of expression by restricting the number of issues discussed, the depth of their exploration, and the size of the audience reached. (687–88)

The Court, however, did not believe that limits on contributions had the same restrictive effects on the free flow of political speech in election campaigns, and so it allowed those limits to stand:

> By contrast with a limitation upon expenditures for political expression, a limitation upon the amount that any one person or group may contribute to a candidate or political committee entails only a marginal restriction upon the contributor's ability to engage in free expression. . . . [C]ontribution restrictions could have a severe impact on political dialogue if the limitations prevented candidates and political committees from amassing the resources necessary for effective advocacy. There is no indication, however, that the contribution limitations imposed by the [Federal Election Campaign] Act would have any dramatic adverse effect on the funding of campaigns and political associations. (688–89)

The belief that contribution limits are essentially content-neutral is accepted by most commentators on *Buckley*, even among those who are skeptical regarding any infringements on political speech and who agree with the Court that expenditure limits offend First Amendment liberties (Smolla 1992, 239).

Yet this study shows that contribution limits do in fact have a "dramatic" and highly selective "adverse effect" on the funding of certain political associations and the "effective advocacy" of certain political interests. Limits on the maximum size of contributions—as well as their institutional sources—inhibit citizen interests and interests typically represented by professionals in the nonprofit sector from participating in elections and thus restrict "the number of issues discussed" and "the depth of their exploration." The Court assumes that contribution limits are neutral in their political effects because the leaders of virtually any cause or political standpoint should be able to mobilize a large number of small contributors rather than a few large supporters or a mixed coalition of contributors. But that simply is not true. The feasibility of different types of contributor coalitions, including the degree of dependence on patrons, is highly correlated with the types of interests represented through collective action. Constraints on the size and sources of contributions will therefore diminish the expression of certain interests no less than limits on expenditures and thus deserve the same strict scrutiny accorded the latter. If, as the Court argued in *Buckley* v. *Valeo*, "the concept that government may restrict the speech of some elements of our society in order to enhance the relative voice of others is wholly foreign to the First Amendment" (1976, 704), restrictions on contributions are no less alien than limits on expenditures.[2]

These first two assumptions—about the equivalence between participatory and representative equality and the distinction between contributions and expenditures—reflect a fundamental, though also mistaken, premise found in most discussions of campaign finance reform: that organization based on purely political aims is not problematic. Reformers and court decisions generally assume that organizations based solely on political motivations are viable, or that their viability will depend on the breadth and intensity of popular support for their demands. Although reformers recognize and even stress that the amount of money raised by a group for electoral action depends on the wealth of the contributors as well as their number and intensity, there is little recognition that the process and logic of collective action are critical and often insurmountable barriers. This premise serves the reform impulse, because it implies that politically interested citizens will always be able to organize for effective political action and that the only real problem for reform is to prevent corporate and other institutionalized interests from "drowning out" the voices of the "people."

This premise emerges, for example, in the Supreme Court's rulings that there is something unfair, extraordinary, or even illegitimate in a situation where the resources generated by economic institutions or transactions are applied to political purposes. In *FEC* v. *Massachusetts Citizens for Life* (1986), the Court argued that the government is justified in preventing corporations from using their treasury funds in election campaigns, since

> [t]he resources in the treasury of a business corporation . . . are not an indication of popular support for the corporation's political ideas. They reflect instead the economically motivated decisions of investors and customers. The availability of these resources may make a corporation a formidable political presence, even though the power of the corporation may be no reflection of the power of its ideas. (556)

Campaign finance regulations that require funding by voluntary, politically motivated contributions are viewed as reasonable since they ensure that "the money collected is that intended by those who contribute to be used for political purposes and not money diverted from another source" (*Pipefitters Local Union No. 562* v. *United States* 1972, 423–24, quoting Representative Hansen) and "that competition among actors in the political arena is truly competition among ideas" (*FEC* v. *Massachusetts Citizens for Life* 1986, 259). An incorporated advocacy group with an exclusively political purpose does not corrupt the political process, because the "resources it has available are not a function of its success in the economic marketplace, but its popularity in the political marketplace" (*FEC* v. *Massachusetts Citizens for Life* 1986, 259). However, a corporation that has nonpolitical as well as political objectives may be legitimately prohibited from using its funds for electoral activities, since contributing members or stockholders may disagree with the political aims of the organization yet not want to withdraw their contributions because of their desire or need for its nonpolitical services. In sum, it is reasonable for government regulations to require that all resources ultimately used for electoral activities be raised through voluntary contributions by individuals in support of purely political aims.

Although these arguments and conditions seem quite reasonable, they fail utterly to recognize the real problems of collective action, and their enforcement creates important inequities in the political system. A central theorem of collective action theory is that many political interests—particularly those that are widespread, or "encompassing," or simply new—will not achieve organization except as a by-product of other, private transactions. Purely political motivations fail to produce enduring political organizations except in very small groups and other limited circumstances. Requiring all organizations to comply with this model of voluntary contributions, provided out of exclusively political motivations, thus prevents the mobilization and articulation of significant political interests. The Supreme Court recognized a part of this truth by arguing that business corporations were more likely to amass great sums of money and dominate political processes than were nonprofit corporations "formed for the express purpose of promoting political ideas" (*FEC* v. *Massachusetts Citizens for Life* 1986, 264). But it did not grasp the broader principle: that political motivations alone do not generate much stable support for any political goal, and that this is true for nonbusiness as well as business interests. By failing to understand this problem, reformers ignore the real prerequisite for a more open and extensive system of group participation in elections—namely, access to a *wider* variety of patrons and institutions that are willing to apply *their* accumulated resources to political aims other than those demanded by business. The citizen-interest PACs organized around small contributors who gave for exclusively political purposes were quite unstable and vulnerable to short-term political conditions, unlike the much stronger and more stable citizen-interest membership associations that were able to draw on a more diverse array of financial sources, including large donors, foundations and other institutional patrons, and fees for goods or services.

This study also undermines a fourth and related assumption found in most discussions of campaign financing: that PACs control enormous sums of money, encompassing most of the money deployed by interest groups to advocate their demands. Journalists and reformers are virtually obsessed with the PAC as the large and potent tool that "special interests" use to frustrate the public interest or majority will. After President Clinton's election in 1992, even as sober a newspaper as the *New York Times* asked, "Having won that support, the question for Mr. Clinton is, can he make it last? Armadas of special interests, armed with rich, sophisticated PAC's, are lying in wait" (4 November 1992, A30).

Although this study does not directly address the question of how much power is exerted by PACs, it certainly throws water on claims about the enormity and centrality of PACs within the national interest group system. The amount of money raised and spent by PACs was only a small fraction of the revenues and expenditures of membership associations active in national policy processes, whether one looked at the individual groups or compared the entire systems; and those fractions were surely much smaller if one were able to measure expenditures for the many other forms of interest group advocacy, such as corporate liaison or public affairs offices, Washington law firms, advocacy-type research organizations, public-interest law firms, and so on. Indeed, most of the large, politically active interest groups in the Walker surveys did not have PACs, and electoral activities were one of the least used methods of advocacy, even among groups lobbying the legislative and executive branches. PACs constitute only one small piece of the interest group picture, and the amount of money they control is minuscule compared to the amounts spent on all forms of interest group representation and advocacy. These findings imply that it is more reasonable to ask why PACs are so small in size and few in number than to assume that too much money is being spent by too many groups, and that it is unreasonable to expect that stronger constraints on interest involvement in elections will reduce the power of interest groups in governmental processes. It is much more reasonable to suppose that additional restrictions will simply force the stronger groups to press their demands in other political arenas, or influence elections in circuitous ways, while diminishing the capacity of the weaker groups to bring about a true expansion in the scope and flexibility of electoral participation.

The tendency to see campaign financing as the locus of interest group power—and the proper target of the most aggressive reforms—seems particularly odd when we compare the dynamics and characteristics of groups involved in different kinds of political activities. As chapter 7 demonstrated, the interest groups that are drawn to electoral tactics are those that are most vulnerable to partisan and electoral changes, that is, those groups that are the least insulated from political changes within broader publics. Why this is so may be found in the basic characteristics of elections as a political institution and campaign contributions as a political resource: the conflict inherent in elections; their public exposure; their sensitivity to so many variables; and the weakness of money, a highly substitutable resource, in building relations between a group and politicians. All these characteristics of elections and the campaign financing system are likely to dissuade the most powerful groups from participating, while drawing those groups that face political conflicts they can no longer contain. Thus, the discrepancy between the relatively strong and complex array of regulations regarding electoral activities and the virtual non-regulation of other political tactics has the perverse effect of restricting the groups that are most vulnerable to partisan and electoral changes, while drawing attention away from the groups that often exercise unchallenged, institutionalized access to government through its administrative and judicial procedures.

These same findings also contradict a fifth assumption found in the debate over campaign financing—that PACs are intrinsically destructive of a competitive party system. This claim certainly misunderstands the correlates of PAC formation and growth. Whether the interest group system as a whole undermines the party system is a question beyond the scope of this study. But our findings show that the interest groups that form PACs—and have the largest receipts—tend to be the ones that are most buffeted by and closely aligned with the political parties and that they are unlikely to emerge among groups involved in stable "sub-governments" insulated from party divisions. PACs do not grow out of the cracks of the party system; they are much more likely to emerge from its strengths. The failure of the PAC system to grow very much in the late 1980s and early 1990s occurred not during a resurgence of our parties but when party government clearly failed—during a time charac-terized by immobility in our national institutions and vacuity in our national elections.

Those who argue that PACs and parties are fundamentally incom-patible may retort, however, that though many PACs may be responding to partisan conflict, their contribution strategies are designed to reduce political uncertainty by supporting incumbents of both parties; that most committees are connected to permanent lobbying operations that pre-vent them from challenging incumbent legislators; and that these contri-bution strategies encourage incumbents to appeal to a diverse array of groups on narrow grounds and to play down their partisan differences in ideology and constituency. However, these premises may mistake institu-tionally induced behavior for inherent qualities of the system. There are no *inherent* reasons why the PAC system as a whole does not reflect the major divisions in the party system even more closely or why more PACs do not contribute in even more partisan ways or show a greater willing-ness to oppose incumbents. Perhaps one of the reasons they do not do so now is because restrictions on fund-raising handicap many of the most partisan and aggressive groups—or, put somewhat differently, the re-strictions prevent the formation of strong, autonomous political organi-zations representing citizen and other noninstitutionalized interests, in-terests that are less likely to accommodate themselves with incumbents of either party. In contrast, the rules bestow considerable advantages on business groups and membership associations, whose institutional base makes them more likely to and more capable of reaching accommoda-tions with members of both parties.

This study therefore undermines several of the presumptions justi-fying the current regulatory regime as well as additional reforms that would impose even greater constraints on interest group involvement in elections and campaigns. Our findings suggest that a regulatory sys-tem requiring contributions to be fairly small and thus of relatively equal size will not produce greater equality but rather create significant biases in the representation of political interests and even prevent cer-tain groups from organizing altogether. The current distinction in con-stitutional law between contributions and expenditures is therefore of little value. Limits on contributions have at least as strong an effect on the articulation of important demands and interests—that is, on political speech—as do limits on candidate and group expenditures. Collective action around even the most intensely held political opinions does not blossom spontaneously; political organization is problematic in most circumstances and often requires patrons and institutional support. The smallness of the current system of PACs—especially when compared with the scope and resources of other forms of political action—suggests that the uniquely strong regulations applying to electoral activities suppress the electoral involvement of many groups. Our findings also suggest that PACs even now show significant alignment with the two major parties and that the extent to which the overall distribution and behavior of PACs fail to be structured around the party system may not be an inherent property but rather is more plausibly a consequence of regulations that place the greatest burdens on the most partisan groups. A remaining question, then, is whether and what kind of regulatory changes are called for under these different understandings of the current system?

Representation and Reform

What is to be done about campaign financing when we assume that political action is problematic, that effective collective action usually requires an institutional base or political patrons, and that restrictions on electoral organizations typically undermine pluralism because rather than constraining the largest, most aggressive political interests they raise barriers to groups that are already hard to mobilize?

Although virtually all proposals to reform the campaign finance system involve additional or stricter restrictions, our analyses make a credible case for eliminating certain regulations. The argument is fairly straightforward. Most restrictions on the size of contributions and institutional patronage or sponsorship have the primary effect of reducing the capacity of new or disadvantaged interests to organize themselves for collective action. Organizationally disadvantaged interests must construct and reconstruct ad hoc coalitions of large individual and institutional patrons—and virtually any restriction limits their capacity to do this—while organizationally advantaged groups can employ their vast institutional powers to mobilize and channel resources in whatever ways still permitted. Thus, allowing contributions or support of any size and from any source—including some public and nonprofit institutions—may help produce a stronger, more representative, and more permeable system of electorally active political organizations than are now found

among PACs, perhaps even as diverse as the elaborate array of membership associations involved in national politics.

Yet deregulation may not be enough to create a more representative system of groups active in campaigns and elections. Because elections are becoming so costly, we may also need to expand the range of
institutions, nonmarket subsidies, or other sources of support available
to groups wanting to enter the electoral fray and play an important part.
That is especially true for groups that seek to represent broader, more
encompassing interests, whether those interests be occupational or
nonoccupational in character. If access to these forms of patronage can
be provided in ways that are open to new and diverse groups—rather
than in ways that create inflexible privileges for keeping old groups
alive—then we may come closer to reconciling Ostrogorski's ideal of an
extensive, open, and highly adaptive array of electorally active groups
(1902, 658–63) with the modern organizational requirements of effective
political action.

Of course, deregulating interest group involvement in campaigns
and elections and providing new subsidies for electoral action only make
sense if one values inclusive, competitive, and vigorous representation
of political interests before governmental institutions—if one wants, in
other words, a diverse system of strong organizations, much like we find
among membership associations. Deregulation is likely to produce more
divisions within the PAC system on more issues and to bring into electoral politics more citizen groups and other encompassing, noninstitutionalized interests that might challenge incumbents and other elements
of the governing coalition. Members of Congress and candidates for
their positions would thus confront a more diverse, conflictual, autonomous, and aggressive array of interest groups in their fund-raising efforts. A more inclusive system would mean that important interests
would be less likely to be overlooked by legislators and candidates,
particularly on issues of intense interest to a group; that political conflicts would be fought out and resolved, as much as possible, within
elections; and that nearly all opponents of government policies could
mount effective electoral attacks against elected officials. A more inclusive system is a reasonable goal if one believes that many of the problems identified with PACs are not the result of group involvement in
elections per se, but rather the consequence of *inequitable* group involvement in elections.

Some might argue that a more open, representative system would
be a less "governable" one in which "majorities" would be harder to
construct. But that is not at all clear. I have argued that the laws regulating participation in elections have reduced the ability of many groups to

use elections to achieve their policy goals and that the restrictions have weighed most heavily on those groups that purport to represent broad, encompassing, even "majority" interests. Many of these groups now avoid elections altogether and use political tactics—such as litigation and administrative or legislative lobbying—where parties and voters *do not* structure competition and conflict and where political closure is usually less clear. The current system may thus diminish elections as a method of democratic government, and majorities may become frustrated as electoral decisions are undermined by groups that use all kinds of nonelectoral means to get what they want.

What can be done to create a more open, representative system of group involvement in elections? How can we expand the size and scope of the PAC system? A two-pronged strategy of selective deregulation (which would allow diverse groups to put together ad hoc coalitions without constraints) and additional subsidies (to ensure that a wide variety of political interests are able to keep up with the rising costs of campaigns and elections) would include four important changes.

First, we should deregulate PAC fund-raising by increasing or eliminating limits on the maximum size of individual contributions to PACs and by allowing membership associations to provide or withhold selective benefits conditioned on support for their affiliated PACs. We saw in chapter 5 that membership associations representing citizen interests were highly dependent on large individual donors or patrons and that citizen PACs relied on relatively large (or moderate-sized) contributors more than did any other type of PAC, especially in their formative stages. Therefore, to ensure that the PAC system includes a wider range of interests and is more open to newly emerging groups, we need to allow individual patrons for political action to perform the same role in establishing and maintaining electoral organizations as they already perform for other forms of political action. This means that the current limit of $5,000 per year on individual contributions should be raised to a point where a single patron could underwrite the group's costs of formation or sustain the committee through periods of political quiescence. The limit should also be large enough to allow potential patrons to determine that their contributions have an appreciable effect on the representation of interests or electoral competition, which greatly increases the chances of obtaining such support.

Although we have less evidence on the biased effects of limits on PAC contributions to candidates, a good case can be made for eliminating those restrictions too. Chapter 7 demonstrated that PACs representing citizen and labor interests were much more likely to run up against those limits than were business committees. The greater difficulties of organizing large numbers of small contributors may imply certain economies of scale or even threshold effects such that organizations mobilizing these sorts of groups need to reach a certain size before they are really viable—a problem that does not affect business groups, with their elaborate institutional base. By imposing the same limits on all PACs, contribution ceilings give an advantage to political interests that can develop a decentralized array of relatively small yet efficient committees—which business groups can surely do—while they constrain larger, more encompassing groups. There is no good normative reason for encouraging groups to proliferate the number of PACs representing their interests—concerns about accountability and clarity in the campaign finance system would argue for precisely the opposite structure. Although limits on PAC contributions to candidates may have been originally justified on the basis of the same vague egalitarianism that underlay limits on individual contributions, their connections to political equality are even more tenuous. There is simply no necessary, positive relationship between equality among organizations—presumably the aim behind contribution ceilings—and equality among individuals (Dahl 1982, 99). And, indeed, whatever correlation does exist may well be negative.

Finally, we should allow membership organizations to use selective incentives to raise money for their PACs, just as we allow them to use such incentives when raising money for legislative lobbying, legal representation, administrative lobbying, public education campaigns, and other political activities. If the by-product method is an important mechanism by which some diffuse groups can organize large numbers of small contributors, then we ought to let groups use it for electoral purposes. As I argued in chapter 2, many large groups are unlikely to benefit from this method; and it is most likely to work when a group's members are already organized in institutional or occupational roles. But it has worked reasonably well for a few groups—such as the Sierra Club and the American Association of Retired Persons—and its proceeds should be available for all kinds of political activities on a neutral basis.

Second among the changes in our deregulation strategy is to relax tax and other laws that prohibit nonprofit, nongovernmental organizations from engaging in electoral activities or from making grants to organizations that conduct electoral activities. Chapter 5 showed that groups that relied on foundation grants, corporate gifts, and other nonprofit subsidies—mostly citizen and nonprofit sector organizations—were unlikely to form PACs even when they were involved in highly complex and partisan political settings and that their underrepresentation in the PAC system was attributable in part to laws restricting the use of nonprofit subsidies by organizations involved in partisan politics. Many nonprofit organizations are prohibited from establishing PACs or engaging in other electoral activities, and some foundations cannot even give grants to groups participating in partisan politics. In contrast, nonprofit groups are allowed to engage in limited legislative lobbying activities and in an unlimited amount of litigational and administrative lobbying activities. These discrepancies should be eliminated by permitting nonprofit organizations and institutions to form PACs and engage in electoral activities, subject to the kinds of limits now imposed on their lobbying activities. This change should not only help reduce the bias found among such groups in favor of nonelectoral activities. More importantly, it should expand the representation of citizen interests and groups representing the nonprofit sector within the electoral system.

Third, we should permit PACs to be set up by multiple institutions, including combinations of different types of institutions, and to relax laws now restricting fund-raising activities by such committees. The PAC system is also biased with respect to groups that span multiple institutions or organizations. Very few PACs draw members from both the profit and nonprofit sectors, and as we noted in chapter 5, PAC formation is much more likely among groups that draw members from a single industry or occupation. The reasons for these biases are not simply legal, but the laws surely contribute. There is, for example, no provision in the FECA for a PAC to be established and maintained by two or more corporations, two or more associations, or two or more cooperatives. Nor is there any allowance for a PAC to be sponsored by different types of institutions, such as a combination of nonprofit organizations and corporations, even though such combinations are sometimes found among membership organizations and represent important interests. The options now available to interests that span institutional affiliations are (1) establishment of a membership association and formation of an affiliated PAC or (2) employees or members setting up a formally independent or unaffiliated committee. But these options are rather restrictive, since trade associations are limited in their fund-raising efforts, and the use of unaffiliated committees limits accountability and disclosure and prohibits the use of institutional funds and facilities to absorb the PAC's establishment and administrative costs. Thus, the regulations now make it relatively hard to establish PACs that span and aggregate the interests of several institutions and combinations of different institutions. To allow the elaboration and expression of more encompassing interests, the laws should be changed to permit PACs to have multiple affiliations and to raise funds as they wish within those institutions, as long as the institutions are willing to authorize them.

Fourth, we ought to provide public subsidies for electoral activities through tax credits and deductions for individual contributions and partial funding for candidates and parties. Even if constraints on contributions were removed altogether, the theory of collective action would suggest that some interests might be underfunded. Nonmarket subsidies are often needed to overcome the problems of collective action, especially for citizen groups that cannot rely on an institutional base to absorb the costs of mobilizing supporters. The first and second recommendations should alleviate the problem, but reducing restrictions on nonprofit organizations is probably not enough to give a wide variety of citizen groups the flexibility and resources they need to establish large and effective PACs; and the problem is made even more acute by the various exogenous factors making elections (and electoral influence) more and more costly.

To address these problems, a public financing system should be established, though one that is partly controlled by the preferences of individual citizens, not just by the parties or candidates, in order to maximize interest representation, innovation, and adaptability. Tax credits for small or moderate-sized contributions could be reinstated for all filers to reduce the costs of participation and encourage the support of PACs, candidates, or parties—whichever potential recipients citizens find most appealing. Deductions for large contributions should be established to encourage political patrons, particularly when they underwrite the costs of administering the organization or soliciting potential contributors. The government might also help to ensure that these credits and deductions are used for citizen as well as corporate and union PACs by requiring employers to give employees the option of designating an independent PAC (or a political party) to receive monies through a payroll deduction plan. If an institutional base is critical in mobilizing small contributors, then a requirement for a more pluralistic system is wider access to at least some of those institutional resources.

By expanding the resources available to a wider variety of PACs, these recommendations should help reduce the disparities in campaign funds between candidates representing different political agendas, policy preferences, and political parties (see chapters 6 and 7). But there still may be groups—especially those that represent citizen interests—that fail to organize, and their failure may mean that certain candidates may not be adequately funded, even if these candidates advocate widespread citizen interests. To deal with this problem, direct subsidies to candidates and parties may be useful in overcoming the problems created by an undermobilization of groups. But these subsidies should be "floors" without "ceilings." They should be helpful in giving all candidates a chance to get their campaigns started, but they should not be used to eliminate group or individual contributions, since a "complete" public funding system may create an even narrower system by suppressing the participation of groups that are hard to activate while exerting relatively little impact on groups with enough institutional resources to evade the restrictions through independent expenditures, bundling, internal communication expenditures, and so on. In fact, complete public funding—that is, public financing paired with absolute restrictions on private contributions—might undermine political equality and democratic control even if it were perfectly implemented. There is no essential connection between the equal funding of candidates (or parties) and the equal representation of citizens or voters (Beitz 1989, 196); and by eliminating candidates' need for private funds, complete public financing may have the effect of strengthening the autonomy of candidates in our political system, which hardly seems to be a central goal in most normative democratic theories.

These changes should have some effect in producing a richer and more responsive array of interests within the PAC system, since they are all designed to permit greater flexibility in PAC formation and resource mobilization. They would permit a wider range of contributor coalitions to emerge, particularly among citizen interests and groups that nonprofit institutions serve and advocate. The changes would also diminish the differences between regulations now applying to electoral activities and those applying to other political tactics, such as litigation, legislative lobbying, administrative lobbying, and public education and media appeals; and this greater neutrality with respect to political tactics should encourage more groups to bring their issues and conflicts to electoral processes for advocacy and resolution. The proposed changes would also encourage greater organizational consolidation—or less decentralization—in the PAC system by giving greater flexibility to PACs spanning two or more institutions and by allowing a single PAC to make a much larger contribution and thus to exert a greater impact on a single election. Finally, the changes ought to enhance the current system of disclosure, since they would reduce or eliminate incentives for contributors to funnel money through loopholes not subject to disclosure laws (e.g., "soft money"), and since the tax subsidies would create positive incentives for disclosure.

Of course, some restrictions are needed to prevent deregulation from threatening its intended objectives, to broaden the base of electoral accountability and reduce the autonomy of elected officials. Allowing federal agencies to use their resources for electoral purposes would create a real danger of giving elected officials the capacity to rely on their authority over such agencies to raise all the funds they need. This would not only threaten to resurrect the corruption of the long-gone urban machines; it would give elected officials even greater autonomy than they already enjoy. Where to draw the line raises some hard questions: Should public educational institutions be permitted to sponsor or help sponsor election committees? Should public hospitals be allowed to do so, or public art or music organizations, such as museums or symphonies? Rather than simply rejecting the idea of allowing such institutions to participate in electoral activities as appalling, the potential problems of corruption and misuse of public funds should be balanced against the representational problems produced by the exclusion of important political interests and institutions from electoral processes.

Some may object to these proposals by arguing that I am treating an end as a means. They may argue that there are good reasons to enforce a grassroots system of small individual contributors as a goal in itself, not because we mistakenly supposed that it would fortuitously produce a more equal representation of political interests. The biases we see in the PAC system may be viewed as appropriate since they reflect which groups have grassroots capabilities. Corporations, unions, and trade and professional associations apparently have those capabilities—while many citizen groups do not. We might wish to create such laws for reasons of normative democratic theory. We might, for example, want to encourage groups to extend and strengthen their membership bases because we want a more participatory political system. Thus, the representational biases in the PAC system may have been intended—or they may have been viewed as unimportant—and so it would be wrong to propose changes in the laws that would reduce the importance of a grassroots structure for the sake of a more balanced system of representation.

Although I would agree that it is reasonable to want to encourage groups to mobilize small individual contributors, I do not think that the current laws actually do that—or at least that they do it in an even-handed way. The laws actually suppress the grassroots capability of some groups, while permitting it among others. As I argued in chapter 2, mobilizing small individual contributors is a costly task. When a group can rely on private economic institutions to facilitate that mobilization, the marginal costs of organizing small contributors are small. But when a group does not have that institutional base, it generally needs individual or institutional patrons to absorb the costs of finding, soliciting, and organizing small contributors. Indeed, there is no logical reason why we would expect that mobilizing large numbers of small contributors would yield *any* surplus that could be used by the group's leadership to fund campaigns. If we want to encourage interest groups to bring small contributors into the political process, we need to accept that many groups need access to a wide variety of patrons to absorb those costs. The rules governing electoral activities therefore do not distinguish groups regarding their grassroots capabilities so much as they inhibit some groups from developing those capabilities while they give other groups full rein.

Another objection to such proposals is that they would not achieve their intended objective—equality in representation—since they would open the dikes to an enormous inflow of resources from organizationally advantaged groups, specifically business firms or other economic institutions, and this inflow would overwhelm any gains from expanding the system. But this objection breaks down under scrutiny. It presumes that contribution limits and other regulations can and do limit business participation in elections, but in fact the real limitations are self-imposed. Many large business firms still do not have PACs, and though there are no limits on the size of PACs, corporate committees are still relatively small and have grown only slowly in recent years. Since American business has hardly exploited the current room for expansion, it seems unlikely that lifting the restrictions will have much effect. Corporations fail to mobilize as much money as they can in elections not because of legal constraints but rather because they believe that their vast resources are better spent elsewhere—including on other political tactics that are more appropriate to their political circumstances and needs—or because they do not want to alienate important elements of the public. Of course, some corporations and industries will exploit deregulation and take advantage of its greater flexibility by acting precisely as they prefer rather than funneling money through loopholes in the current regulatory scheme. For example, the large amounts of "soft money" now given to the parties might be contributed to PACs if contribution limits were lifted, and "bundling" may dwindle away in favor of contributions to the PACs. But this rerouting of contributions does not necessarily mean a large expansion of contributions; and in any case, if full disclosure of contributions is retained, the system of disclosure gains in comprehensiveness by eliminating the need for backyard paths.

Improved public disclosure may itself serve as a selective restraint on large contributions from business groups. Yet we can only speculate about the unique effects of strong disclosure requirements, vigorously enforced, since there has never been a time in the history of federal regulation of campaign financing when we have relied primarily on public reporting and disclosure laws to restrain the behavior of contributors. The most venal contributions by business corporations in the 1972 presidential elections—the contributions and abuses that inspired many of the current laws—were passed along in the expectation that they would *not* be made known to the public. If we did have full disclosure of corporate, industry, and other business activities regarding federal elections, it is at least possible that business organizations would be restrained by their need to maintain good relations with a wide variety of stockholders, customers, and government officials—that is, that institutional caution would induce political restraint.

But we do not now have that sort of disclosure. For example, some of the most savvy and politically aggressive businesses—such as the financial industries and Washington legal representatives and lobbyists—funnel most of their political money not through PACs but through individual contributions delivered directly to candidates and parties (Makinson and Goldstein 1994). This tactic minimizes public knowledge about the contributions, since the FEC does not strictly enforce the requirement that candidate organizations disclose the occupations and places of employment of all major contributors and so many candidates do not (Makinson and Goldstein 1994, 35). Nor does the FEC ever report this sort of information to the public in a readily usable form. If the reporting and disclosure laws were strengthened and enforced in such a way that *all* contributions and their institutional sources were made widely known to the public, they might have the selective restraining effects that would help produce a pluralistic yet relatively uncorrupted system. Political patrons willing and able to explain their large contributions to the public would make those donations, while potential large contributors (and potential recipients) with less commendable motives might feel restrained by the possibility of public disapprobation or even outright hostility. Public disclosure might, in short, serve as a kind of Kantian filter for prospective electoral actions.

Even if disclosure does not have these admittedly speculative effects on the wealthiest, most aggressive political interests, criticisms of deregulation still make little sense when we consider interest group activities as a whole. We tolerate weak regulations regarding contributions to interest groups that use litigation, administrative lobbying, and legislative lobbying to achieve their aims; yet there is little anxiety about the voices of nonbusiness interests being "drowned out" by business interests in these other, unregulated forums. Perhaps there should not be much anxiety, since the funding levels of the less strictly regulated associations that conduct these other tactics show less inequality across the typology of occupational roles than do the funding levels of the more strictly regulated system of PACs.

Yet it is sometimes argued that elections, more than any other form of political participation, must be insulated from the corrupting effects of money and its concomitant, inequality. Thus, limits on the size of individual contributions to political organizations when those organizations are involved in campaigns or elections are viewed as reasonable even though no such limits are applied to organizations employing other forms of political advocacy. Such arguments usually contend that elections occupy a special role in democracies, not only because they perform a central function of allowing citizens to choose their leaders, but also because the vote is the one political resource that is widely distributed. David Cole, for example, argued that "campaign spending regulation is one of the only areas where the [Supreme] Court has recognized the distorting effects of private wealth on constitutional rights" because a "strong strain of equality runs through our collective vision of the electoral process," a vision that is offended by "gross disparities in campaign spending" (1991, 275). Inequalities that may be acceptable in other forums, and that result from weak or nonexistent ceilings on the size of contributions, are therefore unacceptable in elections, since inequality in the latter context means that *no* political mechanism exists where individual citizens have a roughly equal say.

What is strange about this argument is not only its assumption that reliance on small and relatively equal contributions produces greater political equality, an assumption that this study not only disputes but contradicts. It is also odd in the way that it views elections and electoral processes as a kind of isolated institution that must be and can be protected from the inegalitarian operations of other political activities. This view is false because it abstracts elections from their function of giving citizens control over their government's policies and activities—a function that they have always shared with other forms of political activity. If those other activities were to undermine the policy intentions of voters in elections, the pristine, egalitarian quality of electoral processes would be of little consequence. It is not important, therefore, that any particular political activity or institution be insulated or comply with some pure model of democratic equality. Yet it is important to understand where the unregulated political "market" is most likely to threaten democratic or pluralist values, for only then can we know where political regulation is most needed.

If we examine the regulatory problem from this point of view, it is not unreasonable to conclude that elections are the one political institution *least* in need of regulation. Consider, for example, the principles used by the Supreme Court in reconciling defamation or libel law with the First Amendment's protection of free speech (*New York Times* v. *Sullivan* 1964). In that situation, the Court found that First Amendment protections were most compelling to the extent that the potentially defamatory speech involved public issues and was aimed at public figures. Public figures must show, among other things, actual malice to recover for injuries, which means that the speaker or defendant must have known that a defamatory statement was false or that the statement was made in reckless disregard of whether it was false or not. This requirement is much stricter than the standards applying to nonpublic persons, where the plaintiff has only to prove that the defendant's statement was in fact defamatory, injurious, and false. The ruling makes it difficult for public figures to win suits, because libel and similar laws, if easily applied in the public arena, have the potential of creating a chilling effect on precisely the sort of political speech that is central to self-government. It is presumed that a public figure can handle the criticisms and that their access to the media affords them an opportunity to tell their side of the story (Epstein 1984). Also, the salience and significance of public figures are likely to generate a broad array of statements and rebuttals from a wide variety of sources, thereby checking the effects of any one falsehood. Finally, because evaluations of public officials are so important in democratic processes, it is imperative to eliminate as many barriers as possible to a free and open debate regarding such persons, even if that means permitting the flow of a considerable amount of false information.

This example and its underlying rationale form a useful analogy in thinking about the conditions under which constraints should be placed on interest group organization and behavior. Because campaigns and elections are so central to democratic processes, because they command so much public interest and discussion, and because conflict and competition are so intrinsic to their operations, it is reasonable and imperative that they, above all other political forums, be open to the representation of any point of view and to organized attempts to advance that view. And given our empirical findings about the difficulty of mobilizing certain types of interests in the face of constraints on the size and institutional sources of organizational support, this need for openness argues for the deregulation of contributions to political committees and institutional involvement in their formation and maintenance. Much more credible arguments may be constructed regarding the need to impose organizational constraints on, for example, administrative lobbying, where the issues and institutional structures are less likely by themselves to produce a wide-ranging debate and more likely to produce a narrow and highly skewed set of participants, despite the fact that many of the issues have a wide-ranging impact.

In fact, there are many other discrepancies in the regulations and political thought regarding interest group involvement in elections and interest group activities in other political arenas, and they are not easily defended. Among all forms of political advocacy, campaign financing alone has regulations that impose elaborate constraints on fund-raising and other internal organizational matters. We do not seem to care whether large corporations, foundations, government agencies, and wealthy patrons support public interest law firms, policy think tanks, and, with some exceptions, lobbying organizations. Why then are limits on the sources of money so important when it is used for elections? Why are we generally content to impose few regulations on the political and organizational behavior of groups involved in litigation, lobbying, and public education campaigns, while we are intent on organizing the entire campaign financing system around an ideal of small individual contributors? Also, why are we so tolerant of subsidies for political activities by interest groups in certain arenas—such as large class-action awards, direct grants and loans, attorney-fee awards, and other government-controlled sources of financial support available to groups when they take their issues to court (McCann 1986, 66–67)—but so reluctant to subsidize interest group involvement in elections? Why do we seem to want to push interest groups out of elections and force them to press their claims in other forums—why don't we want to see as many conflicts as possible resolved in competitive elections involving as many groups as have a legitimate stake in their outcome? I do not think that these discrepancies are normatively defensible; and rather than calling for equally elaborate constraints on other forms of interest group advocacy, I think that it is much more reasonable to reduce the burdens on group involvement in elections and even to consider some sort of selective subsidies where collective action problems are particularly difficult.

Barriers to a More Open System

It is unlikely that this approach to the problem of representation will command much support. Most recent proposals to amend the federal campaign finance laws would lower contribution limits, not raise them; and most proposals to extend public financing beyond presidential races would provide public subsidies to candidates, not groups.[3] These differences, however, are not surprising. Arguments for a combination of deregulation and subsidies for group electoral involvement depend on assumptions quite different from those common in most discussions of campaign financing—in fact, they rest on a very different conception of the primary political problems to be solved.

Deregulating the PAC system and encouraging a larger, stronger, and more diverse array of electoral organizations makes sense if one wants to ensure that important political interests are not ignored or overlooked and that government officials are held accountable on their positions regarding national issues. Organized interest groups may be vilified as reducing the power of individual citizens over government, but their very organization allows them to oversee and evaluate politicians on the basis of national issues, criteria that are only occasionally important for most congressional voters and even for many presidential voters. To the extent that we strengthen the capacity of a greater number and variety of organized interests to use their resources in elections, we are likely to produce a broader base of accountability on important national issues. Erecting higher barriers to such groups will not only force them to take their demands to less open political arenas; it will diminish the necessity of politicians to be responsive on broad national policies and will emphasize the types of activities that typically influence unorganized voters, such as constituency casework, homestyle, character, scandals, and other aspects of the more personality-based politics emphasized by incumbents and reflected in most congressional voting.

These, however, are not the dominant interests of most political reformers, nor are they even among the major concerns of many public, journalistic, and academic discussions of campaign financing. The more salient concerns regarding the role of interest groups in campaign financing are the issues of equality, immediacy, and generality. The involvement of "special interests" in financing campaigns is viewed as undermining political equality by giving some citizens greater political "weight" than those who do not have the resources to make large contributions or to make any contributions at all. Special interest involvement, however, is also intrinsically troubling in many of these analyses. Because special interest groups are usually organized, they are viewed as diminishing or even destroying the appropriate *unmediated* relationship between citizens and public officials or political candidates. Institutions and organizations are viewed as having little or no legitimacy as political entities in a democracy. To the extent, then, that they perform a role in representation and political processes, they corrupt the direct and exclusively legitimate connections between citizens and their representatives. Finally, the involvement of interest groups in campaigns and elections is perceived as threatening the "public interest" or "common good" by displacing such general assessments with narrow and usually selfish evaluations of candidates and issues. For all these reasons, the primary goal of many reforms—even an unquestioned assumption in some scholarly studies (Magleby and Nelson 1990)—is to reduce or eliminate the role of "special interests" in U.S. campaigns and elections.

These concerns seem to grow in part out of a periodic anxiety in American politics about preserving or recovering the legitimacy of governmental institutions. Major periods of campaign finance reform typically occurred in the aftermath of important scandals—such as the Teapot Dome and Watergate incidents—that seemed to indicate widespread corruption among government officials. In response, the reforms generally enacted constraints in the campaign financing system designed to enforce a nearly Rousseauian conception of the legitimate relationship between citizens and government—a conception that encompasses the desirability of greater equality, immediacy, and generality in the relations between individual citizens and their government and that questions the legitimacy of participation by "special" interests, organized groups, institutions, and wealthy patrons or contributors. The thrust of these reforms owes, of course, a lot to the ideas of the Progressive movement that emerged in the early decades of the twentieth century and that sought to purge American politics of bossism, partisanship, corruption, and any other, usually organizational influences that diminished the capacity of the individual citizen to exercise and impress on government his or her own independent and deliberative judgments regarding the public interest.

In fact, several elements of the Progressive tradition stood in the way of any realistic recognition of the problems of collective action. The movement's individualism and distrust of organization—whether party machines or large corporations—made it unlikely to admit the legitimacy or even the existence of organizational problems in politics. Progressive reformers typically tried to purge politics of organizations by strengthening various forms of direct, immediate connections between citizens and government—such as direct primaries, initiative and referendum, and recall—and by restricting or prohibiting the involvement of corporations, government agencies, parties, and other institutions in elections and campaigns. That certain interests confronted considerable barriers in organizing themselves for the purpose of pressing their demands on government was more likely to be viewed as a symptom of a more general problem—a politics based on competing organizations. The real solution was not to facilitate further organization, or "countervailing power," but rather to establish a new political system based on the judgment and actions of independent, individual citizens.

Indeed, the Progressive movement was reluctant to concede the significance of expanding the range of specific interests represented in politics and elections, since it questioned the legitimacy of representing *any* particular interests. As Hofstadter pointed out, the Progressives sought to empower the "Man of Good Will," who was "abstracted from association with positive interests," and whose "chief interests were negative," in the sense that he was dissociated from all special interests and biases and had nothing but the common weal at heart. . . . He would act and think as a public-spirited individual, unlike all the groups of vested interests that were ready to prey on him. Bad people had pressure groups; the Man of Good Will had only his civic organizations. Far from joining organizations to advance his own interests, he would disassociate himself from such combinations and address himself directly and high-mindedly to the problems of government. (1955, 260–61)

These ideas about the proper roles of citizens and institutions in democratic politics were not only reflected in the Progressive Era reforms of campaign financing, which established limits on individual contributions and prohibitions against corporate contributions; they also influenced later reforms by way of the neo-Progressive "public interest" movement. This movement shares many of the assumptions of the Progressive tradition by emphasizing the need to create a new political system based on individuals conducting spontaneous, "grassroots" campaigns for the public interest, which is usually identified with a general, "consumer" interest that has little in common with private or governmental institutions (McCann 1986). And these ideas found their way into law in part through their acceptance among many, newly elected Democratic members of Congress in 1974 as well as through the persistent efforts of public interest groups like Common Cause in proposing and lobbying for campaign finance reforms (McFarland 1984). Yet the acceptance of these ideas and values extends well beyond the public interest movement and its sympathizers. As Sorauf (1988) points out, the media's conception of politics owes a lot to the neo-Progressive ideal of grassroots politics, a conception that seems to be echoed in the public's view of American politics. It is found among certain political elites who are clearly uncomfortable with pluralistic views of politics and who seek to recover a more direct and individualistic style of politics (Wright 1976). Indeed, the same political individualism and distaste for organizations may even be found among such esoteric intellectual trends as postmodernism, in which the very concept of representation is attacked (Rosenau 1992).

But it is not only the Progressive tradition that gives American reforms their egalitarian, individualist, and antiorganizational thrust; that tendency is reinforced by the interests of elected officials in weakening the capacity of the electoral system to allow the development of strong, autonomous centers of power outside government. It is probably not a coincidence that major campaign finance reforms tended to occur during relatively volatile periods in American politics, usually in the aftermath of a major decline in the strength of political parties. By making it harder for large contributors and institutions to deploy and concentrate their resources for electoral purposes, elected officials may have helped to insulate themselves from potential bases of electoral opposition. Of course, elected officials do not have the same concerns about other forms of political activity, so their interest in constraining the role of large contributors and institutions in elections is perfectly compatible with giving these same political actors relatively free rein in lobbying, litigational activities, and other political channels. Indeed, it is hard to imagine a political system that is more accommodating to career-ist politicians than one that constrains the entry and involvement of institutions and other political patrons in elections while allowing them considerable flexibility in seeking support for their policy aims by lobbying and providing both policy and political information to incumbent legislators.

These factors—occasional crises of legitimacy in American politics, Progressive ideas about the legitimate scope and methods of representation, and elected officials' interest in limiting the organization of power outside government—operate together to strengthen legal constraints inhibiting institutions and other political patrons from using their resources to establish and support autonomous electoral organizations. Of course, the constraints were never totally effective in shutting out institutions and patrons, nor were they ever designed to do so. But they are strong enough to inhibit or even prevent the electoral participation of some groups, particularly those that represent citizen interests and other interests that are not directly embodied in existing institutions. The fundamental problem, therefore, is this: the institutional arrangements most likely to widen the scope of interests involved in elections (i.e., organizational subsidies and deregulation of their behavior) are largely incompatible with the dominant (i.e., Progressive) ideas about legitimacy in political processes, as well as with the interests of elected officials (who must enact the regulations, and who want to inhibit the formation of autonomous centers of electoral power). The consequence is that our electoral reforms pay little attention to the real problems of organizing for collective action and that our electoral system is smaller, less inclusive, and less capable of vigorous opposition than it might otherwise be.

These clashes may help account for some of the dissatisfaction over campaign financing in the United States, even though it is the one aspect of our politics that has changed more than any other in response to deliberate institutional reform. The attempts to bring greater equality to the system by imposing new constraints on contributions has only cre-ated more inequality. The laws that some reformers hoped would give the public greater control over their representatives may have only served to increase the safety of incumbents, by removing the means by which the private campaign finance system would have been able to establish its own autonomy. And though many of the reformers believed that their regulations would produce greater accountability in the most important means by which the public controls its representatives, their measures may have created an even more bewildering, decentralized system than what had existed before, and they may have diminished the importance of elections by causing many important interest groups to take their demands and conflicts to other forums. The persistence of these unintended effects points to the fact that American citizens have simply not come to terms with the existence and necessity of interest groups in democratic politics and thus with the prerequisites for their effective and widespread organization.

Appendixes

Merged Data on Associations and PACs: Sources, Procedures, and Descriptions

Two of the data sets used in this study were constructed by merging U.S. Federal Election Commission data on nonparty committees and their sponsors with data from two mail surveys of membership associations conducted at the Institute of Public Policy Studies of the University of Michigan. The surveys were conducted in 1980 and 1985, under the guidance of Professor Jack L. Walker as principal investigator, and they were designed to encompass major membership associations involved in national policy-making processes. To that end, the investigation chose as samples all membership associations listed in Congressional Quarterly's *Washington Information Directory*. The 1979–80 and 1984–85 (1979, 1984) editions were used, respectively, for the 1980 and 1985 surveys. The *Directory* was useful in identifying the major organizations involved in national policy processes because it was organized around substantive policy areas—such as energy, equal rights, education and culture, economics and business, national security, and employment and labor—and was intended to include the major governmental and nongovernmental organizations involved in these issues at the national level. This policy focus was a clear advantage for my analytic purposes because I was interested in understanding how groups with different policy interests and demands use different political tactics and institutions to advocate their positions and agendas.

These data have been described and analyzed in several publications and papers (for an overview, see Walker 1991). The only major difference between the survey data used in this study and the data reported in most of these other analyses was that labor unions were included in the present study. Although the *Directory* listed labor organizations and though each of the surveys included them, unions were usually excluded in the analyses and reports because of their low response rates and the difficulties they had in responding to some of the questions, particularly those involving member benefits. Although those problems must be kept in mind when evaluating my findings, they are less significant in my study because its focus was on PAC affiliations, the political activities of organizations, their sources of revenue, and other variables that were more meaningful and comparable for unions.

Because I had access to the names of the associations in the survey and their corresponding identification numbers, I was able to go through the entire list of respondent organizations in each survey and determine whether they had one or more affiliated federal PACs in the current or most recent national election cycle. For organizations in the 1980 survey, I checked whether they had any affiliated PACs registered in the 1979–80 cycle; for associations in the 1985 survey, I checked to see whether they had any registered committees in the 1983–84 election cycle. My primary source of information on PAC affiliations was Edward Roeder's *PACs Americana* (1982), which listed connected organizations and their affiliated nonparty committees registered during the 1981–82 election cycle. However, I also searched for affiliated PACs in the FEC's *Committee Master* data tapes for the 1979–80 and 1983–84 election cycles. These tapes capture information from each political committee's "Statement of Organization" (FEC form 1), including the name of any connected organizations. In cases where I thought that a group *might* have a PAC—perhaps because it reported in the survey that it engaged in electoral activities—but where I was unable to find one, I looked up the organization in Gale Research Corporation's *Encyclopedia of Associations* (1980–85), which often listed affiliated organizations, including PACs, under each association. In some cases, I also consulted Columbia Books' *Washington Representatives* (1980–86), which listed some PACs with Washington offices and their connected organizations, and Edward Zuckerman's *Almanac of Federal PACs* (1986), another PAC directory. Although I relied on many of the same sources, I carried out the search processes for the 1980 and 1985 surveys separately.

These search processes yielded a list, for each survey, of nonparty committees, their FEC identification numbers, and the identification numbers of their parent or connected organizations in the Walker surveys. I matched these data records with their corresponding records in the FEC's "spread" and "crosstabs" files for the relevant election cycles: that is, 1980 survey groups were matched with nonparty committees registered in the 1979–80 election cycle, and 1985 survey groups were matched with nonparty committees registered during the 1983–84 cycle. I then merged these data on affiliated nonparty committees with the Walker data sets. In cases where an association had more than one affiliated PAC, the receipts, disbursements, contributions, debts, and other financial information were summed across all nonparty committees. The FEC data are described in its "Data Description Booklets";

TABLE APP. A.1.   Summary of Two Merged Data Sets

Year in which associations were surveyed	1980	1985
Election cycle in which affiliated PACs were sought	1979-80	1983-84
Number of associations in sample	974	1,501
Number of associations responding with usable data	592	828
Percent responding	60.8	55.2
Number of associations with affiliated PACs	112	157
Number of affiliated PACs	201	345
Percent of all PACs registered in election cycle	7.2	7.9
Total receipts of affiliated PACs (in thousands of dollars)	20,151	50,017
Percent of all PAC receipts in election cycle	14.4	17.0

the survey data and questions are described in Walker 1991, appendixes B and C.

Table app. A.1 summarizes the two resulting data sets. A third data set was also created based on the "panel" of surveyed associations in the Walker study. The panel was composed of associations that responded in 1980 and that were resurveyed in 1985. Data on affiliated nonparty committees in *both* election cycles—1979–80 and 1983–84—were matched and merged with this data set. The total number of associations in the panel study was 434—72 of them had a total of 133 affiliated PACs in the 1979–80 cycle, while 90 had a total of 172 committees registered during the 1983–84 elections.

I will provide any or all of these data to interested students and scholars on request.

APPENDIX B

Coding PACs according to Occupational Type: Data Sources and Coding Rules

Information Sources

I relied on several data sources when I coded nonparty political committees according to the typology of occupational roles.

Information Sources Used to Identify a Committee's Connected Organization

If the committee was a separate segregated fund, I had to identify its "connected organization," which may have been a corporation (including one without capital stock), a trade or other membership association, a labor organization, or a cooperative that was itself not a political committee but that directly or indirectly established, administered, or financially supported the political committee. It was usually possible to determine the name of the connected organization from the name of the separate segregated fund, since SSFs are required to incorporate the name of their connected organizations within their official names, but sometimes the references were unclear or incomplete. In the latter cases, I relied on the Federal Election Commission's *Committee Master* data tapes for the 1979–80 and 1983–84 election cycles. These tapes listed the information obtained by the FEC from each political committee's "Statement of Organization" (FEC form 1), which included the complete names of all connected organizations as well as their mailing addresses and designated treasurers.

Sources Used to Identify a Connected Organization

In some cases, I found a connected organization but I was not sure about what types of members belonged to it. This was true for PACs affiliated with a few membership associations as well as for those affiliated with some lobbying or law firms. In these situations, I used Congressional

Quarterly's *Washingtion Information Directory* (1979, 1984), Gale Research Corporation's *Encyclopedia of Associations* (1980–85), Columbia Books' *Washington Representatives* (1980–86), and other sources to find more information about the connected organization.

Sources Used to Determine the Contributors to Committees without Connected Organizations

The contributor or membership base of committees with no connected organizations was harder to assess, but several sources of information were helpful. The committee's name was usually useful in understanding the occupational roles of its supporters, as was the case with, for example, the Osteopathic Political Action Committee, the National Small Business Political Fund, or the California Agricultural Producers Political Action Committee. Some of the committees with "no connected organization" status nonetheless indicated an organizational affiliation on their "Statement of Organization," and that affiliation often aided coding. For example, the BPW/PAC listed a connection with National Women's Clubs, Inc., and the W F C Political Fund indicated an affiliation with Women for Change—connections that suggested that the committees belonged to the citizen group category (issue-related subcategory). And the Hispano Political Action Committee of Sante Fe reported a connection with the Hispano Chamber of Commerce, implying that that it belonged in the profit sector category (multifirm subcategory), not in the citizen group category as an ethnic group without an occupational base.

In many cases, however, committees without formal connected organizations were harder to code, usually because their names were not very precise. My primary resource for discerning the organizational base of these committees was Edward Roeder's *PACs Americana* (1982), which listed more than 3,100 nonparty committees registered during the 1981–82 election cycle as of May 1982. Roeder contacted the PACs' treasurers and, in some cases, their major contributors to determine their organizational affiliations and the types of interests they represented; and he and his team listed as many codes as were applicable under each PAC. For example, under Free Enterprise PAC, the "interests" included

Oil and Gas Extraction (1300); Traditional Conservative (8600); Limit Federal Domestic Spending (9420); Limit Fed Regulation of Business (9430); General Pro-Business (9460). (Roeder 1982, 171)

Even though contributors to this committee clearly had certain broad, citizen interests in mind when supporting this committee, it was eventually placed in the profit sector category (multifirm subcategory), since it had an occupational base in the energy industry.

In mixed or ambiguous cases, or in cases where Roeder's data did not include a certain committee, I looked up the "major" contributors of PACs in government records to see whether they showed any occupational patterns. These contributor listings—available on-line from the FEC—reported data from schedule A, FEC form 3, including the name, address, occupation, and employer of individuals who contributed over $200 to a committee during a calendar year.

Finally, in cases where a PAC had few or no major contributors and I was not able to get enough information from the sources already mentioned, I used a wide variety of data sources before coding the group or giving up and relegating the group to "missing data." I used newspaper indexes and newspaper articles from the *National Journal, Congressional Quarterly Weekly Report, Wall Street Journal, New York Times, Los Angeles Times,* and *Washington Post.* In some cases, I looked up the name of the treasurer in the reference work by Columbia Books, *Washington Representatives* (1980–86), to see whether he or she specialized in representing certain types of interests or industries; however, this information was only used to confirm other indications that a PAC had a specific occupational base.

Coding Rules

Although the typology of occupational roles is discussed extensively in chapter 3, a few additional coding rules and decisions should be noted.

First, only in cases where a *clear and consistent* occupational pattern emerged from the data—such as when the occupations of all major contributors had the same occupations or worked for employers in the same industry—did I code a committee as having an occupational base. In cases where I found any deviation from such a pattern, the committee was coded as having a nonoccupational base or as "missing data" (where too little information was available). This coding rule probably had the effect of underestimating the importance of economic institutions in structuring the mobilization of PACs, a potential bias that only strengthens many of the conclusions about the overall weakness of citizen PACs. For example, a committee like Lewis Lehrman's Fund to Keep America #1 showed a strong base in the New York financial industry, with numerous contributors from Wall Street firms like Lehman Brothers Kuhn

Loeb and Morgan Stanley and from major real estate firms, but since its base extended beyond those bounds and since it was clearly created to further Lehrman's political future, it was coded as a citizen PAC in the candidate/party subcategory.

Second, law and lobbying firms were placed in the profit sector, corporate/single firm subcategory. Although some of these firms may at times act as conduits for their clients, I assumed that most of the contributions were given primarily to further the objectives of these firms or partnerships, which were not necessarily the same as the needs of the clients.

Third, in cases where a nonprofit institution had profit sector businesses for members, I coded the committee according to the sector of the group's immediate membership. Thus, PACs established by agricultural cooperatives—like Sunkist Growers, Inc.; Mid-America Dairymen, Inc.; Sunsweet Growers, Inc.; and Florida Citrus Mutual—were placed in the profit sector, multifirm category, since their members and contributors were for-profit businesses. However, PACs affiliated with trade associations of cooperatives were coded as belonging to the nonprofit sector, since their members were nonprofit institutions. Examples included the National Council of Farmer Cooperatives PAC and the Action Committee for Rural Electrification (connected with the National Electric Cooperative Association).

Fourth, PACs connected with credit unions and credit union associations were placed in the nonprofit sector, while committees affiliated with savings and loan associations and mutual insurance companies were coded as belonging to the profit sector.

Fifth, even though many citizen groups were incorporated—often as nonprofit corporations without capital stock, as was the Women's Political Caucus—their PACs were placed in the citizen interest category, because they did not organize members or supporters around occupational roles in the nonprofit sector.

I will provide any or all of these data to interested students and scholars on request.

APPENDIX C

Explanation of the Interactive Model of PAC Affiliation

To obtain the results displayed in figure 5.1, I estimated the following equation using ordinary least-squared regression:

$$Y = a + b_0 M^{(IC=0)} + c_1 D^{(IC=1)} + b_1 M^{(IC=1)} + c_2 D^{(IC=2)} + b_2 M^{(IC=2)} + c_3 D^{(IC=3)} + b_3 M^{(IC=3)} + e$$

where

Y = 1 if the group has one or more affiliated PACs
      = 0 otherwise

$M^{(IC=i)}$ = a group's estimated motivation to form a PAC (based on the predicted values from the equation reported in table 4.3), if the group satisfies i "institutional conditions" (where i = 0, 1, 2, or 3)
      = 0, if the number of "institutional conditions" a group satisfies is not equal to i

$D^{(IC=i)}$ = 1 if the group satisfies i "institutional conditions" (where i = 0, 1, 2, or 3)
      = 0 if the number of "institutional conditions" a group satisfies is not equal to i

This equation yielded the same slope and intercept coefficients as we would have obtained by estimating four separate regression equations— one for each subset of PACs satisfying a certain number of institutional conditions (ranging from 0 to 3). The only difference was that the overall intercept term (i.e., a) must be added to the subgroup intercepts (i.e., c_1, c_2, and c_3) for groups satisfying one or more institutional conditions (ICs) in order to obtain the true intercept for that subgroup (i.e., the intercepts used in the figure). The estimated coefficients are displayed in table app. C.1.

The number of "institutional conditions" was calculated simply by counting how many of three institutional criteria a group satisfied. These criteria, based on the most important institutional factors emerging from the estimated equation reported in table 5.2, were (1) less than five percent of a group's membership worked in nonprofit institutions; (2) the group reported that the statement "Members of this association are affiliated with a single profit-making industry or occupation" was a good description of their association (i.e., four or five points on a five-point scale); and (3) the group did not receive significant funding from foundations, individual gifts or bequests, corporate gifts, or churches.

This last condition was measured by a variable created by a principal components analysis of four variables indicating the percentage of total revenues received from foundations, individual gifts, corporate gifts, and churches. Only the first component was used, which was correlated with all four item variables. I then divided the groups in two subsets at the median value of this first component, which was *negatively* related to reliance on gifts and grants. Groups with scores that were greater than the median met the institutional criterion (facilitating PAC formation), while those that fell below the median did not. The mean percent of revenues obtained from these four sources among groups that met the criterion was 0.1; the mean for groups that did not meet the insitutional criterion was 28 percent.

I tested the hypothesis that this unrestricted model—in which slopes and intercepts may vary across subgroups identified by these

TABLE APP. C.1.   Regression of PAC Affiliation on Summary Motivational Score, Allowing Intercepts and Slopes to Vary across Subgroups Differing in the Number of Institutional Conditions They Satisfy, 1985 Survey

Subgroup; i.e., Number of Institutional Conditions Satisfied (i)	Subgroup Intercepts	Subgroup Slopes on Motivation Scores (Standard Errors in Parentheses)	Number of Cases in Each Subgroup
0	.027	.165 (.139)	239
1	(.027 + (-.064)) = .037	.897 (.148)	185
2	(.027 + (-.067)) = .040	1.490 (.171)	137
3	(.027 + .126) = .154	1.216 (.177)	137

Number of cases = 698
F-ratio = 43.8
R^2 = .31

three institutional criteria—fits the data significantly better than a more restricted model, such as one in which slopes and intercepts are required to be the same for all subgroups. To conduct this test, I estimated a restricted model of the relationship between PAC formation and our summary motivation score, one in which all groups were forced to have the same intercept and slope. To test whether the unrestricted model produced results that were significantly different from the restricted model, I used an *F*-test that compared the explained variance of each model, correcting for differences in degrees of freedom:

$$F = \frac{(R^2_{\text{full model}} - R^2_{\text{restricted model}}) \,/\, (\text{difference between number of parameters in full model and restricted model})}{(1 - R^2_{\text{full model}}) \,/\, (\text{number of cases minus number of parameters in full model})}$$

$$= ((.307 - .174)/(8 - 2)) \,/\, ((1 - .307)/(698 - 8))$$

$$= 21.2$$

This *F*-ratio is significant well beyond the 0.01 level. We can therefore reject the restricted model, in which institutional factors are assumed to have no impact.

NOTES

Chapter 1

1. Labor wanted express authority for its PACs because it felt threatened by an Appeals Court decision in 1970 that upheld the conviction of a union and three officers for controlling a segregated fund for which solicitations were routinely made at job sites (*Pipefitters Union Local No. 562* v. *United States* 1970). However, the decision was eventually overturned by the Supreme Court, though after the FECA recognized such funds as a legitimate mechanism for union and corporate political activities (*Pipefitters Union Local No. 562* v. *United States* 1972).

2. The advisory opinion was requested by Sun Oil Company, which asked the FEC to give it permission to use corporate treasury funds to establish "a trustee payroll deduction plan (SUN EPA), which would act as a conduit for political contributions to candidates designated by the donor, and a political action committee (SUN PAC), through which contributions would be given to candidates at the discretion of company officials" (Cantor 1982, 43–44).

3. A lot of attention has been given to the problems of disentangling different paths of causation: are statistical relationships between PAC contributions and legislators' votes a result of PAC influence, or are they a consequence of PACs giving money to friendly legislators who would have supported their interests anyway? I have only cited the studies that addressed this problem by testing credible, multiequation models that seek to express and estimate these different effects. But many problems still remain, such as the crude and indirect measures of legislators' ideological and other predispositions to vote a particular way regardless of contributions (Smith 1995).

4. See Malbin 1984, 249–52, for a criticism of this second assumption.

5. Grier, Munger, and Roberts (1991)—following Zardkoohi (1985)—are aware of this problem, and they claim that they discriminate between the effects of these factors in their analyses. However, they do not measure political incentives in a direct way; the different political agendas of corporations are inferred indirectly from measures of industrial structure.

6. The term *political action committee* is not a legal term used in FEC records. The search procedure encompassed all registered "non-party political committees" in FEC computer files for the relevant election cycle. This broad category is the operational definition of *PAC* in this study. Data on affiliated "non-party

political committees" were included whether or not the committees showed any receipts or disbursements during the election cycle. Thus, the data on affiliated PACs are as inclusive as possible.

7. See appendix A for a description of the coding procedure and the sources of information used.

Chapter 2

1. The calculations rely on Jacobson's ordinary least-squared linear regression estimates of the effects of campaign spending on House elections (1984, 62).

2. For a discussion of increasing decentralization in the Senate, see Ornstein, Peabody, and Rohde 1993; of multiple referrals as one aspect of this complexity, see Young and Cooper 1993; and of more complex trends in the House, see Dodd and Oppenheimer 1993.

Chapter 3

1. The concept of a "separate segregated fund" was first codified in the Federal Election Campaign Act of 1971, when it was applied to corporations and labor unions, but the underlying idea may be traced to the Supreme Court's attempts to reconcile First Amendment freedoms of speech and assembly with the statutory prohibition on union political activities. See, for example, the importance the court attached to the question of whether certain political advertisements were "paid for out of the general dues of the union membership" or "obtained on a voluntary basis" (*United States* v. *UAW* 1957).

2. For a description of the procedures and sources used, see appendix B.

3. See, for example, Anthony Lewis' complaints (*NYT,* 30 November 1992, A15). Also see Robert Sullivan's article (*NYT,* 25 April 1993, s. 6, 34).

4. I eliminated small, financially insignificant committees because they probably had not yet developed any sort of predictable organizational structure or a presence that might yet appeal to potential contributors, large or small. The smallest committees, of course, could not by definition secure support from moderate-sized contributors.

Chapter 4

1. For a description of the procedure and materials used to create these data sets, see appendix B.

2. Other surveys of Washington interest groups and group representatives have also found that electoral activities are a relatively infrequent form of political advocacy. See, for example, Schlozman and Tierney 1986, 150–51; and Heinz, Laumann, Nelson, and Salisbury 1993, 99.

3. The questions regarding the relative importance of different political tactics were different in the 1980 and 1985 surveys, and the data suggest that the criterion used to distinguish whether an activity was important was less inclusive

in the latter survey, since all the percentages were lower in 1985. Thus, the apparent shifts between 1980 and 1985 in the percentages of groups indicating that these tactics were important probably stem in large part from changes in measurement, particularly in light of the stability in the percentages of groups that engage in these activities regardless of their importance.

4. As we saw in chapter 3, the PAC system has grown relatively little since the 1984 and 1986 election cycles, especially PACs affiliated with membership associations, so it is unlikely that a similar sample of groups in the early 1990s would produce figures much different from these.

5. Though the data suggest that more groups of the mixed type had PACs in 1980 than in 1985, the difference may be due to better coding of the typology variable in 1985, which tended to reduce the proportion of groups in this category.

6. I estimated this ratio by assuming that the revenue numbers reported by respondents in the 1985 group survey referred to the 1984 calendar year. The survey question actually asked groups to report the total revenues for the last fiscal year, but in some cases that is coincident with the calendar year, and in most others, the differences in revenues are negligible. Since PAC receipts are recorded on a biennial basis (calendar year), I also had to estimate the revenues raised by associations in 1983. I simply assumed that revenues increased for all groups by 10 percent between 1983 and 1984—a fairly high figure—and I thus estimated that 1983 revenues equaled 1984 revenues times 1/1.1 or 0.91.

7. Forty-six percent of the associations providing usable data (N = 818) reported that legislative lobbying was one of their most important activities—the highest level in a six-point scale. Of these 374 associations, 113 (30 percent) had affiliated PACs in the 1983–84 election cycle, and 261 (70 percent) did not. The results from the merged 1980 FEC/Walker data were similar, even though the relevant questions and scales were different. Out of a total of 586 associations, 121 (21 percent) reported that "working for the passage of needed legislation at the local, state, or national level" was "not very important" or not an activity in which the organization was engaged. Of these groups, only 1 (1 percent) had a PAC. At the other end of the scale, 354 associations (60 percent) said that legislative activities were "very important" in the organization's work. Of these, 104 (29 percent) had PACs, while 250 (71 percent) did not. For similar results using a different methodology, see John Wright's (1990) study of agriculture and tax legislation, where he reports that *most* of the interest groups lobbying members of two congressional committees on these issues did *not* have PACs.

8. On the distinction between representational roles, see Hannah Pitkin 1967. On caucus organizations, see James Q. Wilson 1973, 217–18.

Chapter 5

1. Note that the measure of reliance on moderate-sized contributors in this chapter differs from the measure used in chapter 3. Here, I am measuring the percentage of *total receipts* accounted for by contributions of more than $500,

while in the last chapter I measured the percentage of *contributions from individuals* that came from these relatively large contributors.

2. Congress revised the Hatch Act in 1993 and loosened some of the restrictions on federal employees' political activities. The new law tightened on-the-job restrictions regarding the political activities of most federal and postal employees, while it eased off-duty limits. While off duty, employees may participate in parties and campaigns and may publicly endorse candidates and raise funds from within their agency's PAC. However, the law prohibits them from soliciting political contributions from the general public. Not incidentally, previous attempts to loosen these restrictions have been blocked by Republican presidents. Presidents Ford and Bush vetoed similar legislation in 1976 and 1980, while President Reagan's veto threat stopped another bill in 1988.

3. Of course, all logistic regression analysis presumes some interaction among the explanatory variables. The marginal impact of each explanatory variable depends on the levels of all other variables, since the probability curve is nonlinear. However, I am concerned here with a more specific, structural type of interaction between motivational and institutional factors.

Chapter 6

1. Groups coded in the mixed category—that is, those with members from the profit and nonprofit sectors—were deleted because of the small numbers of groups in each of these policy areas.

Chapter 7

1. For analysis of a similar measure in the 1980 survey, see Gais, Peterson, and Walker 1984.

2. Financial industry PACs that had already been established by the 1980 elections increased their receipts enormously by 1984—again, probably in response to the partisan conflicts over reform and deregulation. Bear, Stearns and Co. PAC grew, for example, from $30,000 in receipts in 1980 to $585,000 in 1984, while the Action Fund of Shearson Lehman Hutton Inc. increased its receipts from $8,000 to $147,000 over the same period.

3. These averages were means for committees whose total contributions in the 1983–84 election cycle were greater than or equal to $25,000. The calculations were based on 612 PACs in the profit sector, 74 labor PACs, and 99 citizen PACs.

Chapter 8

1. Although my argument about the effects of contribution limits is based on an analysis of contributions to PACs, it might also apply to limits on contributions to candidates. But I am not ready to make that claim. Extending the domain of my argument to encompass individual contributions to candidates raises methodological and conceptual problems that deserve a book all by themselves.

2. Although the Supreme Court has yet to recognize the selective effects of contribution limits, lower courts have begun to explore their impact. See, for example, *Day* v. *Holahan* 1994, a decision by the federal eighth circuit court of appeals, which found that the $100 annual state limit on contributions to PACs like the Minnesota Concerned Citizens for Life "significantly impairs the ability of individuals and political committees and funds to exercise their First Amendment Rights" (1366).

3. The final version of S. 3, which failed in the final weeks of the 103d Congress, would not have directly affected contributions to PACs, but its supporters hoped it would diminish their overall role in federal elections by reducing the maximum contributions by PACs to candidates from $10,000 per election cycle (i.e., $5,000 in the primary and $5,000 in general election) to $6,000 over the entire cycle (with a maximum of $5,000 in the primary). The bill would also have capped total PAC contributions at one-third of the spending limit for House candidates and 20 percent for Senate candidates—for those candidates who would opt for the bill's spending limits, discounted television time, and other potential benefits (*Congressional Quarterly Weekly Report* 1, November 1994). An earlier version of the bill would have prohibited PACs from contributing to any federal campaign.

Works Cited

Books and Articles

Adamany, David W., and George E. Agree. 1975. *Political money: A strategy for campaign financing in America.* Baltimore: Johns Hopkins University Press.

Alford, John R., and David W. Brady. 1993. "Personal and partisan advantage in U.S. congressional elections, 1846–1990." In *Congress reconsidered,* 5th ed., edited by Lawrence C. Dodd and Bruce I. Oppenheimer. Washington, DC: CQ Press.

Axelrod, Robert. 1972. "Where the votes come from: An analysis of electoral coalitions, 1952–1968." *American Political Science Review* 66:11–20.

Baker, Ross. 1989. *The new fat cats: Members of Congress as political benefactors.* New York: Priority Press.

Bauer, Raymond A., Ithiel de Sola Pool, and Lewis Anthony Dexter. 1963. *American business and public policy.* New York: Atherton.

Bauer, Robert F., and Doris M. Kafka. 1984. *United States federal election law: Federal regulation of political campaign finance and participation.* Seattle: Oceana Publications.

Beitz, Charles R. 1989. *Political equality: An essay in democratic theory.* Princeton: Princeton University Press.

Berry, Jeffrey M. 1977. *Lobbying for the people: The political behavior of public interest groups.* Princeton: Princeton University Press.

Boies, John L. 1989. "Money, business, and the state: Material interests, *Fortune 500* corporations, and the size of political action committees." *American Sociological Review* 54:821–33.

Bosso, Christopher J. 1995. "The color of money: Environmental groups and the pathologies of fund raising." In *Interest group politics,* 4th ed., edited by Allan J. Cigler and Burdett A. Loomis. Washington, DC: CQ Press.

Boyle, Larry, and Paul R. Reyes. 1986. "The hard facts about soft money." *Federal Bar News and Journal* 33:339–45.

Brody, Richard A. 1978. "The puzzle of political participation in America." In *The new American political system,* edited by Anthony King. Washington, DC: American Enterprise Institute.

Cantor, Joseph E. 1982. *Political action committees: Their evolution and growth and their implications for the political system.* Washington, DC: Congressional Research Service, Library of Congress.

Chappell, Henry. 1982. "Campaign contributions and congressional voting: A simultaneous probit-tobit model." *Review of Economics and Statistics* 62:77–83.

Cigler, Allan J., and Anthony J. Nownes. 1995. "Public interest entrepreneurs and group patrons." In *Interest group politics*, 4th ed., edited by Allan J. Cigler and Burdett A. Loomis. Washington, DC: CQ Press.

Clawson, Dan, Alan Neustadtl, and Denise Scott. 1992. *Money talks: Corporate PACS and political influence.* New York: Basic Books.

Cobb, Roger W., and Charles D. Elder. 1972. *Participation in American politics: The dynamics of agenda-building.* Boston: Allyn and Bacon.

Cole, David D. 1991. "First amendment antitrust: The end of laissez-faire in campaign finance." *Yale Law and Policy Review* 9:236–78.

Columbia Books. 1980–86. *Washington representatives.* 4th–10th editions. Washington, DC: Columbia Books.

Congressional Quarterly. 1979. *Washington information directory, 1980–1981.* Washington, DC: CQ Press.

———. 1984. *Washington information directory, 1984–1985.* Washington, DC: CQ Press.

Corrado, Anthony. 1992. *Creative campaigning: PACs and the presidential selection process.* Boulder: Westview.

Crenson, Matthew A. 1971. *The un-politics of air pollution.* Baltimore: Johns Hopkins University Press.

Cyert, Richard M., and James G. March. 1963. *A behavioral theory of the firm.* Englewood Cliffs, NJ: Prentice-Hall.

Dahl, Robert A. 1982. *Dilemmas of pluralist democracy.* New Haven: Yale University Press.

———. 1989. *Democracy and its critics.* New Haven: Yale University Press.

Dallek, Robert. 1991. *Lone star rising: Lyndon Johnson and his times, 1908–1960.* New York: Oxford University Press.

Davis, Frank. 1993. "Balancing the perspective on PAC contributions: In search of an impact on roll calls." *American Politics Quarterly* 21:205–22.

Denzau, Arthur, and Michael C. Munger. 1986. "Legislators and interest groups: How unorganized interests get represented." *American Political Science Review* 80:89–106.

Dodd, Lawrence C., and Bruce I. Oppenheimer. 1993. "Maintaining order in the house: The struggle for institutional equilibrium." In *Congress reconsidered,* 5th ed., edited by Lawrence C. Dodd and Bruce I. Oppenheimer. Washington, DC: CQ Press.

Downs, Anthony. 1957. *An economic theory of democracy.* New York: Harper and Row.

Drew, Elizabeth. 1983. *Politics and money.* New York: Macmillan.

Edelman, Murray. 1964. *The symbolic uses of politics.* Urbana: University of Illinois Press.

Edsall, Thomas B. 1984. *The new politics of inequality.* New York: W. W. Norton.

Eismeier, Theodore J., and Phillip H. Pollack III. 1988. *Business, money, and the rise of corporate PACs in American elections.* New York: Quorum Books.

Eldersveld, Samuel. 1964. *Political parties: A behavioral analysis.* Chicago: Rand McNally.

Epstein, Anthony C. 1984. "Lobbying and defamation." In *Federal lobbying*, edited by Jerald A. Jacobs. Washington, DC: Bureau of National Affairs.

Epstein, Edwin M. 1980. "Business and labor under the Federal Election Campaign Act of 1971." In *Parties, interest groups, and campaign finance laws*, edited by Michael J. Malbin. Washington, DC: American Enterprise Institute.

Etzioni, Amatai. 1984. *Capital corruption.* New York: Harcourt Brace Jovanovich.

Fenno, Richard F. 1973. *Congressmen in committees.* Boston: Little, Brown.

Fleisher, Richard. 1993. "PAC contributions and congressional voting on national defense." *Legislative Studies Quarterly* 18:391–409.

Foley, Edward B. 1994. "Equal-dollars-per-voter: A constitutional principle of campaign finance." *Columbia Law Review* 94:1204–57.

Foundation for Public Affairs. 1988. *Public interest profiles, 1988–1989.* Washington, DC: CQ Press.

Freeman, Jo. 1975. *The politics of women's liberation.* New York: David McKay.

Friedman, Milton. 1962. *Capitalism and freedom.* Chicago: University of Chicago Press.

Gais, Thomas L., Mark A. Peterson, and Jack L. Walker, Jr. 1984. "Interest groups, iron triangles and representative institutions in American national government." *British Journal of Political Science* 14:161–85.

Gale Research Corporation. 1980–85. *Encyclopedia of associations.* 14th–19th editions. Detroit: Gale Research Corporation.

Gardner, John W. 1972. *In common cause.* New York: W. W. Norton.

Gelb, Joyce, and Marian Lief Palley. 1987. *Women and public policies.* Princeton: Princeton University Press.

Ginsberg, Benjamin. 1984. "Money and power: The new political economy of American elections." In *The political economy*, edited by Thomas Ferguson and Joel Rogers. Armonk, NY: M. E. Sharpe.

Goedert, Paula C. 1989. "Lobbying by charitable organizations." In *Federal lobbying*, edited by Jerald A. Jacobs. Washington, DC: Bureau of National Affairs.

Goidel, Robert K., and Donald A. Gross. 1994. "A systems approach to campaign finance in U.S. House elections." *American Politics Quarterly* 22:125–53.

Green, Donald Philip, and Jonathan S. Krasno. 1988. "Salvation for the spendthrift incumbent." *American Journal of Political Science* 32:884–907.

———. 1990. "Rebuttal to Jacobson's 'New evidence for old arguments.'" *American Journal of Political Science* 34:363–72.

Grenzke, Janet. 1989. "Shopping in the congressional supermarket: The currency is complex." *American Journal of Political Science* 33:1–24.

Grier, Kevin B., and Michael C. Munger. 1993. "Comparing interest group PAC contributions to House and Senate incumbents, 1980–1986." *Journal of Politics* 55:615–43.

Grier, Kevin B., Michael C. Munger, and Brian E. Roberts. 1991. "The industrial organization of corporate political participation." *Southern Economic Journal* 57:727–38.

Hall, Richard L. 1987. "Participation and purpose in committee decision making." *American Political Science Review* 81:105–27.

Hall, Richard L., and Frank W. Wayman. 1990. "Buying time: Moneyed interests and the mobilization of bias in congressional committees." *American Political Science Review* 84:797–820.

Handler, Edward, and John R. Mulkern. 1982. *Business in politics.* Lexington, MA: D. C. Heath.

Hansen, John Mark. 1991. *Gaining access: Congress and the farm lobby, 1919–1981.* Chicago: University of Chicago Press.

Hardin, Russell. 1982. *Collective action.* Baltimore: Johns Hopkins University Press.

Heard, Alexander. 1960. *The costs of democracy.* Chapel Hill: University of North Carolina Press.

Heinz, John P., Edward O. Laumann, Robert L. Nelson, and Robert H. Salisbury. 1993. *The hollow core: Private interests in national policy making.* Cambridge: Harvard University Press.

Hershey, Margorie R., and Darrell M. West. 1983. "Single-issue politics: Prolife groups and the 1980 Senate campaign." In *Interest group politics,* edited by Allan J. Cigler and Burdett A. Loomis. Washington, DC: CQ Press.

Hirsch, Fred. 1977. *Social Limits to Growth.* London: Routledge and Kegan Paul.

Hofstadter, Richard. 1955. *The age of reform: From Bryan to F.D.R.* New York: Vintage.

Hopkins, Bruce R. 1987. *The law of tax-exempt organizations.* New York: Wiley.

Huntington, Samuel P. 1981. *American politics: The promise of disharmony.* Cambridge: Harvard University Press.

Jackson, Brooks. 1990. *Broken promise: Why the Federal Election Commission failed.* New York: Priority Press Publications.

———. 1988. *Honest graft: Big money and the American political process.* New York: Knopf.

Jacobson, Gary C. 1980. *Money in congressional elections.* New Haven: Yale University Press.

———. 1984. "Money in the 1980 and 1982 congressional elections." In *Money and politics in the United States,* edited by Michael J. Malbin. Chatham, NJ: Chatham House Publishers.

———. 1985. "Money and votes reconsidered: Congressional elections, 1972–1982." *Public Choice* 47:7–62.

———. 1990. "The effects of campaign spending in House elections: New evidence for old arguments." *American Journal of Political Science* 34:334–62.

————. 1992. *The politics of congressional elections.* 3d ed. New York: HarperCollins.

Johnson, Cathy Marie. 1992. *The dynamics of conflict between bureaucrats and legislators.* Armonk, NY: M. E. Sharpe.

Kau, James B., Donald Keenan, and Paul H. Rubin. 1982. "A general equilibrium model of congressional voting." *Quarterly Journal of Economics* 97:271–93.

Kenny, Christopher, and Michael McBurnett. 1992. "A dynamic model of the effect of campaign spending on congressional vote choice." *American Journal of Political Science* 36:923–37.

Kingdon, John W. 1984. *Agendas, alternatives, and public policies.* Boston: Little, Brown.

————. 1989. *Congressmen's voting decisions.* 3d ed. Ann Arbor: University of Michigan Press. First edition published in 1973 by Harper and Row.

Langbein, Laura I. 1986. "Money and access: Some empirical evidence." *Journal of Politics* 48:1052–62.

Latus, Margaret Ann. 1984. "The operations of ideological political action committees: Thirteen liberal and conservative PACs in the 1982 elections." Ph.D. diss., Princeton University.

Lindblom, Charles E. 1977. *Politics and markets.* New York: Basic Books.

Lowi, Theodore J. 1979. *The end of liberalism: The second republic of the United States.* 2d ed. New York: W.W. Norton.

Luntz, Frank I. 1988. *Candidates, consultants, and campaigns.* New York: Basil Blackwell.

Magleby, David B., and Candice J. Nelson. 1990. *The money chase: Congressional campaign finance reform.* Washington, DC: Brookings.

Makinson, Larry. 1990. *Open secrets: The dollar power of PACs in Congress.* Washington, DC: CQ Press.

Makinson, Larry, and Joshua Goldstein. 1994. *The cash constituents of Congress.* Washington, DC: CQ Press.

Malbin, Michael J. 1984. "Looking back at the future of campaign finance reform: Interest groups and American elections." In *Money and politics in the United States,* edited by Michael J. Malbin. Washington, DC: American Enterprise Institute.

————. 1993. "Campaign finance reform: Some lessons from the data." *Rockefeller Institute Bulletin,* 47–53.

Masters, Marick F., and Gerald D. Keim. 1985. "Determinants of PAC participation among large corporations." *Journal of Politics* 47:1158–73.

Matthews, Donald R., and James A. Stimson. 1975. *Yeas and nays: Normal decision-making in the U.S. House of Representatives.* New York: Wiley.

McCann, Michael W. 1986. *Taking reform seriously: Perspectives on public interest liberalism.* Ithaca: Cornell University Press.

McCarty, Nolan, and Keith Poole. 1993. "A test of two-candidate competition using political action committee contributions." Graduate School of Industrial Administration, Carnegie-Mellon University. Typescript.

McFarland, Andrew S. 1984. *Common Cause: Lobbying in the public interest.* Chatham, NJ: Chatham House Publishers.

Mitchell, Robert Cameron. 1991. "From conservation to environmental movement: The development of the modern environmental lobbies." In *Government and environmental politics*, edited by Michael J. Lacey. Washington, DC: Woodrow Wilson Center Press.

Moe, Terry M. 1980. *The organization of interests.* Chicago: University of Chicago Press.

Morris, Dwight, and Murielle E. Gamache. 1994. *Handbook of campaign spending.* Washington, DC: CQ Press.

Morris, Roger. 1990. *Richard Milhous Nixon: The rise of an American politician.* New York: Henry Holt.

Mutch, Robert E. 1988. *Campaigns, Congress, and courts: The making of federal campaign finance law.* New York: Praeger.

Nicholson, Marlene A. 1974. "Campaign financing and equal protection." *Stanford Law Review* 26:815–54.

Olson, Mancur. 1965. *The logic of collective action: Public goods and the theory of groups.* Cambridge: Harvard University Press.

———. 1982. *The rise and decline of nations.* New Haven: Yale University Press.

Olson, Mancur, and Richard Zeckhauser. 1966. "An economic theory of alliances." *Review of Economics and Statistics* 48:266–79.

Olson, Susan M. 1990. "Interest group litigation in federal district court." *Journal of Politics* 52:854–82.

Ornstein, Norman J., Thomas E. Mann, and Michael J. Malbin. 1994. *Vital statistics on Congress, 1993–94.* Washington, DC: CQ Press.

Ornstein, Norman J., Robert L. Peabody, and David W. Rohde. 1993. "The U.S. Senate in an era of change." In *Congress reconsidered*, 5th ed., edited by Lawrence C. Dodd and Bruce I. Oppenheimer. Washington, DC: CQ Press.

Ostrogorski, M. 1902. *Democracy and the organization of political parties.* Volume 2. Translated by Frederick Clarke. New York: Macmillan.

Peterson, Mark A., and Jack L. Walker, Jr. 1986. "Interest group responses to partisan change: The impact of the Reagan Administration upon the national interest group system." In *Interest group politics*, 2d ed., edited by Alan J. Cigler and Burdett A. Loomis. Washington, DC: CQ Press.

Petrocik, John R. 1981. *Party coalitions: Realignment and the decline of the New Deal party system.* Chicago: University of Chicago Press.

Pitkin, Hannah F. 1967. *The concept of representation.* Berkeley: University of California Press.

Poole, Keith T., and Thomas Romer. 1985. "Patterns of political action committee contributions to the 1980 campaigns for the U.S. House of Representatives." *Public Choice* 47:63–111.

Pratt, Henry J. 1976. *The gray lobby.* Chicago: University of Chicago Press.

Raskin, Jamin B., and John Bonifaz. 1994. *The wealth primary: Campaign fundraising and the Constitution.* Washington, DC: Center for Responsive Politics.

Rawls, John. 1993. *Political liberalism*. New York: Columbia University Press.

Ripley, Randall B., and Grace A. Franklin. 1987. *Congress, the bureaucracy, and public policy*. 4th edition. Chicago: Dorsey Press.

Roeder, Edward. 1982. *PACs Americana*. Washington, DC: Sunshine Services Corporation.

Rosenau, Pauline Marie. 1992. *Post-Modernism and the social sciences: Insights, inroads, and intrusions*. Princeton: Princeton University Press.

Rothenberg, Lawrence S. 1992. *Linking citizens to government*. New York: Cambridge University Press.

Sabato, Larry J. 1984. *PAC power: Inside the world of political action committees*. New York: W. W. Norton.

Salisbury, Robert H. 1969. "An exchange theory of interest groups." *Midwest Journal of Political Science* 13:1–32.

———. 1984. "Interest representation: The dominance of institutions." *American Political Science Review* 78:64–76.

———. 1990. "The paradox of interest groups in Washington, D.C.: More groups and less clout." In *The new American political system*, 2d version, edited by Anthony King. Washington, DC: American Enterprise Institute Press.

———. 1992. *Interests and institutions: Substance and structure in American politics*. Pittsburgh: University of Pittsburgh Press.

Saltzman, Gregory M. 1987. "Congressional voting on labor issues: The role of PACs." *Industrial and Labor Relations Review* 40:163–79.

Sandler, Todd. 1992. *Collective action: Theory and applications*. Ann Arbor: University of Michigan Press.

Schattschneider, E. E. 1960. *The semi-sovereign people*. New York: Holt, Rinehart, and Winston.

Scheppele, Kim Lane, and Jack L. Walker, Jr. 1991. "The litigation strategies of interest groups." In *Mobilizing interest groups in America*, by Jack L. Walker, Jr. Ann Arbor: University of Michigan Press.

Schlozman, Kay Lehman. 1984. "Political equality and the American pressure system." *Journal of Politics* 46:1006–32.

Scholzman, Kay Lehman, and John T. Tierney. 1986. *Organized interests and American democracy*. New York: Harper and Row.

Shaiko, Ronald G. 1991. "More bang for the buck: The new era of full-service public interest organizations." In *Interest group politics*, 3d ed., edited by Allan J. Cigler and Burdett A. Loomis. Washington, DC: CQ Press.

Sinclair, Barbara. 1989. *The transformation of the U.S. Senate*. Baltimore: Johns Hopkins University Press.

Smith, Richard A. 1984. "Advocacy, interpretation, and influence in the U.S. Congress." *American Political Science Review* 78:44–63.

———. 1995. "Interest group influence in the U.S. Congress." *Legislative Studies Quarterly* 20:89–139.

Smolla, Rodney A. 1992. *Free speech in an open society*. New York: Alfred A. Knopf.

Sorauf, Frank J. 1984a. *What price PACs?* New York: Twentieth Century Fund.

———. 1984b. "Who's in charge? Accountability in political action committees." *Political Science Quarterly* 99:591–614.

———. 1988. *Money in American elections.* Glenview: Scott, Foresman.

———. 1992. *Inside campaign finance: Myths and realities.* New York: Yale University Press.

Stratmann, Thomas. 1991. "What do campaign contributions buy? Deciphering causal effects of money and votes." *Southern Economic Journal* 51:606–20.

Sundquist, James L. 1968. *Politics and policy: The Eisenhower, Kennedy, and Johnson years.* Washington, DC: Brookings Institution.

U.S. Federal Election Commission. 1986. *Campaign finance law 86.* Report prepared by James A. Palmer and Edward D. Feigenbaum. Washington, DC: Federal Election Commission.

U.S. General Accounting Office. 1987. *Tax administration: Information on lobbying and political activities of tax-exempt organizations.* Washington, DC: General Accounting Office.

U.S. House Committee on House Administration. 1991. *Campaign finance reform: Hearings held before the Task Force on Campaign Finance Reform of the Committee on House Administration.* 102d Cong., 1st sess., 23 and 28 May. Washington, DC: U.S. Government Printing Office.

U.S. House Committee on Ways and Means. 1987. *Lobbying and political activities of tax-exempt organizations.* 100th Cong., 1st sess., 12 and 13 March. Washington, DC: U.S. Government Printing Office.

U.S. Merit Systems Protection Board. 1988. Political activity and the federal employee. Washington, DC: Office of the Special Counsel, Merit Systems Protection Board.

U.S. Senate Committee on Rules and Administration. 1986. *Proposed amendments to the Federal Election Campaign Act of 1971.* 99th Cong., 1st and 2nd sessions, 5 November 1985, 22 January and 27 March 1986. Washington, DC: U.S. Government Printing Office.

Walker, Jack L. 1983. "The origins and maintenance of interest groups in America." *American Political Science Review* 77:390–406.

———. 1991. *Mobilizing interest groups in America: Patrons, professions, and social movements.* Ann Arbor: University of Michigan Press.

Wayman, Frank. 1985. "Arms control and strategic arms voting in the U.S. Senate: Patterns of change, 1967–1983." *Journal of Conflict Resolution* 29:225–51.

Weisbrod, Burton A. 1988. *The nonprofit economy.* Cambridge: Harvard University Press.

Welch, William P. 1982. "Campaign contributions and legislative voting: Milk money and dairy price supports." *Western Political Quarterly* 35:478–95.

Wilhite, Allen, and John Theilmann. 1987. "Labor PAC contributions and labor legislation: A simultaneous logit approach." *Public Choice* 53:267–76.

Wilson, James Q. 1973. *Political organizations.* New York: Basic Books.

Wolman, Harold, and Fred Teitelbaum. 1985. "Interest groups and the Reagan presidency. In *The Reagan Presidency and the Governing of America*, edited by Lester M. Salamon and Michael S. Lund. Washington, DC: Urban Institute Press.

Wright, J. Skelly. 1976. "Politics and the Constitution: Is money speech?" *Yale Law Journal* 85:1001–21.

Wright, John R. 1985. "PACs, contributions, and roll calls: An organizational perspective." *American Political Science Review* 79:400–414.

———. 1990. "Contributions, lobbying, and committee voting in the U.S. House of Representatives." *American Political Science Review* 84:417–38.

Young, Garry, and Joseph Cooper. 1993. "Multiple referral and the transformation of House decision making." In *Congress reconsidered*, 5th ed., edited by Lawrence C. Dodd and Bruce I. Oppenheimer. Washington, DC: CQ Press.

Zardkoohi, Asghar. 1985. "On the political participation of the firm in the electoral process." *Southern Economics Journal* 51:804–17.

Zuckerman, Edward. 1986. *Almanac of federal PACs*. Washington, DC: Amward Publications.

U.S. Federal Election Commission

All campaign finance data were obtained from the U.S. Federal Election Commission. Except for the computer files discussed in the appendixes, data on PACs were obtained from the biennial report *FEC Reports on Financial Activity: Party and Non-Party Political Committees* (Washington, DC: Federal Election Commission); and data on candidate committees were found in the biennial series *FEC Reports on Financial Activity: U.S. Senate and House Campaigns* (Washington, DC: Federal Election Commission). Only the reports entitled "Final Report" were used in constructing the tables, except for the report for the 1977–78 election cycle, which was called "Interim Report No. 5." Data on the 1992 elections were obtained directly from the FEC's on-line service.

Court Decisions

Austin v. *Michigan Chamber of Commerce*. 1990. 494 U.S. 652.

Buckley v. *Valeo*. 1976. 424 U.S. 1.

Day v. *Holahan*. 1994. 34 F.3d 1356.

Faucher v. *FEC [Federal Election Commission]*. 1991. 928 F.2d 468.

FEC v. *Massachusetts Citizens for Life*. 1986. 479 U.S. 238.

FEC v. *National Right to Work Committee*. 1982. 459 U.S. 197.

Hammerstein v. *Kelly*. 1964. 235 F.Supp. 60.

New York Times v. *Sullivan*. 1964. 376 U.S. 254.

Pipefitters Local Union No. 562 v. *United States*. 1970. 434 F. 2d 1127.

Pipefitters Local Union No. 562 v. *United States*. 1972. 407 U.S. 385.

United States v. *UAW*. 1957. 352 U.S. 567.

Index

Access, legislative, 11–14, 90–93, 130
Action Fund of Shearson Lehman Hutton, Inc., 216
Aerospace industry, 55
AFL-CIO, 9
Agenda, political, 130, 173
Agriculture Committee, U.S. House of Representatives, 12
Agriculture industry, 10, 56–57
Agriculture policy, 130–34, 137–38, 140–42
Airline industry, 10
Akin, Gump, Hauer and Feld, 56
American Association of Retired Persons, 184
American Bankers Association, 56
American Council of Life Insurance, 134
American Dental Association, 56
American Family Institute, 114
American Federation of Home Health Agencies, 57
American Federation of State, County, and Municipal Employees' PAC, 162
American Hospital Association, 56–57
American Medical Association, 6, 48, 56
American Physical Therapy Association, 57
American Security Council, 68
Americans for Democratic Action, 58
American Space Frontier Committee, 162

Amoco PAC, 48, 55
Amsouth PAC, 161
Archer-Daniels-Midland Corporation, 35
Arnold and Porter, 56
Associated General Contractors of America, 56
Associated Milk Producers' Committee for Thorough Agricultural Political Education, 48
Association of General Contractors, 9
Association of Trial Lawyers of America, 56
Austin v. Michigan Chamber of Commerce, 174
Auto Dealers for Free Trade PAC, 49, 54, 56, 162
Automobile industry, 55
Autonomy in PAC system, lack of, 21, 61, 82, 171

Bear, Stearns and Company PAC, 48, 216
Bias among PACs: compared to other political tactics, 122–26; defined, 17–18, 81–82; with respect to occupational roles, 45, 77–79, 81–82, 100–101, 119–21, 126–27; with respect to policy interests, 4, 42, 129, 131, 141–45. *See also* Collective action; Occupational roles; Political parties; Political action committees, formation of
Blue Cross/Blue Shield PACs, 57
Boeing Company PAC, 162